Better Homes and Gardens.

quick color gardening

WILEY

John Wiley & Sons, Inc.

Better Homes and Gardens® Quick Color Gardening

Contributing Writer: Julie Martens
Contributing Project Editor: Deb Wiley
Contributing Designers: Sundie Ruppert, Lori Gould, Cathy Brett
Editor, Garden Books: Denny Schrock
Editorial Assistant: Heather Knowles
Contributing Copy Editor: Susan Lang
Contributing Proofreaders: Fern Marshall Bradley, Kate Carter Frederick
Contributing Indexer: Don Glassman
Contributing Photographers: Dean Schoeppner, Denny Schrock
Contributing Photo Manager: Deb Wiley

Meredith® Books
Editorial Director: Gregory H. Kayko
Editor in Chief, Garden: Doug Jimerson
Art Directors: Tim Alexander, Gene Rauch
Managing Editor: Doug Kouma
Business Director: Janice Croat

John Wiley & Sons, Inc.
Publisher: Natalie Chapman
Associate Publisher: Jessica Goodman
Executive Editor: Anne Ficklen
Assistant Editor: Heather Dabah
Senior Production Editor: Jacqueline Beach
Production Director: Diana Cisek
Manufacturing Manager: Tom Hyland

This book is printed on acid-free paper.

Better Homes and Gardens Magazine
Editor in Chief: Gayle Goodson Butler

Meredith National Media Group
President: Tom Harty
Executive Vice President: Doug Olson

Meredith Corporation
Chairman of the Board: William T. Kerr
President and Chief Executive Officer: Stephen M. Lacy

In Memoriam: E. T. Meredith III (1933–2003)

Library of Congress Cataloging-in-Publication Data

Better homes and gardens quick color for your garden.
p. cm.
Quick color for your garden
Includes index.

Summary: A comprehensive guide to quick color for your garden that combines the categories of container gardening, beds and borders, annuals, perennials and bulbs.

ISBN 978-1-118-18239-0 (pbk.)

1. Color in gardening. 2. Gardens--Design. I. Better homes and gardens. II. Title: Quick color for your garden.

SB454.3.C64B48 2912

635--dc23

2012031076

Printed in the United States of America
10 9 8 7 6 5 4 3 2 1

Paint your yard with the living hues of quick color plants. Inspiring images and easy-to-follow advice help you design and maintain plantings featuring these bold, beautiful performers.

table of contents

p.**6**

CELEBRATE COLOR
Quick color bursts from annuals, tender perennials, tropicals, and other plants during a single growing season.

p.**18**

PLAYING WITH COLOR
Use these hue clues to transform a ho-hum landscape as easily as an artist daubs color on a picture.

p**28**

SEASONAL SHOW
Quick color makes it easy to create attractive displays that keep pace with the seasons.

celebrate color

Give your outdoor spaces a color boost using plants that peak in a single growing season. These one-season wonders can transform a ho-hum yard into a spectacular showpiece.

p.8
WELCOME COLOR
Ignite your landscape with the explosive color of annuals, tender perennials, and tropical plants. From front yard finery to backyard beauty, quick color plants make every space a garden destination.

p.14
OUTDOOR ROOMS
Decorate outdoor living areas with the alluring beauty of colorful plants. On decks and patios, and around pools and spas, learn the tricks for adding living color so it enhances daily life.

p.16
COLOR IN THE LANDSCAPE
Transform spaces from functional to fabulous by including pockets of pretty color. Dig in, using fences, blank walls, and narrow side yards as a location for plantings.

Plug into quick color

Transform your landscape into a seasonal showpiece.

You don't need a big budget to turn a cookie-cutter landscape into a showplace. All you need is quick color from plants that please for a single season. These speedy growers inject intense color into a yard, then fade with the frost.

Whether you garden where winter lingers for months or merely a matter of weeks, capitalize on frost-free seasons by filling your yard with eye-catching beauty. Fast-growing, single-season color offers versatility and the option to change your scenery with the flip of the calendar.

Meet the quick color players

Annuals and tender perennials grown as annuals headline the quick color theater. The stars of the show include traditional favorites, such as cosmos, zinnia, and impatiens as well as uncommon beauties, such as Mexican petunia, bidens, and nierembergia.

A true annual sprouts from seed and matures to a seed-producing plant in a single growing season. These fast-track plants feature a wide array of blossom colors, from black-purple to lemon yellow to watermelon pink to everything in between. You can choose annuals with a skyscraping stature, such as sunflower or castor bean, or focus on shorter bloomers, such as marigold. Whatever your passion, you can find an annual that's right for you.

Tender perennials also play a prominent role in the quick color cast. Surviving as perennials in warmer climes, these plants infuse the summer garden with exuberant hues, then die with the frost in colder areas. Tender perennials include familiar faces like geranium, coleus, and lantana, as well as newer introductions, such as grassy sedges, Bolivian begonia, and angelonia.

Above: **Design an entry with impact by filling pots and planting beds with hot-hued quick color plants. Good container choices include zinnia, black-eyed Susan, and blanket flower.**

Opposite top: **Foliage plants with bold hues, like red 'Big Judy' coleus, add snap to summer plantings. More punch comes from 'Vancouver Centennial' geranium, 'Denver Daisy' black-eyed Susan, little bluestem, and zinnia.**

Tropical plants with exotic blooms and safari-style leaves add over-the-top color to a seasonal landscape. This group includes banana, mandevilla, and canna, which introduce rain-forest flair to garden settings. Most tropicals can't withstand even the lightest freeze and must be stored in a frost-free location to ensure winter survival in all but the warmest locales.

Many gardeners, however, happily sacrifice their tropical treasures as the growing season ends and simply purchase new plants the following year.

That's quick color.

Stage a show

Quick color makes an impact in the landscape. The splash of color, whether from flowers or foliage, captures attention and directs the eye. You can use color intentionally to command attention or guide foot traffic, or you can just have fun with it, positioning it to fill the growing season with sizzle. Consider some of these uses for quick color:

On a patio or deck. Cheery pots of pretty blooms and patterned leaves add warmth and coziness to the outdoor setting.

Tucked in a planting bed. Count on fast-growing beauties to fill in a bare spot, brighten a dull corner, or dress an empty wall with appealing splendor.

Where you need screening. Position quick color plants—especially tropical plants or tall grasses—to create a seasonal privacy screen.

At an entry. Colorful plants elevate an entry from functional to fabulous.

What you do with quick color is limited only by your imagination. Dream up your own garden schemes and be bold enough to take a risk. Above all, get ready to be inspired. Ready, set, grow!

Not your grandmother's annuals
Breeding breakthroughs have transformed common plants grown as annuals into garden all-stars. Add these colorful newcomers to your shopping list.

SUNPATIENS
SunPatiens makes it possible to grow shade-favorite impatiens in sun-splashed spots. These sun-worshiping cuties boast nonstop flower power.

VARIEGATED SNAPDRAGON
Snapdragons aren't just for cool-season color. 'Snap Happy' snapdragon won't swoon as the mercury soars, and it unfurls fun, variegated foliage.

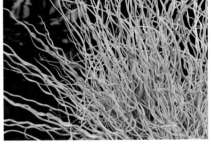

CORKSCREW RUSH
Foliage plants can star in leading roles when you select quirky, colorful candidates like 'Twister' corkscrew rush.

PETUNIA WITH PANACHE
Celebrate color by planting an uncommon hue of a traditional botanical friend, like 'Rhythm and Blues' petunia.

STRIPED CORN
Use edibles as ornamentals when you plant 'Tricolor' zea (corn, *above*), Bright Lights Swiss chard, or burgundy basil.

FLASHY FOLIAGE HIBISCUS
Bloomers prized for exquisite flowers now are grown for outstanding foliage such as 'Mahogany Splendor' hibiscus.

A touch of the tropics

As you learn about quick color plantings, you'll learn to draw on tropicals again and again. These one-season wonders boast larger-than-life growth and possess the power to transform an everyday setting into an exotic oasis. With flamboyant foliage and intensely hued blooms, these plants present captivating drama whether they're tucked into pots or planting beds.

Tropicals are a natural choice for growing in containers. Just be sure to give them enough elbow room to spread their roots. They're hardwired to grow and won't thrive for long in 10- or 12-inch pots. Plants like cannas will outgrow—and possibly crack—even 14-inch pots in a single growing season. Some tropicals achieve significant height during the growing season and will quickly topple too-small pots.

In the landscape, the easy-growing habits of tropicals make every gardener feel like an expert. Tropicals tend to produce luxurious growth with

Above: **Elephant's ear dress a garden with equatorial flair. Solid foliage pairs well with colorful coleus and caladium.**

Opposite top: **Trailing 'Blackie' and 'Marguerite' sweet potato vines, burgundy cordyline, and 'Pretoria' canna complement geraniums and New Guinea impatiens with tropical punch.**

record-breaking speed, so you savor the fruits of little labor yet garner sincere compliments from neighbors.

Don't want to wait? You can create an instant tropical paradise by purchasing larger plants in 3-gallon pots. Most often, you'll find these larger pot sizes at independently owned garden centers. If you're happy to start with gallon-size pots and watch your tropical garden grow, check out the offerings at discount stores and home centers.

The secret to bigger, bolder beauty

Tropicals need heat to thrive. For the most part, they don't demand heavy-duty coddling to achieve lush growth. They typically leap from the ground when summer heat builds. For most tropical plants, simply providing full sun and ample water yields jungle-size leaves and showstopping flowers.

It's worth digging into the exact fertilizer needs of specific plants to be sure you're delivering the right nutrition. In general, a nitrogen-rich fertilizer or aged compost worked into the soil ensures a steady supply of larger, more numerous leaves. Choose this regimen for plants prized for their glorious foliage, such as canna or elephant's ear.

A bloom-booster fertilizer encourages abundant blossoms and is a must with flowering tropicals, such as angel's trumpet, mandevilla, and Chinese hibiscus. Using a liquid fertilizer allows you to control the application frequency. Typically a dose every two weeks is more than sufficient to fuel a fantastic flower show.

Tropicals respond quickly to temperature, and as night temperatures begin to dial down, growth slows. The first frosty night melts leaves and flowers into watery mush.

At this point, some gardeners dig roots to overwinter the plant indoors. Others just celebrate the end of another growing season and let the plant die. In warmer climates, the end of a tropical plant's life simply signals the end of warm-season color and the beginning of cool-season quick color.

Accessories set the mood

When growing tropicals for a backyard escape, accent the plantings with accessories that infuse the garden with equatorial ambience. A trickling fountain, tiki torches, and even pink flamingoes fit the mood. Consider wicker furniture, a hammock swing, or a rattan rug to cultivate a vacation paradise outside your own back door.

Tropical blooms or foliage? Wondering what to choose for tropical beauty? Any of these quick color favorites makes a bold statement.

TROPICAL BLOOMERS

ABUTILON Pretty bell-shape blooms dangle from stems.

ANGEL'S TRUMPET Exotic flowers exude intense fragrance.

CANNA Large blossoms boast rich, sizzling hues.

CHINESE HIBISCUS Striking flowers open in many colors (shown, *above right*).

MANDEVILLA Twining vines open large, flared blooms (shown, *above left*).

TROPICAL FOLIAGE PLANTS

BANANA Tall, lush leaves may be variegated (shown, *above left*).

CANNA Leaves offer eye-catching variegation (shown, *above right*).

CORDYLINE Upright, spiky plants bear strappy leaves.

ELEPHANT'S EAR Mammoth leaves in various color choices.

NEW ZEALAND FLAX Strong upright plants with wide, grasslike leaves in many hues.

Make a grand entrance

Eye-catching plantings packed with quick color

help your home extend a friendly welcome. First impressions count, and when you preface a front door with floral and foliage fireworks, you create an atmosphere of gracious warmth.

A colorful entry also adds curb appeal, which enhances home value. The trick is to arrange plantings that blend fuss-free style with traffic-stopping beauty. Quick color plants fit the bill.

Entry gardens fill many roles in the landscape. On a busy street, a well-executed fence garden or bermed planting bed can muffle traffic noise and foster a sense of privacy.

Tall ornamental grasses, statuesque tropical plants, and vines trained on arbors can form living screens that shield front yard living spaces from passersby.

Add a trickling fountain and the surrounding sounds all but disappear.

Instead of using a picket fence, create small-town welcome by focusing on billows of blooms. Planting beds brimming with flowering annuals and tender perennials dress up a home with alluring color and make it the talk of the block.

Even the tiniest dooryard can support pretty plantings. If your entry has hard surfaces, group together container gardens to fill the space with waves of beauty.

A mailbox perched at the edge of a yard provides a classic invitation for a colorful garden design. To save your mail carrier from painful encounters with stinging insects, remember not to pack plants too close to the mailbox.

Whenever you trade turf for quick color, you reduce lawn-mowing duties—cause to cheer.

Using seasonal color in a front yard works well for several reasons. It provides a loom on which you can weave different planting patterns

Above: **Create a porch with personality by slipping traditional annual favorites—geraniums—into containers painted with vibrant designs and complementary hues.**

Opposite top: **Zinnias kick off a parade of color flanking an entry. These old-fashioned annuals offer ample flowers for picking and placing into vases.**

year to year. For a gardener who enjoys designing plantings, an entry garden furnishes endless opportunities to satisfy the craving for staging something new. In areas with rugged winters and ample snowfall, quick color that disappears with the frost means no worries about plant damage from road salt or piles of snow.

Tips for success

When designing entry garden plantings, adapt these techniques and you'll make your home the toast of the neighborhood.

Consider scale. Design planting areas and select plants so they don't overpower a small space. By the same token, select plants and designs that won't get lost against an imposing multistory facade.

Use structures. An entry arbor, pergola, bench, or birdbath transforms a planting bed into a focal point and destination. Choose structures to complement your home's architectural details and motifs. Position them to accent or emphasize the entry, not to overwhelm it.

Define a path. Don't allow plantings to obscure or block an entry path. Leave ample walking space—4 feet wide is ideal. If a path branches toward another part of your yard, define public and private areas with an arbor or gate.

Be artistic. Choose plants that match or complement your home's color scheme. Or, if you find a plant you can't live without and it clashes with your exterior color scheme, try giving your front door or window trim a new color that bridges the gap between offending shades.

Screen with care. In a small entry space, achieve privacy with latticework or vine-covered trellises. This type of peekaboo screen creates a shield that doesn't feel confining.

Count on containers. Prepare potted plants to provide a punch of color during seasonal downtimes. Select containers that are lightweight and easy to move. Keep them stocked with seasonally appropriate plants, or grow them elsewhere and pop them into place when the plantings look their best.

Favorite front yard flowers
Some quick color annuals have what it takes to survive life on the street. If you're designing roadside plantings, choose a few of these tough-as-nails beauties. They withstand heat and drought without missing a blooming beat.

PROFUSION SERIES ZINNIA
This mounding grower is blanketed with daisylike blooms.

PETUNIA
Groundcover types available in many colors boast true flower power.

LANTANA
Lantana stands up to intense heat and drought. Its blooms beckon butterflies.

PURPLE FOUNTAIN GRASS
Burgundy leaves add texture and movement to plantings.

AFRICAN DAISY
Flowers sparkle and shine above drought-resistant foliage.

COSMOS
Cheery blooms in bright colors dance atop feathery leaves.

ALTERNANTHERA
Colorful foliage can steal the spotlight or accent other blooming plants.

SALVIA
Choose bedding types or drought-tolerant shrubby forms.

Live large
in the great
outdoors

**Keep water
on hand**

Potted plants look their best when you provide ample water. If a hose bib isn't located near the containers in your outdoor room, add a Y-connector on the closest faucet and use a length of hose that's handy for your space.

Count on quick color to accent outdoor living areas

with inviting beauty. Nothing transforms a plain patio, an empty deck, or a poolside setting like colorful plantings placed in containers or growing in beds. A lush abundance of flowers and foliage can turn an ordinary outdoor scene into an everyday escape.

In outdoor living areas, family and friends view plantings up close, so ponder the plant combinations carefully. Seating areas are perfect places to enjoy fragrant or tiny flowers as well as unusual variegated foliage or bicolor blooms. As you select plants for outdoor living, consider size, growing conditions, insects, and color blending.

Think about plant size

When you're dreaming up plant combinations for a patio, deck, or pool, keep a few things in mind. Quick color comprises a host of plants, from toe-tickling groundcovers to towering tropicals. As you scan your outdoor living area, try to match plant size to the space. A too-large plant easily overpowers a small patio or modest deck, and a too-small plant disappears when plopped beside an Olympic-size pool.

Dig into plant information in the encyclopedia section of this book (see page 124) to focus on appropriate size choices.

With container gardens, it's somewhat easier to narrow the field of options, particularly if you purchase full-grown plants to create instant color. Research mature plant size to ensure you're not placing a too-tall plant in a too-short pot, or vice-versa. On elevated decks, avoid a top-heavy container planting, especially if your deck

faces prevailing winds. Elevated decks expose plants to intense sun and heat. Shade-loving plants like impatiens don't thrive in that type of setting.

Water gardens work well on a deck or patio, but ensure the deck load capacity can withstand the heavy weight of water.

Blossoms lure pollinators, such as butterflies, hummingbirds, and insects. Keep this in mind when selecting plants to grace seating areas, barefoot zones, or play spaces.

Mix and match

Match flower or leaf colors to fabric hues, and invest in containers that suit an outdoor room's style. For a formal note, fill several pots with the same plant. To create a casual, playful scene, mix lush, full plants and patterned foliage.

Perk up a pool

When selecting plants to grow near a swimming pool, keep the palette tight. Concentrate on a few plants, then repeat them around the pool area. Place bee-beckoning plants at least 4 feet from pool coping and seating areas to avoid accidental stings. For large pools, use tall plants and baskets hung from freestanding hooks to interject vertical interest in an otherwise level setting.

Be container savvy

Consider container alternatives. Built-in planters can be crafted to include seating. On a deck, a built-in container helps overcome wind issues. Deck rail planters provide perfect housing for seasonal color. Stand-alone containers offer endless options in terms of size, shape, material, and color. Planting in pots allows you to swap fresh seasonal color for spent plants and move freestanding containers to suit various gatherings. In narrow garden rooms, consider wall or fence planters, or explore vertical gardens, which grow as living walls.

Above left: **A trio of containers with colorful plants embraces a deck table and chairs. Staging pots together transforms individual plantings into one larger "garden."**

Above middle: **Dress a blank fence with quick color plants. When space is tight, select plants with a tidy habit so they don't sprawl from the bed into nearby lawn or outdoor living areas.**

Opposite: **Stock a small outdoor living space with quick color plants in containers. Plants, from front to back, include pink-leaf iresine, yellow black-eyed Susan, blue salvia, and tall purple fountain grass.**

Enliven the landscape

Quick color plants are the quick-change artists of landscaping, transforming existing spaces into cherished views and destinations. When incorporating annuals, tender perennials, and tropicals into your yard, you can place plants directly into the soil or let them shine in containers. Either method produces great results.

Often, your setting dictates how to proceed. In a tight side yard, for instance, you may lack space for in-ground planting beds, so you'll have to draft containers to supply quick color. Alternatively, spacious lawn flanked with a fence can easily be augmented with planting beds.

Certain areas in a home landscape lend themselves to quick color adornment: fences; walls of garages or sheds that face outdoor living spaces; narrow, unused side yards; and spots between existing plantings, such as shrubs and vegetable gardens.

Blank walls and fences
When your backyard includes the empty wall of a garage or storage shed or an expanse of fence, dress it up with wide planting beds (at a minimum, 2 feet wide) edged with curves, not soldier-straight lines. Think of that wall or fence as a backdrop.

Your job is to create a garden that steals the spotlight and relegates that structure to a supporting role.

Count on taller plants, such as tropical canna, angel's trumpet, or towering ornamental grass, to give the planting vertical appeal.

Above: **Dot the landscape with pots and planting beds brimming with color. Choose bright outdoor furnishings to enhance the display.**

Opposite left: **When there's no room for planting beds, group containers stuffed with flowers to make a splash.**

Opposite right: **Dress a fence with festive color by attaching planters. Monochromatic petunias create a formal mood.**

On a wall, add a trellis for height or stir interest by hanging cast-off window frames. With a fence, train vines to complement or camouflage the structure. Consider using hanging wall planters where you can place pockets of color. Stairstep planting heights, placing taller plants near a wall or fence and shorter ones near the bed's outer edges. Where curves swoop outward creating beds wider than 2 feet, add a stepping-stone or two to provide easy access into the bed for planting and maintenance chores.

Side yard savvy

Many homes feature a narrow side yard. Frequently, homeowners consider this tight squeeze of a space too small to merit serious landscaping, and it's demoted to a suburban no-man's-land. Despite the small square footage, this area can become a family favorite when you focus on color and comfort.

Count on containers to host quick color plants that will splash head-turning hues into the space and soften the angular edges. If you're dealing with a shadowy space, select plants with blooms and leaves in neon tones and white to give the area a sense of expanse.

Choose outdoor furnishings that suit your style and physically fit the space. You might even add a trickling wall fountain to enhance a sense of privacy and seclusion.

Accenting shrubs and vegetables

Small groups of quick color plants can skirt shrubs with a happy flounce of flowers and foliage. Avoid cultivating the soil too deeply beneath shrubs or you risk disturbing roots.

But you can tuck annuals into place to extend a shrub's season of interest and improve its contribution to the landscape. This is especially effective with spring-blooming shrubs that shift into foliage mode once flowers fade. For instance, pansies partner well with flowering quince or Japanese kerria and extend the color show into early summer.

Summer-blooming shrubs get a boost from quick color plants. Surround June-blooming mock orange with a ruffle of sweet alyssum for a pretty scene from early spring until late June.

If you're short on garden space, placing annuals around shrubs gives you another place to satisfy your green-thumb itch and experiment with color, flower form, and leaf texture.

In the vegetable garden, including quick color plants elevates a hard-working edible production to a work of art. Flowering plants also draw pollinators that help many food crops produce an abundant harvest.

ASK THE GARDEN DOCTOR

Which annuals attract pollinators?

ANSWER: Many quick color plants have nectar-rich blooms. Plant a mix of flower types to attract butterflies, hummingbirds, and bees. Single flowers: bidens, gomphrena, Mexican petunia, scaevola, and wishbone flower. Clustered blooms: ageratum, lantana, pentas, phlox, and verbena. Flower spikes: angelonia, cleome, flowering tobacco, salvia, and snapdragon.

playing with color

Blending colorful plants is a fun, exciting way to transform a landscape. Best of all, it doesn't demand painterly skill. Master a few simple tricks, then turn your inner artist loose.

p.20
COLOR CUES
Blue, red, yellow, green—designing artful plant partnerships starts with understanding the basics about color. Learn how to position color like a pro to create beautiful spaces.

p.22
DESIGN WITH COLOR
Design color-coordinated plantings using simple techniques. Choose a favorite shade, repeat hues, focus on a single color, or complement exterior surfaces.

p.26
MIX AND MATCH
Color can go monochromatic, or it can add creative tension when you pair bold opposites such as dark-hued foliage and flowers with fiery plantings.

First steps with color

As you begin to experiment with quick color plants

and call on them to accent your landscape, the first thing you'll probably be drawn to—and the first thing you'll probably wrestle with—is color. While it's easy to select plants that reflect your favorite shade or your home's exterior hue, it's much more challenging to mix and match colors to craft an eye-pleasing scene. Discover some building blocks of color and how to make hues work for you.

Responses to color

Different colors produce distinct responses. Red can be exciting, passionate, and stimulating. It can also irritate and invoke feelings of anger or violence. Yellow energizes and lifts spirits, but when used in intense shades it can also overwhelm. Blue frequently soothes and cools but may also depress or discourage. Green may induce a state of relaxation.

Above: **Pink variegated iresine and orange zinnia lay a brightly tinted foundation for a morning glory vine blanketed with blue blooms.**

Opposite: **Let colorful containers fuel plant selection. Bring a red-orange pot to life with blue-violet lobelia tumbling over its edges.**

Let these responses guide you as you select color schemes for your outdoor spaces. Calming blue, purple, and green hues are ideal for a spot where you like to relax after work or sip morning coffee on the weekends. Plan swaths of red and yellow bloomers for play spaces, swimming pools, or areas where you frequently work out or study.

Perception and color

To make the most of color in the garden, it helps to understand how we perceive different hues and tones.

For example, the human eye sees yellow faster than other colors, which is why warning signs and school buses display this color. When choosing where to place yellow in the garden, think of it as a blinking light that will quickly draw attention.

Site yellow near any possible hazards, such as steps or a pond, or position it as a subtle guide along a path or to draw the eye to a key feature such as a fountain or bench. In a bed, sprinkling yellow throughout leads the eye through the planting.

When using yellow, red, and orange colors, realize that they leap out of a scene, making things appear closer than they really are. In a large garden, these shades can foster a sense of intimacy. In smaller garden spaces, place these hot colors with care to avoid making the area appear even smaller.

An effective way to incorporate these spicy colors in a small space is to use them sparingly as accents in flower or leaf colors. Coordinate the colors with any patio furniture fabrics or containers.

Blue, green, and purple recede in the distance. They make a large garden seem even larger and can help a small garden feel like it has some serious elbow room. However, in deeply shady corners or areas with little natural or reflected light, these hues tend to disappear.

Color wheel basics
A goofproof way to design color combinations with eye appeal is by using a color wheel. This classic art tool displays the colors of a rainbow in a circle. By mixing and matching colors that are complementary, analogous, or in a triad, you'll arrange plantings with artistic ease.

Complementary colors: Located across from each other on the wheel. Examples: Blue and orange, violet and yellow, green and red.

Analogous colors (also called harmonious): Located beside each other on the color wheel. Examples: Blue and blue-violet, red and red-orange, and green and yellow-green.

Color triad: Separated by three other colors on the wheel. Examples: Red, yellow, and blue; blue-violet, red-orange, and yellow-green.

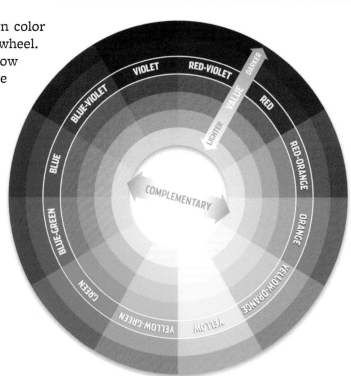

Cool colors

Blue and green create a restful, peaceful planting. An urn holding blue browallia skirted with variegated ivy and lobelia floats above boxwood hedges and blue perennial campanula.

When working with color, it helps to understand that some colors are cool while others are hot. Cool colors fall on the purple-blue-green side of the color wheel and also encompass white, gray, and silver. Warm colors include red, orange, and yellow tones. You can design a garden that caters to cool or warm colors or that melds both with artistic ease. In certain situations it's best to plant cool colors, as explained below.

Classic cool color combinations include blue and pink, a range of blues arranged in a monochromatic scheme, or purple and silver. Pastel forms of traditionally warm colors such as pink, yellow, salmon, and apricot also fit into a cool-theme garden plan.

Don't overlook leafy plants when pondering quick color groupings. Many annuals and tropicals feature foliage in blue tones, pastel hues, or white variegation patterns.

Grass or grasslike plants frequently offer cool tones, including pinkish 'Field of Dreams' or 'Tricolor' ornamental corn, ruby grass, or 'Vertigo' ornamental millet. Many coleus varieties sport leaves splashed with pink. In general, cool-color foliage plants present a well-choreographed garden when partnered with orange or yellow tones in either blooms or leaves.

White: A lone tone

White, used on its own, also falls into the cool-color category. You can partner white with warm colors to give combinations a little zest, although white tends to recede when placed with yellow. Or use white as a quiet yet robust punctuation in cool arrangements. When planted with soft blue-tone foliage or flowers and silvery hues, white absolutely sparkles. The effect is magical and enchanting, ideal for a garden viewed at dusk or by starlight.

Above: **Tresses of silver dichondra vine cascade in a cool-tone waterfall. Pair silver with pink, blue, or white to arrange a soothing scene.**

Below: **Palest pink geraniums place cool color next to violet-blue petunias, effectively turning down the visual thermometer.**

Cool-color dos and don'ts
Cool colors have their place in the garden, and when you master them, the effect is fabulous. Follow these guideliines to evoke the most impact from your quick color cool-tone plantings.

WITH WHITE AND LIGHTER HUES OF COOL COLORS:

DO PLACE PLANTS
In dark corners or shady garden situations to reflect light and illuminate the area.

In themed evening gardens or areas where night lighting dances across plants.

Against a dark backdrop such as a bank of evergreens or a deep red brick wall.

DON'T PLACE PLANTS
In beds that are primarily viewed during early to midafternoon when light is harshest, because they will appear faded.

Thickly in poolside plantings if your pool is located in full sun, for the same reason.

WITH MORE SATURATED HUES OF COOL COLORS:

DO PLACE PLANTS
Where morning sun or dappled high shade prevails.

DON'T PLACE PLANTS
In dark corners or other places where shadows linger. The colors will disappear into the darkness.

Red-hot color

Ignite your garden with quick color plantings

in warm colors: red, orange, yellow, and nearly black. These colors set outdoor scenes ablaze with fiery hues that command attention. Warm shades are frequently the colors of high summer, when heat chases the mercury upward and full sun spills freely through the garden.

When blending warm hues, stage theatrical combinations by placing full, saturated hues side by side. Smoldering red with neon chartreuse, deep wine-purple with flaming orange, deep burgundy with sassy red—these colors festoon any setting like a fiesta.

As you dream up plant blends, don't overlook orange. This color offers a range of shades from bronze to copper and tangerine, which mingle happily with other warm hues. Orange embodies versatility and manifests subtle changes depending on its partner. For instance, with a darker burgundy, a citrus orange glimmers; placed with a blue-ink tone, it merges and presents a pleasant tableau.

Color hybrids

On the color wheel, blends result where cool and warm colors meet, such as green and purple. Depending how much of a warm (or cool) hue comprises these blends, their character can shift from cool to warm. For example, a strong kelly green has more blue in it, making it a cool green. A neon lime green boasts a large yellow component, which renders it sharp and sizzling.

As you design plantings, you'll get the most pop when you pair opposites, such as a warm-tone chartreuse or yellow-green with a deep cool blue, or a red-violet with a clear yellow. The effect is vivacious and vibrant and can even convey a sense of being alive with movement.

You might not want an entire bed planted with these types of combinations, but when tucked into containers and placed in outdoor living areas or spaces viewed from indoors, these duets can make a garden sing.

Black: Another lone tone

In a recent trend for gardens, dark colors are taking center stage in the form of foliage plants with very dark leaves. These not-quite-black beauties feature deep burgundy or purple leaves that add snap to quick color plantings.

In containers or beds, darkleaf plants disappear when used in shadowy settings. Keep them in full sun and sited against a lighter background for best effect. For a never-fail pairing that gives the garden a jolt, team these dark introductions with golden-leaf plants.

You can find deep-tone leaves on many kinds of plants. Groundcovers include 'Midnight Lace' sweet potato vine and alternanthera. Look for 'Black Pearl' ornamental pepper and 'Purple Lady' iresine to fill midheight roles in color groupings. 'Mahogany Splendor' hibiscus, cordyline, and 'Purple Majesty' millet add height to plantings.

Tips for warm-color success

Like their cool-hued cousins, warm colors look their best when used in certain places in the garden. In general, warm colors strut their stuff best in full sun locations.

In shadier, low light conditions or against a dark backdrop, the more saturated (darker) versions of these hues can appear washed out and flat and even recede into the background. This is especially true of deep wine red, burgundy, brown-beige, or rusty orange, shades traditionally considered fall colors.

Above left: **Shades of yellow and green create a heat-loving display with 'Pineapple Splash' coleus, 'Taishan Gold' marigold, 'Sweet Caroline Light Green' sweet potato vine, and 'Benary's Giant Lime' zinnia.**

Above middle: **'Black Pearl' ornamental pepper and purple angelonia stage a dark backdrop that contrasts neatly with yellow lantana.**

Above right: **Celebrate orange with a monochromatic salute to this varied color. Include orange 'Zahara Double Fire' zinnia, coppery 'Henna' coleus, 'Mahogany Splendor' hibiscus, and 'Silky Scarlet' butterfly weed.**

Opposite: **Hot colors sizzle, like this blend of orange zinnia, burgundy coleus, orange-red coleus, red geranium with lime green foliage, and 'Blackie' sweet potato vine.**

Combine colors with confidence

Working with a color wheel can take

guesswork out of blending colors in the garden. You can also adopt painterly techniques to mix and match plants. For an easy way to start creating quick color plantings, focus on a favorite shade and build combinations around it.

Maybe you have a container with a unique finish or cast. Select annuals and tender perennials that complement the colors of the pot to elevate it from casual container to work of art.

In a furnished garden space or patio, let outdoor fabric guide your plant choices. Gather and arrange flowers and foliage that harmonize with the fabrics so your outdoor room shines with a polished look.

For planting areas located near your home or other structures, accessorize quick color with surrounding surface hues. You always serve a visual feast when you design with a nod to the entire view.

Above: **Color draws the eye. Here, bright pink, orange, and yellow keep the hues on the hot side of the color wheel. A few splashes of white cool down the scene.**

Opposite: **The gray of 'Icicles' licorice plant draws out the cool shades of the African daisy, phlox, and flowering cabbage.**

Repeat after me

Whether you're staging quick color in a landscape bed or in containers, repetition always wins. With a planting bed, daubing the same hue at intervals throughout the bed accomplishes several things. It serves as a rhythmic pulse that moves the eye through the bed, as well as a special accent that encourages a casual glance to become a lingering gaze. That resonating tone also acts as a unifying note, orchestrating diverse plants into a cohesive symphony of color.

In containers, using identical plants in different pots has the same effect as in a planting bed, drawing the eyes through an outdoor space or tying separate areas together. Repeating every detail of a container garden combination, especially in a pair of matching pots, fosters a formal feel.

Color-echo designing promotes your gardening efforts to a new level of artistry. A color echo occurs when you match leaf or petal hues of different plants. For instance, pairing a white-flowered New Guinea impatiens with the white spots on green leaves of 'Splash Select White' polka-dot plant outfits a striking combination. Add pink or purple sweet alyssum and you have a pot dressed in its Sunday best.

This technique offers a simple way to design with variegated leaves. 'Fireworks' fountain grass sports leaves striped in white, green, burgundy, and hot pink. Pair this upright grower with a mounding zinnia in shades of pink for a gorgeous duet. The leaves of variegated 'Tropicanna' canna paint a burgundy backdrop with stripes of pink, red, gold, and green. Echo any of those hues in a nearby plant—such as a gold black-eyed Susan or pink petunia—to ignite real summer sizzle.

The benefit of following a monochromatic theme with quick color plants is that you can design an area that's blue one season and red the next. Change is easy when the plants are single-season showstoppers.

Color values vary

For head-turning results, select a group of plants that unfurl leaves or flowers in different shades, tints, and tones of the same color. If your passion is purple, outfit an area with plants in various shades of lavender, lilac, blue-violet, eggplant, and mauve. Gardeners who love red can combine plants in tones of pink, burgundy, wine, cerise, scarlet, and other red-based hues.

You should also pay attention to a color's saturation. A saturated hue is pure and strong. In essence, it's the truest version of that color. Saturated colors carry a bold presence and even a sense of liveliness, appearing to dance as you view them. Saturated hues are clear, not muddied with tones of other colors. For instance, a pure blue is bright and bold, whereas a steel blue has more gray tones in it. As colors become less saturated, they shift toward gray.

TEST GARDEN TIP

Shop and mix

When shopping at a garden center, make a trial run of color pairings. Place plants next to one another in your cart and see what you think. Move your cart to check out the color blending in light conditions similar to those in your garden.

White, silver, and gray
Rely on white, silver, and gray to coax other colors into peaceful coexistence. These plants can act as a foil for bolder shades, casting a solid backdrop that lets strong colors shine. In small gardens or containers, these neutral-tone plants serve as fillers that complement other colors without competing.

FLOWERS

BACOPA White flowers that thrive in full sun blanket green leaves.

DIAMOND FROST EUPHORBIA The nonstop blooms are actually tiny white strappy petals.

IMPATIENS Choose white varieties for color in a shade garden.

NEMESIA During cool weather, select white nemesia as a neutral.

VINCA During hot seasons, white varieties of vinca, with flat, five-petaled flowers, seem to turn down the temperature.

FOLIAGE

CALADIUM Heart-shape leaves feature solid color veins or splotches.

'SILVER FALLS' DICHONDRA Kidney-shape silver leaves grow along cascading stems.

DUSTY MILLER Soft, silver foliage stands up to both heat and late-season frosts.

FLOWERING CABBAGE Scalloped or ruffled leaves boast silver or white splashes.

LICORICE PLANT Vining stems sport feltlike silver foliage.

seasonal show

Count on quick color to dress the growing season with ever-changing beauty. Design plantings with short-term success in mind, and you'll find every season offers new scenes to savor.

p.30
SEASONAL BEAUTY
As the seasons unfold, different plants step into the garden spotlight. Use quick color plants to make every season and planting bed consistently bright and beautiful.

p.32
SPRING
Jumpstart spring with cool-season color: presprouted bulbs and annuals that thrive despite frost. Dress spring with cheery quick color plants that linger until summer's arrival.

p.36
SUMMER
Summer coaxes a bold, incredible show from quick color plants. Tropical plants soar, and annuals explode with flower power. Learn ways to pump up the color when the mercury soars.

p.38
FALL
Continue the color in autumn by choosing plants that shine brighter as the season shifts. In planting beds or pots, switch out spent color with ready-to-grow substitutes.

p.40
WINTER
The coldest season doesn't have to stop the color display. Discover easy ideas for setting the stage for a winter show—no matter where you garden.

p.42
SEASONAL SWAPS
As seasons end, quick color plants can falter and fizzle. Make a little garden magic by dressing faded scenes with fresh plants that are rarin' to grow.

Seasonal
color

Even in gardens brimming with quick color,
the march of the seasons draws out different plants to take the spotlight. Spring's sunny afternoons and frosty nights favor annuals that can withstand cold night air. Sweltering summer days and sultry nights serve up ideal conditions for tropicals and tender perennials to thrive. Shorter days and sweater weather make autumn the season for cool-weather color. In mild-winter regions, chill-tolerant annuals can paint the town through the year's coldest months.

In each season, bulbs, perennials, shrubs, and trees also color the landscape with fabulous flowers and appealing foliage, but this show lasts only a short time compared to quick color plants. These season-long charmers supply nonstop sizzle once they're established. The performers in the quick color chorus—annuals, tender perennials, and tropicals—can sound steady notes of flower or foliage splendor throughout the season even as other plants peak and fade.

Bridge the gap
Draft quick color annuals into your arsenal of garden problem solvers. Tucked into containers or planting beds, these enthusiastic growers can fill gaps throughout the garden year when other performers are warming up in the wings or cooling down after a vigorous show.

After spring's beautiful bulb chorus takes a bow, for instance, withering foliage can range from easily ignored to eyesore status. Slip some quick color annuals, such as pansies or nemesia, among the bulbs. The fading leaves—which you should leave until they're completely dry to allow the bulb to rejuvenate—disappear amid a glee club of cheerful blooms.

The same scenario frequently unfolds throughout the growing season whenever perennials complete their bloom period. Quick color annuals sprinkled near and among perennials mask the passing splendor of perennial blooms. Tropical plants that come into their own in midsummer easily draw attention away from late-spring and early-summer growers melting in July heat.

Plan ahead
Using quick color in companion with other plantings and fillers for a strong, season-long show requires planning and forethought. Begin with annuals of the correct size so they won't overpower existing plantings or be overwhelmed by those same plantings.

It's also wise to consider flower or leaf hues when you're leaning on annuals or tender perennials for season-bridging color. Choose quick color plants intentionally, adding those that will complement or pleasantly contrast with existing beds or plants that flower later in the season. Count on quick color plants to steal the scene when other performers fade, and you'll make your garden a botanical showstopper.

Above left: **For striking summer color, count on a trio of heat-tolerant performers: variegated 'Pretoria' canna, orange lantana, and trailing golden creeping jenny (*Lysimachia nummularia*).**

Above right: **Autumn splendor holds with planters sprouting mums, dusty miller, and flowering kale.**

Opposite: **Dress spring containers and beds with floral finery that thrives in cool weather, such as viola, tulip, ranunculus, blue daisy (*Felicia*), tufted poppy (*Eschscholzia caespitosa*), and snapdragon.**

Early spring bloomers

Chilly air and cold, wet soil—hallmarks of early spring growing conditions—cause many plants to experience sluggish growth or stall completely. The annuals that grow best in spring are known as cool-season plants. These bloomers typically tolerate frost and like moist (but not soggy) soil.

This group of plants thrives when nighttime temperatures plunge. Some, like snapdragon or pansy, tolerate light freezes (29°F to 32°F). As their name implies, cool-season plants grow best during the chilly seasons: spring and fall in four-season climates, as well as winter in regions where freezes are few and far between. In areas with cool summers, these beauties shine from June through fall. Plants start to fizzle when temperatures hover in the 80°F range.

Seeds vs. seedlings

In early spring, the longest season of strongest color comes from chill-chasing bloomers grown in cell packs or 4-inch or larger pots. When temperatures are low, plants grow slowly and need little to keep them looking good.

You can start many early-season favorites

Above: **Violas earn star status when it comes to early spring color. These cheery bloomers greet the season in many shades. Perky flowers perch upon sturdy stems and withstand light frosts.**

from seed. The seeds for many plants need a chilling period to germinate. Some must freeze before seed coats crack open. Because of these requirements, certain seeds should be planted outdoors in late fall in warm regions or in very early spring—while chances of frost still linger—in colder regions. Examples of plants that germinate following a frigid period are poppy, larkspur, and bachelor's button.

Other early spring growers do best when started indoors. This group includes pansy and snapdragon. The timing for indoor sowing depends on your region's average last frost date. Follow seed packet instructions to time your plantings correctly.

X marks the spot

By siting early spring bloomers in specific locations, you'll make the most of the seasonal show. For earliest plantings in colder areas where late freezes and snow are real possibilities, tuck plants into portable containers so you can safely shift them out of harm's way should a late storm threaten. If temperatures prohibit spending time outdoors, place early spring color near entrances to your home or in areas that you frequently view from indoors.

Another great place for early spring quick color is beneath deciduous trees. Before trees leaf out, the area beneath offers full to dappled sun, making ideal growing conditions for early spring bloomers.

Perennials and early bloomers blend beautifully. Quick color plants can infuse a perennial bed full of bare shoots and young leafy growth with much-needed splashes of flowery good looks.

Consider using spring bulbs as planting partners for early spring color. They form a natural pairing in complementary colors with quick color plants. Pansies in particular provide a wide palette of bloom colors that make mixing and matching petal shades a delightfully artful endeavor.

Some plants, such as sweet alyssum and lobelia, boast both short stature and lilliputian blooms. Showcase these plants in containers or small planting areas that are viewed from a close vantage point. Unless they're planted en masse, these smaller plants disappear when inserted in a large planting bed.

Many early spring performers, including stock, sweet pea, and sweet alyssum, feature fragrant blooms. Yellow pansies and violas also often carry a strong, sweet scent. Site these perfumed bloomers in places where you can savor the aroma.

TEST GARDEN TIP

Spring pests

Pests seem to be always on the move, even in spring. Keep an eye out for aphids and slugs, which damaged the leaves of this red salvia (*Salvia splendens*). To control them, handpick the slugs or use slug bait. Wash aphids off plants with a strong spray of water.

Cool-weather beauties
Dress your garden with spring color by planting these early bloomers. Some self-sow if allowed to set seed that will sprout in following years. The success of self-seeding can vary by region, so consider saving a few seeds to sow in case nature's crop doesn't materialize.

SELF-SOWERS
CALENDULA, CALIFORNIA POPPY, NASTURTIUM, AND SWEET ALYSSUM (near right)
CORNFLOWER
FORGET-ME-NOT
LARKSPUR (far right)
LOVE-IN-A-MIST
NEMESIA

NOT SELF-SOWERS
DIANTHUS
MIMULUS
PANSY
STOCK
SWEET PEA
VIOLA

Combining with spring bulbs

Drifts of daffodils and troops of tulips

paint gorgeous spring scenes. Use that classic spring color to fill containers and small planting beds by purchasing presprouted bulbs. Tuck bulb bloomers into pots and patio gardens to jump-start the gardening season with a floral flourish of instant color.

Look for these spring harbingers in grocery stores, home centers, and discount stores. For outdoor plantings, purchase bulbs with short shoots and tightly closed buds, which won't be disturbed by an early spring chill.

If you must buy plants that have reached the ready-to-flower stage, slowly acclimatize them to frosty spring air by holding them in a cool but above-freezing garage or enclosed porch for a few days before planting outside. Otherwise, flower petals may experience cold burn, which will manifest as white splotches or brown edges.

Timing is critical for early spring bulb color. Hold off planting presprouted bulbs outdoors if their bulb siblings aren't already up for the season. For instance, if the tulips in your neighborhood aren't in bloom, the presprouted bulbs you tuck into planting beds or pots may not survive. Time your presprouted bulb plantings with existing bulb plantings. You might be able to push the season a few days, but don't expect to gain weeks.

Above: **Pansies thrive in containers or beds and make perfect partners for tulips. The blue, yellow, and pink colors selected for the plantings and furnishings seem to scream "spring."**

Two key considerations when planning quick color bulb gardens are flower color and number. Because you're purchasing budded plants, you won't know petal color for certain until blooms open. You'll have to rely on plant tags for color cues, and tags are sometimes inaccurate.

The other factor to take into account is how many plants you'll need. If you want large sweeps of color, it's more economical to plant bulbs in your garden in fall. But for containers and small bed spaces, such as entry, patio, and mailbox gardens, presprouted bulbs offer an affordable investment.

Planting companions

Pair your spring bulb quick color with other early spring bloomers. Seasonal beauties such as bachelor's button, nemesia, pansy, and viola all marry well with bulbs in pots or mixed borders. Count on sweet alyssum, ivy, creeping phlox, and dianthus to spill gracefully out of containers in a colorful cascade.

Insert clipped branches from shrubbery, such as forsythia, pussy willow, and redtwig dogwood, into containers to add height to bulb plantings.

Place a trellis in a presprouted bulb garden—either a small one in a pot or a large one in a bed—and sow sweet peas around it for fragrant, cold-tolerant vines.

Many herbs thrive in early season conditions, as do decorative edibles, such as lettuce, parsley, and chard. Blend these functional plants with bulbs for unexpected early season color.

When blossoms fade

After presprouted bulbs finish flowering, snip the bloom stems. To allow the bulb to rejuvenate itself, wait to remove the foliage until it naturally turns brown and dies.

In containers, most bulbs—except tulips, which won't readily rebloom—can be planted into your garden for future spring shows. Wait until the leaves fade before transplanting the bulbs. You can also store the bulbs in a location that's protected from extreme temperature swings, then plant them in autumn.

If you don't plan to keep presprouted bulbs, gently pull them out if you can do so without damaging nearby plants, or just cut off the leaves at soil level. Toss spent bulbs into the compost bin.

Spring fling Dress early spring with a flowery flounce of color courtesy of presprouted bulbs.

1 FILL
For best growth, fill your container with a commercial potting mix. If your container is deep, save space by placing a wad of plastic in the bottom. Blend a slow-release fertilizer into the soil. Follow label instructions carefully on fertilizer rates. Plant growth is slow in early spring; don't risk burning roots with too much fertilizer.

2 CAREFULLY PLACE
Handle quick color plants and potted bulbs carefully to avoid damaging flower buds that may be present. Plant bulbs at the same depth as they are in their existing pots.

3 WATER
Water the container after planting. Soak the soil thoroughly until water runs out the bottom of the pot. Consider mulching the soil surface if squirrels or chipmunks typically ravage your container gardens. The finished planter won't require much maintenance. Water when the soil is dry to the touch 1 inch deep; remove dead blooms so the planting looks its best.

Summer color

Summer absolutely sizzles with flamboyant flowers and foliage

when you stock your yard with quick color annuals, tender perennials, and tropicals. Many of these showstopper plants come into their own when summer heat builds, filling the garden with waves of bold color. Cool-weather beauties swoon, but heat-loving tropicals take center stage to showcase their stunning personalities.

The summer palette explodes with strong shades—bright tones of red, orange, neon pink, and gold glow against deeper, saturated purple, burgundy, wine, and russet. White blooms seem to disappear in the harsh light of day but glow during summer's evenings. Variegated leaves sparkle in sunbeams and enhance the season's tropical ambience.

Summer's all-stars include classic quick color favorites, such as sunflower, marigold, geranium, and zinnia. Advances in breeding offer the formerly unthinkable: sun-loving coleus and impatiens, branching vinca, and heat-tolerant snapdragon.

Tender perennials with tropical origins thrive as the mercury soars. This group includes butterfly attractors lantana and Mexican petunia, sprawling

Above: **Let hot colors shine as the temperatures climb. Blend New Guinea impatiens with 'Margarita' sweet potato vine, coleus, and purple scaevola, also called fanflower.**

sweet potato vine, strappy New Zealand flax, and colorful cordyline. Look for tropicals to steal the spotlight during summer's peak. Foliage favorites, such as canna, elephant's ear, and banana thrive when ample water combines with hot nights. You can almost see these plants spurt overnight when growing conditions are right.

Volunteer color

Some of summer's performers self-sow readily when allowed to ripen seeds. The roster includes cleome, flowering tobacco, cosmos, zinnia, and Texas sage (*Salvia texana*). In cool-climate gardens, many of these volunteers don't appear until early to midsummer, especially in partially shaded beds where the soil warms slowly. Some late-summer bloomers, such as flowering tobacco and scarlet sage, may not sprout until after July 4.

If you depend on any of these self-sowers to contribute a colorful presence, it's wise to purchase a few seedlings in cell packs or small pots to jump-start the flower show. By the time these plants finish flowering and ripen seeds, the self-sowers will be revving up to run their own colorful race.

Secrets to success

Coax the most color from heat-loving plants by supplying them with consistent moisture and sufficient nutrients.

Remove faded flowers to keep blossoms forming.

Keep stakes handy for tall plants not staked at planting time, such as cleome, Magilla perilla, tall ornamental pepper varieties, sunflowers, and Mexican bush sage. Summer storms can instantly batter and flatten tall quick color plants.

TEST GARDEN TIP
Spur regrowth

Revive tired, leggy annuals with a midsummer haircut. Remove up to one-half of growth by pinching or cutting. Candidates include petunia, sweet alyssum, polka-dot plant, and snapdragon.

Annuals for cool-summer locations
In some regions, summer doesn't dish up record-breaking heat and intense humidity but instead offers cool days and even cooler nights. For these areas, try these annuals that thrive when temperatures swing between 60°F and 80°F.

ANNUAL PHLOX (*Phlox drummondii*) Clustered flowers feature pink, red, white, or lavender; deadhead older varieties for continuous bloom; 6 to 9 inches tall.

DIASCIA Spurred blossoms unfurl in pink, coral, white, and lavender; 8 to 18 inches tall.

NEMESIA Self-seeding plants produce snapdragon-like blooms in a rainbow of hues; some blooms provide clove scent; 8 to 24 inches tall.

PANSY Look for flowers in hues from pastel to black; deadheading extends bloom season; 6 to 8 inches tall.

STOCK Spicy, clove-scented blooms come in shades of red, pink, white, yellow or purple; 12 to 18 inches tall.

SWEET ALYSSUM Sweetly scented flowers attract pollinators and beneficial insects; plants in white, pink, and mauve self-sow; 4 to 9 inches tall.

Fall finery

No matter where you garden,

the end of summer doesn't have to signal the end of color in the garden. Many quick color plants continue to step out with a strong flower and foliage presence deep into autumn. Some even withstand early frosts to grace Indian summer with bright and bold drama.

Reliable fall color performers include many tropical plants, such as canna, elephant's ear, ornamental peppers, and Bolivian begonia. After these heat lovers sail through a toasty summer, they coast into fall at the height of their glory until frost knocks them back. As long as they're deadheaded, tender perennials like Mexican bush sage, heliotrope, and scarlet sage continue producing flowers well into fall.

Grasses earn top billing as autumn starlets. Their foliage burnishes bronze, gold, and other fall tones. Seed heads steal the spotlight. Mexican feather grass, ruby grass, and fountain grass contribute to garden beauty as fall unfolds. Ornamental millets strut their stuff in autumn if you allow plants to ripen their stiff bottlebrush seed heads, which appeal to hungry birds.

Bloom-stopping chill

The footfall of Jack Frost on the garden's doorstep begins to close out the color season. Tropical plants and tender annuals are the first to bow out of the scene. This includes ageratum, celosia, cosmos, gomphrena, marigold, sunflower, and

Above: **Ornamental grasses steal the spotlight in fall quick color plantings. Purple fountain grass is a favorite for its dark stems and wheat-hued seedheads.**

zinnia. Half-hardy annuals—such as flowering tobacco, gazania, petunia, and salvia—can withstand a light frost (29°F to 32°F), but cease taking curtain calls when temperatures tumble to 28°F.

Typically, most plant tissue freezes when temperatures remain at 28°F for five consecutive hours. Hardy annuals, which can withstand a hard freeze (25°F), are exceptions. Bloomers in this group include baby's breath, cleome, dianthus, pansy, snapdragon, stock, and sweet pea.

It's important to note that mature hardy annuals—plants that experienced the gradual cooldown of autumn prior to frost—survive a hard freeze better than newly purchased ones accustomed to a greenhouse-sheltered life.

Plants may appear wilted and look worse for wear the morning after a hard frost, but be patient. They typically revive as the day unfolds and temperatures swing away from the freezing mark. If frost does occur, check plants early in the morning, before the sun strikes them. If you spot any frost on leaves, using water to wash it off can prevent tissue damage.

After a frost, then what?

Once a hard freeze wipes out quick color annuals and tropicals, shift into cleaning mode. Simple cleanup chores help prevent diseases and insects from overwintering in the garden and attacking next year's plants.

Pull any dead or otherwise unsightly plants and toss them on the compost pile. The exception is impatiens. If you had downy mildew disease this year, do not compost impatiens. Bag and destroy this plant matter. Read more about downy mildew on page 170.

If you plan to save tropical tubers or bulbs, such as elephant ear's, canna, or caladium, cut down damaged stems and dig roots. Learn more about overwintering tropicals on page 123.

Snip ripe seed heads of annuals that tend to self-sow (see list below). Scatter seeds in new areas of the garden.

ASK THE GARDEN DOCTOR

What can I do other than cover plants when frost is predicted?

ANSWER: Water the soil around garden plants, especially just before sundown. The water evaporates overnight, raising air temperature near the plants. Be careful with containers, however. Saturated soil in a pot packed with plants could spell disaster if the water in soil freezes. It could expand and break your container.

Self-sowing annuals
Color your garden with ease by stocking it with self-sowing beauties. If allowed to ripen and drop seeds, these plants sprout year after year, splashing serendipitous color throughout your garden. Hybrid plant seedlings won't come true to the parents. The results may prove a pleasant surprise or not worth the effort.

AGERATUM Fringed blue, buttonlike flowers are a butterfly magnet; crinkled leaves contrast in bright green; 6 to 30 inches tall.

BLACK-EYED SUSAN (*Rudbeckia hirta*) Heat- and drought-tolerant plant bears yellow flowers atop sturdy stems; 2 to 3 feet tall.

BLANKET FLOWER (*Gaillardia*) Deer-resistant flowers appear in bright shades on heat- and drought-tolerant plants; 1 to 2 feet tall.

CLEOME Tall stems sport large blossom spikes of whiskery flowers in white and shades of rose and purple; 2 to 4 feet tall.

FLOWERING TOBACCO (*Nicotiana*) Star-shape blooms come in red, white, chartreuse, pink, or purple; 1 to 6 feet tall, depending on type.

PETUNIA A bedding favorite with trumpet-shape blossoms in a host of hues; plants trail, ideal for planters or beds; 6 to 12 inches tall.

SWEET ALYSSUM Sweetly scented white, pink, or mauve flowers; plants self-sow readily; 2 to 10 inches tall.

VERBENA BONARIENSIS Lavender-pink flowers top tall, willowy stems; butterflies can't resist blossoms; a wonderful cut flower; 2 to 4 feet tall.

Winter show

Even the coldest season can host a color transformation. After freezes wipe out quick color plants, you may want to leave some areas of the garden empty as you head into winter.

In containers and planting beds in highly visible areas, consider replacing tender annuals with chilly-weather favorites. What you use to stage a winter color display largely depends on where you live.

In regions with mild winters, fill the garden and containers with hardy annuals that can withstand frost or even a hard freeze. Flowering cabbage and kale continue to display arresting leaves as cold weather lingers. Nemesia, pansy, snapdragon, stock, sweet alyssum, and viola persist as temperatures tumble. These colorful plants can dress wintry scenes with summer-worthy hues.

Above: **Stir some holiday spirit by decking a window box with festive elfin shrubs, including dwarf cedar, false cypress, 'Rheingold' white cedar, and winter heather.**

Employ grasses to fill roles in the winter color production. With or without seed heads, grasses can dress a garden or container throughout the cool months, adding color, movement, and texture.

Succulents and herbs show strong staying power after frost arrives, especially when they're tucked into planting beds. In a mild climate, rosemary, oregano, and scented geraniums infuse the winter garden with living greenery.

When winter brings snow

In frigid areas, celebrate the garden's quiet season by stuffing containers and window boxes with materials that stand up to snowfall. Gather a mix of needled evergreen boughs, berried branches, bristly pinecones, and waving grain seed heads to create an attractive display.

Leafless branches of cardinal or yellow dogwood give winter container arrangements colorful height. Clip broadleaf evergreens, such as holly, mountain laurel, boxwood, and rhododendron, to introduce different textures. Branches of trees that hang onto leaves through winter—like beech and some oaks—infuse containers with added structure and interest.

Creating winter pageantry

Follow these tips to make the most of winter creations composed of garden gleanings.

Place cuts carefully. When gathering branches from living plants, remember that you're pruning. Don't leave stubs; place cuts just beyond side branches. Try to prune evenly.

Plunge stems into water. If you won't arrange immediately, store stems in a bucket of tepid water in a cool place like an unheated shed.

Limit water loss. Spray evergreens with an antidesiccant (sometimes called an antitranspirant), which slows water loss from stems. This keeps greens fresher longer.

Create holes in soil. If the soil in containers is a solid root mass, shove a screwdriver into the soil to create holes to hold stems.

Thaw frozen soil. When an early freeze turns soil into stone, pour warm water for a gentle thaw. To avoid cracking the container, thaw just enough to permit shoving stems into the soil.

TEST GARDEN TIP

Dress up soil

In winter containers, cover bare soil with material that enhances the display when snow isn't present. Try sphagnum moss, pine straw, reindeer moss (from crafts stores), pinecones, or stones.

Quick winter color
Set the stage for garden drama by filling containers with winterproof materials. Choose a container that's equally winter-hardy. Concrete, stone, cast iron, wood, and fiberglass fit the bill. Moss-lined metal hayracks and baskets also survive winter weather.

FOR THE BIRDS Design a beak-pleasing buffet in a metal stand overflowing with seedy treats. Create a background of evergreen boughs so seed heads stand out.

ABUNDANT BEAUTY Red winterberry branches shine in an arrangement of mixed broadleaf and needle evergreens. Scarlet rose hips contribute to the textural creation.

FORMAL FINERY Classic four-part harmony sings in an elegant container featuring a miniature boxwood, evergreen branches, pinecones, and moss.

Bridging the seasons

Cool-season plants like viola and sweet alyssum inject color into a garden during that awkward time between the finale of spring perennials and the debut of summer plants.

The change in seasons spells occasional gaps

in color. Public gardens, theme parks, and city landscapers rely on seasonal renovation to ensure a botanical show guaranteed to turn heads. Adapt this technique to suit your yard's planting areas, and stage a magic show of bud and bloom that looks terrific in every season.

Spring to summer changeouts

In spring, quick color plants can camouflage fading bulb foliage. These companions display flowery ribbons in places where summer perennials have yet to join the summer tapestry.

Trailing or sprawling plants such as sweet alyssum, bacopa, or Swan River daisy earn their keep between seasons, filling in holes until summer plants, including tropicals and perennials, establish an eye-catching presence.

Early season annuals may rebound in summer if cut back by one-half to one-third. Others won't survive sultry summer days and should be sliced at soil level and composted.

To learn which tactic to use, check with your local cooperative extension office or garden center, or simply wait and see what happens. Spreading perennials and tropicals often shade early season annuals, which quietly disappear.

Summer to fall

For fall plantings in chilly regions, invest in the largest plants you can afford because once you plant them, they're not likely to grow much bigger. Growing conditions aren't suitable for plant size to increase. Pansies and sweet alyssum will flower to beat the band even when night temperatures regularly tumble into the upper 20s, but they won't increase much in size.

When you're making any garden swap between seasons, toss discarded plants on your compost pile. If you have a soft heart and can't stand throwing out good plants, gently set them on the top of the pile, give them a quick drink of water, and then let them swoon gracefully into botanical oblivion.

A seasonal pause in pots

Containers planted with small annuals in early spring will probably experience a bit of awkwardness in late spring to early summer when pots show a few bare spots.

During this intermission, it's wise to protect bare soil from birds or rodents, such as chipmunks and squirrels. They can dislodge and even toss plants with their excavations.

For a severe problem, cover the soil with a physical barrier, such as netting or chicken wire. In most cases, disguising the bare soil surface with a layer of composted leaves or shredded bark is sufficient.

TEST GARDEN TIP

Plant and pinch

At planting time, pinch the growing tips of annuals to increase branching. Pinching also increases the number of future flowers.

Gap-filling color Avoid awkward pauses in your garden's symphony of color as it plays through the seasons. Slip a few of these bloomers into planting beds to bridge the gaps.

SPRING
LOVE-IN-A-MIST
MIMULUS
NASTURTIUM
SHIRLEY POPPY
SNAPDRAGON

SUMMER
AFRICAN DAISY
CALIBRACHOA
IMPATIENS
NIEREMBERGIA
TUBEROUS BEGONIA

FALL
BLACK-EYED SUSAN
DUSTY MILLER
ORNAMENTAL GRASSES
SALVIA
ZINNIA

NASTURTIUM

SUPERBELLS GRAPE PUNCH CALIBRACHOA

ZINNIA

Seasonal swaps

Recruit annuals, bulbs, and perennials as quick-change
artists to help a front-and-center container garden segue gracefully through the seasons. Entry gardens take many forms, and you don't need vast square footage to display head-turning color. A large planter or a pair of planters can extend a cozy welcome.

To succeed with a year-round front porch container garden, think big. A large container easily weathers the seasons, even frigid winters, and has enough legroom for a small, slow-growing evergreen. In cold regions,

Above: **A mix of boxwood and pine boughs skirts a dwarf Alberta spruce with in this entry planter. A red-berried garland stirs holiday spirit. See the next page for other seasonal suggestions.**

focus on containers that stand up to winter weather, such as stone, concrete, wood, or resin.

Think green

Building a year-long design around a living evergreen ensures steady color no matter where the calendar lands. To headline your container, select an evergreen that's hardy to at least two Zones colder than where you garden.

For instance, if you're in Zone 5, the evergreen needs to be hardy to Zone 3 to guarantee winter survival. Slow-growing evergreens that can thrive in containers include dwarf Alberta spruce, 'Sky Pencil' holly, topiary juniper, mugo pine, and Japanese umbrella pine.

Growing evergreens in containers is challenging, but you can improve your odds of success by providing proper winter care.

Because evergreens don't go dormant, they need water until the soil freezes. During a thaw, irrigate again. Resume spring watering as soon as the soil thaws. In the coldest regions, this will likely occur before you garden outdoors.

Insulate the container with bubble wrap, straw, or burlap stuffed with leaves to improve winter survival. It also helps to give container evergreens light shade. Spraying them with an antidesiccant helps reduce winter moisture loss through needles or leaves.

Making the switch

Refresh a container whenever plants look tired. Follow these tips when renovating:

Remove spent plants. Use a sharp or serrated knife to slice through roots to free them. Try not to cut too deeply into the root ball, which is likely to hold the interlaced roots of plants you want to save.

Add fresh potting soil. Fill holes and refresh the footing for all plants. Mixing compost with the soil is a good idea.

Prune existing plants as needed. Take care when you prune tall plants in fall. In cold regions, they lack sufficient time to rebound if cut back severely.

Fertilize plants after repotting. Mix a slow-release organic fertilizer into the soil to give plants a nutritional boost without the risk of burning roots.

An all-year show Embrace seasonal shifts by replacing spent plants with fresh beauties that celebrate the new season. An anchor plant, such as this dwarf Alberta spruce, provides continuity.

SPRING Tulips, daffodils, and pansies contrast nicely with the dark spruce. Leaf lettuce offers an edible treat that adds texture and beauty to the container.

SUMMER A simple plant palette stages a lavish production. Colorful additions include New Guinea impatiens, celosia, and 'Troy Gold' plectranthus.

FALL Purple-tinted garden mums pair artfully with the gold plectranthus. Flowering cabbage infuses another layer of purple-pink tones into the scene.

design tips

Every quick color success starts with simple tenets that take the guesswork out of garden design. Adapt these basics to reflect your personal flair and make plantings sing.

p.48
BASIC PRINCIPLES
Design eye-pleasing plantings by relying on simple tricks of the trade. Plant by height, and learn tips for creating planting beds. Use focal points to command attention.

p.52
TEXTURES AND SHAPES
Elevate quick color plantings to artistic levels by blending plants based on leaf and flower texture. Discover how to integrate and play with plant shapes to produce beautiful plantings.

p.56
FABULOUS FOLIAGE
Discover the wonderful world of foliage plants. These leafy beauties can steal the spotlight with their colors, patterns, textures, and shapes. Glean tips for success with foliage.

p.58
SUMPTUOUS SUCCULENTS
Count on succulents to infuse quick color plantings with sculptural flair. These thick-leaved plants are ideal candidates for containers. Get inspired by a showcase of succulents in pots.

p.60
QUICK AND EASY VINES
Celebrate fast-growing beauty by including vines in your quick color plantings. Climbers add vertical interest to beds and containers, and they don't need much ground to strut their stuff.

Plant by height

Whether you're planting in beds or containers, you create harmonious, eye-pleasing scenes when you arrange plants by height. The simplest approach is following a short-to-tall format, with ground-hugging plants tucked along bed edges and taller plants anchoring the back of the border. This tried-and-true method works wonderfully in planting areas with a distinct front and back.

For containers or island beds viewed from all sides, tweak the technique by placing the tallest plants toward the center of the planting. Then stairstep plantings outward from the center, placing the shortest plants along pot or bed edges.

Choose plants in scale

When selecting plants, keep them in scale with their surroundings. For instance, if a bed skirts a 4-foot-tall fence, add plants that will stretch a little above the fence posts. If you select plants that don't even reach the top of the fence, the structure will seem more prominent and may even appear to cage plants in.

Once you select the tallest plant, stairstep heights down from there. A general rule is to step down the heights by half. So, underplant a 6-foot 'Pretoria' canna with a 3-foot-tall orange-flowered zinnia. Purple-tone ageratum or a gomphrena that

Above: **Stairstep plant heights in beds to craft classically beautiful designs. With its lofty size, canna is an ideal back-of-the-border plant. Marigolds work well as edging plants.**

Opposite: **Trailing plants, like yellow lantana and 'Blackie' sweet potato vine, work well along pot edges. 'Tropicanna' canna anchors the center or the back. Orange marigolds occupy the middle height.**

tops out at 18 inches strike a pretty pose next to the zinnia. To supersize the planting, place an even taller castor bean or sunflower behind the canna.

If you don't have a structure to influence your plant height selection, select the tallest plant so it is equal to half the width of the planting area. When choosing plants to surround a birdbath or sculpture, pick plants no more than two-thirds the height of the object they will surround.

When you purchase plants at the garden center, try to find large plant specimens to stage side-by-side comparisons. You can still purchase smaller plants to save money, but you'll be able to see their scale in relationship to one another.

If you goof on scale and pair a tall banana with a creeping verbena, the look may be more cartoonish than attractive. Luckily, it's easily remedied. You can always pull and replant or add more midsize plants between the two.

Less-forgiving scale mistakes occur when choosing an arbor or sculpture. If you err on the too-big side, you'll have to live with an object that looks like it escaped from a giant's garden, and it will overshadow your plantings. If you select an item that's too small, plantings will overwhelm it, and it will struggle to be seen.

TEST GARDEN TIP

Trailers as groundcovers

When you need to cover ground, consider trailing plants. While they look great cascading out of a container, they apply that same growth habit to create a colorful carpet in planting beds. Good choices include spreading petunia (such as Wave), bidens, creeping zinnia, and purple heart.

Size it up
While size is relative, in general you can count on these quick color annuals and tender perennials to fill holes in a planting design for tall, medium, and short plants.

TALL (48 TO 72 INCHES)
ANGEL'S TRUMPET
'MAHOGANY SPLENDOR' HIBISCUS
SUNFLOWER

MEDIUM (18 TO 48 INCHES)
CLEOME
COLEUS
MAGILLA PERILLA

SHORT (4 TO 18 INCHES)
IMPATIENS
PETUNIA
VINCA

CASTOR BEAN

BLUE ANISE SAGE

AGERATUM

ORNAMENTAL MILLET

ZINNIA

CREEPING ZINNIA

Planting beds and focal points

Designing a planting area to host quick color

plants doesn't have to be difficult. Sometimes nearby elements such as a driveway, sidewalk, or patio define the bed dimensions. Other times, you're free to create. Just remember to consider your own budget and time available for maintenance.

You should also think about the ambience you're trying to create. A formal bed typically features straight lines, while an informal look needs curves.

In formal gardens, the layout of planting beds and the way those clearly defined lines interact plays almost as important a role as the plantings. In an informal garden, the plants themselves shine in beds of any shape.

Your yard's dimensions influence how large planting areas can be. Those, in turn, dictate the types and number of plants you can use. If you're working with a narrow bed area—less than 2 feet deep—you'll be limited to arranging plants in two tiers. If you can squeeze out another foot, the potential for plant combinations increases because you can work with at least three layers of plants to fill the bed. Add stepping-stones in beds wider than 2 feet so you have easy access for plant maintenance.

Focal points

A focal point in the garden acts like a traffic light, commanding attention and directing visual traffic. When placed in the front of a planting bed, a focal point draws the eye to the bed and hints at more to come. Sited in the rear of a planting area, that same focal point beckons the eye to travel the bed, taking in all plantings along the visual journey. You can apply the philosophy of focal points to a patio, porch, or outdoor room, using one object within the space to capture and target interest.

Above: **Quick color plants underscore a focal point in a planting bed. In this setting, pale pink wax begonias complement a bright pink tree rose.**

In a typical garden, a focal point might be an object such as an arbor, trellis, fountain, or sculpture. It could be a small tree or planting bed. An outdoor living area or bench could function as a focal point, especially if it creates a place to pause in the midst of a larger space such as a backyard. A planting bed, whether an island floating on a sea of lawn or a classic fence-skirting area, can equally lure the eye and forge a frame of focus.

You can recruit plants to fill the role of focal point. Make sure your selection is a standout beauty. Quick color plants, with their flamboyant personalities, are ideal choices. A focal-point plant should provide a strong and steady flower show or striking foliage that contrasts with its surroundings. Typically these commanding plants blend stature and beauty, especially if placed among other plantings or rising from an island bed.

Plantings play a role in showcasing a structural focal point. When you surround a focal point with quick color that complements its hue or shape, you magnify the object's size. In the same way, if you select plants that create an artful friction, the focal point appears larger because the plantings become part of the view. Color or texture contrasts easily achieve this effect. Consider the leaf texture of caladiums surrounding a latticework trellis or a fiery coleus against a copper obelisk.

Pots as focal points

Use a container packed with quick color plantings as a focal point. The container may stand alone or hold court over other colorful plantings in a bed. Either a showy container or its plantings can take center stage. A container may offer the only solution for growing plants in a particular spot. Whatever the reason, it's okay to give a container top billing. Adapt one of these ideas for focal-point pots in your garden.

PASTELS ON A PEDESTAL Elevate a pot in a planting bed to create a striking focal point. The easiest way to lift a pot above the surrounding plantings is with a pedestal. You may have a formal stone or concrete column, or you could improvise your own lift device using an inverted pot or bricks. Make sure any pedestal used is sturdy enough to support the weight of your fully planted container.

BASKET OF BLOOMS Hanging baskets always cause a stir in the garden when they hoist color heavenward. Display baskets from arbors, porches, tree limbs, or dedicated display posts. Baskets grow best when plants receive even amounts of light. If the sun strikes your basket from only one side, give the basket a half-turn every three days. A swivel makes this task easy.

FLOWERS IN VIEW Window boxes transform every outward glance into a garden view. Choose window boxes that are as wide as your window, or wider. For a window with shutters, boxes should reach from the middle of one shutter to the other. Fill your box with plants in hues that complement your home's exterior. Learn about hanging window boxes on page 73.

Plant textures
and shapes

The big selling point with quick color plants

is—no surprise—their color. Brightly hued petals and luxuriously tinted leaves make them welcome additions to any outdoor setting. No matter what palette you favor, you can find quick color plants to complement it. But when you dig into the wonderful world of texture and plant shape, you really fill your yard with botanical drama.

Texture

When referring to plants, texture encompasses multiple aspects. The visual appearance of a plant as it relates to touch—how it appears to feel—is one facet of texture. Ageratum blooms, for example, have a soft, fuzzy appearance and feel. Wax begonia leaves look like they've been dipped in molten wax and feel cool, slick, and slippery to the touch. 'Silver Lace' dusty miller leaves tickle with delicate featherlike divisions.

The size of individual leaves or flowers also helps define a plant's texture. Plants with large leaves or flowers, such as elephant's ear or hibiscus, contribute a bold texture to plantings. The small leaves or blooms of plants such as bidens and viola convey a fine texture.

In general, plants fall into three textural classes: coarse, fine, and medium.

Coarse-texture plants feature big leaves and blooms. Canna, elephant's ear, and banana are quintessential examples.

Fine-texture plants boast delicate, diminutive leaves and blossoms. Leaves may have a ferny look or be finely divided. Nierembergia and sweet alyssum typify classic fine-texture plants, as do thinner-leaf grassy plants, like Mexican feather grass and sedges.

Medium-texture plants produce flowers and foliage somewhere in between coarse and fine, and can often go both ways. Beside some plants,

they appear fine textured; alongside others, they show their coarse side. For instance, a black-eyed Susan appears coarse textured beside a fine-texture cosmos. But use it as a flounce around a stocky castor bean, and it appears light and airy.

The stage of a plant's growth also plays a role. From a foliage standpoint, strawflower seems to be fine textured, but when the chunky, papery blooms open, it appears coarse. Other plants, like airy Diamond Frost euphorbia or cleome, or chunky New Zealand flax or caladium, offer reliably steady textures, no matter the season or growth stage.

One secret to arranging stunning quick color plantings lies in combining different textures. When you place contrasting textures side by side, the result is plant magic. You can also manipulate space with plant texture. Place fine-texture plants in the rear of a planting bed to lend a sense of spaciousness. Conversely, you can shrink the appearance of a large space by using coarse-texture plants at the far side of a bed.

Plant shape

As you blend plant colors, sizes, and textures, consider plant shape, as well. Some plants hug the ground while others form a rounded mound in the garden.

Brazilian verbena, for example, appears to float through other plantings as a colorful cloud. Spiky plants offer strongly upright, sturdy forms. Fountainlike plants rise and fall like their namesake, creating a cascade effect. Larger-than-life, in-your-face plants are the ones you can't miss.

Mix and match plant shapes to infuse quick color plantings with lively interest. When you blend shapes, you design aesthetically pleasing planting areas that boast artistic flair and ooze with charm.

Above left: **Canna and sweet potato vines both feature broad leaves, but they work well together because of the differences in plant height.**

Above middle: **Spiky 'Duet' New Zealand flax contrasts artfully with the small, narrow leaves of Callie Yellow calibrachoa and Profusion Fire trailing orange zinnia.**

Above right: **The long, narrow stems of purple Brazillian verbena wend through and between other plants.**

Opposite: **Varying leaf textures of asparagus fern, coleus, canna, and Magilla perilla create a pleasing planting.**

Quick color plant shapes

Use this handy shape guide to create

showstopping designs with quick color plants. Follow the suggestions for mixing and matching shapes, or come up with your own groupings.

Sprawlers

Sprawlers hug the ground or trail over the edge of a container. They form pools of color. In the landscape, they spread across the soil and offer a firm foundation for other plants. They look terrific paired with short spikes or short rounded mounds. For intense combinations, focus on sprawling plants with consistent color such as bright foliage selections or nonstop bloomers.

Rounded mounds

These plants form orbs that play counterpoint to spiky plants and harmonize with sprawlers. A rounded mound typically has a height and spread that are nearly equal. A mounding plant may be short, such as pansy or shamrock, or it may be knee-high or taller, like lantana or blanket flower. Some form dense clumps; others grow in a looser shape.

Misty plants

These plants appear to float, showcasing the silhouettes of nearby plants. Misty plants make good fillers because their airy stems form a pool of color in midair. Their hazy growth softens the rigid lines of spiky plants and the intensity of bold plants. A large misty plant can provide a resting place for the eye.

Spiky plants

Spikes have an upright form that directs the eye upward. Typically, their growth is more up than out. They may require staking; sometimes stems don't stay rigid, especially when flowers form. Group them to make a statement. Pair them with rounded mounds, fountains, or bold plants for a good-looking planting.

Fountain plants

Fountain plants erupt from the soil with a cluster of stems that rise and bow at the ends. Stems create a cascade of foliage, or blossoms form a fountain effect. These plants pair well with bold plants or spikes. They look lovely in complementary or contrasting hues as they stand above from sprawling plants. Place them in tall pots to showcase the flowing effect.

Bold plants

Bold plants have ambitious attributes such as height, leaf size, or vivid hues. These plants quickly command attention no matter where they're placed. Some are small but mighty due to dramatic coloration. Choose partners in colors and forms that complement these grand growers.

SPRAWLERS

CREEPING ZINNIA Miniature sunflowerlike blooms on a heat-tolerant plant; 4 to 12 inches tall, 10 to 14 inches wide.

LOBELIA Small fan-shape flowers in purple, white, lavender, or rose; sun or part shade; 5 to 12 inches tall, 8 to 12 inches wide.

MOSS ROSE Bright hues of pink, orange, yellow, rose, white and more on a drought-tolerant, heat-loving plant; 8 to 12 inches tall, 10 to 16 inches wide.

ALSO:
DICHONDRA
NIEREMBERGIA
PETUNIA

ROUNDED MOUNDS

COLEUS Foliage for sun or shade in various shades, including bi- and tricolor patterns; 6 to 36 inches tall, 12 to 28 inches wide.

IMPATIENS Shade favorite; the double form of *Impatiens walleriana* grows roselike blossoms in pink, red, orange, or white hues; 8 to 16 inches tall, 8 to 20 inches wide.

LANTANA Butterfly-luring flowers in shades of gold, pink, lavender, or red; blooms change color as they age; 12 to 36 inches tall, 12 to 36 inches wide.

ALSO:
BLANKET FLOWER
BROWALLIA
MELAMPODIUM

MISTY PLANTS

BABY'S BREATH Airy, deer-resistant beauty with fine leaves and abundant flowers in pink tones; 6 to 12 inches tall, 8 to 12 inches wide.

COSMOS Ferny foliage topped with daisylike flowers in white, pink, or red shades; 1 to 6 feet inches tall, 1 to 2 feet wide.

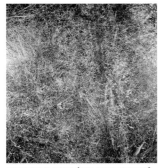

LOVEGRASS (ERAGROSTIS) Drought-resistant native grass with blue-green leaves topped with tan- to straw-color wispy seed heads; 3 to 4 feet tall and wide.

ALSO:
CLEOME
BRAZILIAN VERBENA

SPIKY PLANTS

CORDYLINE Straplike burgundy leaves for part sun to sun locations; 18 inches to 5 feet tall, 18 inches to 8 feet wide.

MEALYCUP SAGE Purple, blue, or white blooms top plants in full sun; 18 to 24 inches tall, 12 to 18 inches wide.

SNAPDRAGON Snapping blossoms in tones of maroon, red, pink, white, yellow, orange, or bicolors; most flower best in cool weather; 18 to 20 inches tall, 12 to 18 inches wide.

ALSO:
ORNAMENTAL CORN
PERSIAN SHIELD
NEW ZEALAND FLAX
WHEAT CELOSIA

FOUNTAIN PLANTS

BOLIVIAN BEGONIA Red-orange blooms blanketing narrow green leaves in full sun to part shade; hummingbird lure; to 20 inches tall and wide.

FIBER OPTIC GRASS Soft, green leaves tipped with a beadlike structure; for part to full sun; 6 to 8 inches tall, 18 to 20 inches wide.

PURPLE FOUNTAIN GRASS Purple seed heads rise from bronze-burgundy leaves; 2 to 5 feet tall, to 4 feet wide, depending on variety.

ALSO:
ACACIA
ELEPHANT GRASS
SLENDER HAIR GRASS

BOLD PLANTS

AFRICAN MARIGOLD Large, rounded flower heads in gold, yellow, or orange; ideal for mass plantings; 10 to 36 inches tall, 8 to 10 inches wide.

CASTOR BEAN Reddish or purple palmate leaves on towering plants; extremely poisonous seeds borne in prickly capsules; 3 to 15 feet tall, 3 to 5 feet wide.

ELEPHANT'S EAR Large leaves that resemble the ear of an elephant in green or purple tones or variegated patterns; tropical looking; 2 to 6 feet tall, 18 inches to 4 feet wide.

ALSO:
BANANA
CANNA
CARDOON

Fabulous foliage

Focus on flowers when designing quick
color beds and containers and you'll come up with inspiring, exciting plantings. Add a few colorful foliage plants, and your designs become compelling. Brightly or darkly tinted leaves inject quick color plantings with a strong dose of steady color that enriches over time as plants mature and fill in.

A shade for every palette
You can find a leaf in any hue you desire, from deep, dark shades of near-black to glowing golds, elegant silvers, sizzling pinks, and cool blues. Sedges sprout leaves in metallic tones of copper and bronze. Of course, there are greens aplenty.

Above: **Foliage plants like sweet potato vine and variegated coleus infuse a planting with color that won't dissipate through the growing season.**

For adventure, dip into variegated leaf offerings. Look for classic green stripes paired with gold, white, pink, or red. Blood banana leaves feature maroon splotches on a green background. 'Tropicanna' canna foliage unfurls with stripes of chartreuse, red, pink, gold, and green.

Try the infinite colorwheel choices of coleus, which mix and match hues in innumerable combinations. Pink, green, gold, near-black, red, bright chartreuse, and multiple blends of those shades outfit coleus leaves with style.

Working with foliage

At times you may want to focus solely on leaf color when planting pots or landscapes. For instance, a variegated canna underplanted with the fresh green of asparagus fern and a dark sweet potato vine ignites an explosive, season-long color show.

At other times, you may want to place a foliage favorite as the focal point of the planting. Match its tints with blooms or foliage in complementary colors for stunning combinations.

Leafy plants can also serve as accents. This technique works well with gold-foliage plants. Their bright, attention-grabbing leaves pop when paired with darker blooms or foliage. In a shade garden, gold foliage shines and is smartly visible.

Variegated plants offer patterns that can be difficult to partner in the garden, but you'll never go wrong using a petal in a complementary hue.

'Field of Dreams' ornamental corn underplanted with saturated pink impatiens composes a pleasing melody in a pot or planting bed. Marry a tangerine African daisy with purple fountain grass and a deep purple trailing verbena, and you have a flamboyantly fun planting.

Site them right

As you make plans to incorporate quick color foliage in your garden designs, double-check plant tags to determine light needs. Some plants only develop and maintain bold leaf colors in full sun. Others require part shade or even deep shade for their tones to shine.

In general, plants with leaves bearing white or creamy patterns tolerate shady conditions. Leaves with gold, purple, or reddish hues stage a stronger color show in sun but frequently thrive in light shade. With some plants, especially the ones that color most in sun, tucking them into a bit of light shade can slightly tone down the pigment. Take care in placing golden-leaf charmers in full sun in sandy or dry soil. If plants dry too much, leaves are likely to scorch.

No matter where they are planted, foliage plants benefit from a nitrogen-rich fertilizer, unless they're growing in a pot with flowering annuals. In that case, if you're encouraging flower bud formation with a bloom booster, that also is sufficient for leafy beauty.

Love those leaves
Foliage plants daub consistent pigments into quick color plantings. Like many other plants, they also come in three basic categories: thrillers, which introduce height to plantings; fillers, which grow at a medium height and have a rounded shape; and spillers, which cascade out of containers or happily ramble along the soil surface.

CORDYLINE

THRILLERS
BANANA
CANNA
NEW ZEALAND FLAX
ORNAMENTAL CORN
ORNAMENTAL MILLET
PERSIAN SHIELD

IRESINE

FILLERS
ACALYPHA
CALADIUM
COLEUS
RUSH
SEDGE
VARIEGATED GERANIUM

PLECTRANTHUS

SPILLERS
DICHONDRA
FIBER OPTIC GRASS
LICORICE PLANT
PURPLE HEART
SWEET POTATO VINE
TRAILING COLEUS

Sumptuous
succulents

When you plant succulents,
you dress outdoor spaces with living
sculptures. Succulents are the camels of the
plant world, bearing thick, fleshy leaves that store
water. These textural beauties hail from regions
as diverse as tropical Mexico and cooler Europe.

Low-maintenance color

Succulent leaves showcase a variety of subtle
hues: gray, green, blushing pink, blue-green,
and silver. In many plants, the leaves form tidy
pincushions perched on nonexistent (or nearly
so) stems. Other types have leaf-studded stems
that sprawl along the soil and sometimes tumble
over pot edges in cascades of foliage.

The leaves aren't just colorful. They vary
immensely in form and texture. Some leaves are
waxy while others resemble smooth stones. Still
others are furry or shiny and smooth while some
bear long hairs that blanket leafy rosettes with
what appear to be ancient, thick cobwebs.

Succulent savvy

These water hoarders boast undemanding
dispositions, producing leaves that store water,
reducing the plants' irrigation needs. Roots don't
sink too deeply, giving succulents versatility
in growing sites. Not only can they survive in
shallow soil, but they do so in spots where the soil

is inhospitable and temperatures sizzle, such as
planting areas near the street or along concrete
paths or driveways.

Succulents are ideal candidates for containers,
especially unglazed terra-cotta, which permits air
flow to roots. Many plants grow no higher than
4 to 8 inches, another reason they're well-suited
to containers.

These water-storing jewels aren't difficult to
grow, and a tough-as-nails constitution makes
killing them a feat. The surest way to premature
death is via overwatering. Irrigate plants sparingly
but before the leaves shrivel.

In containers, tuck succulents into a mixture
blended with equal parts enriched potting soil and
sand. For a decorative touch, top the soil mix with
polished stones, river rock, or sand.

Succulents reproduce themselves in various
ways. Some types generate tiny plantlets at or near
their base. Others produce runners that form small
plants at their tips. Over time, as succulents form
miniature versions of themselves, the original
planting can become crowded to the point of
overflowing. When tiny new plantlets appear
firmly rooted in the soil, snap or cut the runner
stem near the tiny plant, then dig and transplant.

Above left: **Succulents
in containers add color to
areas on decks and
porches where the sun
bakes other plantings.**

Above middle: **The low-
maintenance nature of
succulents lends itself to
success when the plants
are unusual forms, like a
living wreath.**

Above right: **Succulent
plant forms embody
diversity, from rose-
suffused, ruffled cups to
trailing stems with button
leaves or spiky blades
edged in glowing gold.**

Opposite: **Shallow-rooted
succulents can thrive—
and even flower—in
containers with little
room for soil.**

Quick and easy vines

If you're looking for a stellar return on investment in the garden, buy a packet of annual vine seeds. Once these gravity-defying plants wrest their way through soil, they rocket toward the sun, gaining inches by the day. Some vines grow so quickly that they barely stop to unfurl their leaves before resuming their mad dash toward open sky.

Vines don't gobble lots of garden real estate. You can grow most in a modest spot—less than a foot wide—and they still reach mature heights and create exclamation points of living color. As vines blanket their supports, they form seasonal hedges that can disguise unsightly views, shield a spa or swimming pool, or supply a little privacy for a patio.

Above: **Morning glory twines its way up supports as it heads skyward. Pretty trumpet-shape blooms greet the day in many hues, including purple, pink, blue, white, and bicolors.**

Lend some support

As vines hoist themselves heavenward, their limber stems twine, twirl, and twist along the nearest support. When you add quick color vines to your garden, you must also consider a support system for these acrobatic beauties.

A structure can be as simple as a bamboo tepee or prefabricated trellis. You might choose to create a custom support made of cedar or copper or invest in an elaborate three-dimensional structure, like a tuteur or pergola.

Narrow your choices by understanding how the vine you intend to plant scrambles skyward. Some vines, like morning glory and moonflower, wrap stems around supports on their trek to the sun. Sweet pea and cup-and-saucer vine climb by twirling tendrils around supports.

At times, any of these climbers will also grab onto nearby plants and quickly cover them in their quest for upward mobility. Keep an eye on nearby shrubs, trees, perennials, and other quick color plants when you are growing vines. Physically move all vine stems toward the support system and away from plant neighbors to protect them from a hostile takeover.

Firmly anchor the vine's support into the soil. When a simple bamboo trellis is blanketed with leaves, stems, and blossoms, it offers substantial wind resistance. If trellises aren't firmly footed, summer storms can easily wrestle them to the ground.

Vines in pots

Consider growing quick color vines in containers. You can create or purchase trellis forms suited to a container. Make sure your pot is large enough so that when the plant covers the trellis, the container won't easily tip in wind gusts. The height of the vine should equal, at maximum, two times the pot height.

TEST GARDEN TIP

Trellis height formula

In a planting bed, you'll always achieve a pleasing scale when the vine or trellis height is equal to or less than one-half the bed width.

Vines for vertical interest
Count on vines to take your garden to new heights—literally. True quick color champions, flowering vines stage a strong season-long performance. These climbers thrive in full sun. All take summer heat except sweet pea, which craves cool weather.

BLACK-EYED SUSAN VINE (*Thunbergia alata*) Cheerful gold, red, orange, or lemony blooms feature brown-purple throats; 6 to 8 feet.

CARDINAL CLIMBER (*Ipomoea × multifida*) Dazzling scarlet blossoms dance above divided leaves; hummingbird favorite; 15 to 20 feet.

MORNING GLORY (*Ipomoea* spp.) Choose sunrise-greeting blooms in hues of white, deep purple, hot pink, blue, or shades in between; bicolors available; 6 to 10 feet.

CUP-AND-SAUCER VINE (*Cobaea scandens*) Unusual flowers open light green, develop purple stripes, then slowly fade to deep purple; 10 to 20 feet.

MOONFLOWER (*Ipomoea alba*) Exquisite white flowers open at dusk, close at dawn, and emit a heavy fragrance; 6 to 8 feet.

SWEET PEA (*Lathyrus odoratus*) Petals are painted in hues from dark purple to delicate pink, maroon, and bicolor blends; older types are heavily fragrant; 5 to 6 feet.

pockets of color

Celebrate color in the smallest spaces by filling pots to the brim with gorgeous flowers and foliage. Dabble with a couple of containers or dazzle with dozens.

Container
gardens

TEST GARDEN TIP

Which pot?

Purchase the best-quality container you can afford if it's a focal point or filled with upright plantings that won't hide the pot. If you're planning to fill the container with trailing plants and cascading growth that quickly obscures the pot, you can use plain plastic pots and direct more of your budget toward plants.

Container gardens package versatility, mobility, and beauty. They provide a chance to showcase your signature style. Gardening in pots also offers easy opportunities for seasonal change.

Planting in containers stirs creative expression. It's a green light to mixing and matching flowering and foliage plants. Containers can be used as small proving grounds for quick color combinations to consider for a bed. A pot also provides the ideal spot to grow a plant you've never tried before so you can see how it really performs in your garden.

Growing pots of color gives you a chance to own plants that otherwise wouldn't survive in your existing beds or do much in a short growing season. For tropical plants, containers provide the added advantage of warm soil, a boon in cool regions and at higher elevations where a short growing season restrains growth.

Use container gardens to dress up patios, porches, or decks. Position one in a planting bed as a focal point. Grouped together, mixed containers stage a potted garden or create a screen. A pair of matching containers flanking an entry interjects a formal note and helps create a balanced, eye-pleasing scene.

Winnow the choices

Finding the right container is almost as much fun as filling it. Look for pots in a variety of materials, from traditional terra-cotta to weighty concrete to fiberglass, metal, ceramic, and plastic. The right material depends on your budget and the plants you intend to grow.

Some quick color plants prefer soil on the drier side and need a container that's more porous, such as terra-cotta. Just be aware that porous pots tend to crack if stored outdoors during freeze-thaw cycles. Stone and concrete planters are long-lasting but can be challenging to move. Plant these heavy players where you intend to display them.

You can find stone look-alikes among synthetic containers made from a variety of materials including fiberglass, plastic, foam, and other resins. These materials cost less than stone and the other high-end materials they mimic. Some fade with prolonged sun exposure; others may crack following freezing temperatures. Look for pots labeled UV-resistant for strong materials that are resistant to fading and cracking.

Growing tips

Drainage. Every pot needs a drainage hole to allow water to escape and prevent roots from drowning.

Soil. Use a commercial bagged product, frequently called a soilless mix. Most contain a high percentage of peat moss, which provides an ideal environment for roots growing in a container.

Water. Consider mixing water-retention crystals into soil so it retains moisture between waterings. Some bagged mixes contain these crystals; read the bag carefully to avoid double dosing.

Fertilizer. Many bagged mixes have slow-release fertilizer that feeds plants for several months. If you use a mix lacking this, consider adding your own fertilizer before planting.

Above left: **Containers take many different forms. Buckets hanging on lattice become living works of art and a built-in planter box edges a wall with flowers.**

Above middle: **A row of planters adds a living wall to an outdoor seating area. Match plant size to container size. For large shrubs like arborvitae, you need containers that hold plenty of soil.**

Opposite: **A wide urn with a tangle of flowering plants steals the spotlight. This planting mix features strong summer performers: trailing purple and magenta petunias, yellow calibrachoa, and yellow marguerite daisies.**

Design tips for containers

Working with quick color destined for containers

can be one of gardening's most enjoyable tasks. By applying the principles of color blending and mixing leaf textures and plant shapes, you can create winning combinations by following one simple recipe. Three ingredients are all it takes to plant one gorgeous pot after another. It's as easy as one, two, three.

One: Thriller

The first ingredient is an attention-grabbing plant, also called a thriller. This plant takes

Above: **Red cordyline plays the thriller role in this container, surrounded by filler New Guinea impatiens and three spiller plants: asparagus fern, dark sweet potato vine, and green ivy.**

center stage in a container, serving as the star of the design production. All other plants relate to this player in some way.

Usually the thriller plant features an in-your-face shape with a strong upright growth habit. Thrillers typically unleash flower power by blooming nonstop all season, or they unfurl dramatic leaves.

In containers viewed from all sides, place a thriller in the center. In containers placed against a wall, position it in the back.

Two: Filler

The second ingredient, known as the filler, complements the thriller in some fashion, but never steals the spotlight. Filler plants are supporting players. These plants typically have rounded mound or misty shapes.

Fillers accomplish several tasks. These pretty plants complement the thriller with leaf or flower color, texture, or other special characteristic. They help disguise the thriller's base and add colorful substance in the space between soil and thriller. Aim for fillers that grow to one-third to two-thirds the height of the thriller.

Place fillers around the thriller between it and the pot rim. For a pot that looks instantly full, use three fillers in a 14-inch pot. If you're willing to let plants slowly fill in, you can plant just two fillers: one in front and one in back, or, if they are in pots that will be shown in a corner or against a all, one on each side of a thriller.

Three: Spiller

The third ingredient is a plant that trails over the edge of the container and helps tie it to its surroundings. It's called a spiller plant. When you're looking for a spiller, seek plants with a sprawling shape. Leaf or flower color should contrast or echo that of the thriller and/or filler.

Plant spillers along pot edges in the openings left between filler plants. It may be a tight squeeze. Feel free to shove and shoehorn plants into place. Anticipate using two spillers for a 14-inch pot viewed from one side, or two or three spillers for a container viewed from all sides.

Other keys to success

Get inspired. Look for container ideas in plant catalogs or garden magazines. Choose colors that match your outdoor furnishings or home's exterior. Or simply find a plant you like, and build a custom design around that.

Test it out. Give your design a dry run at the garden center. When gathering plants, arrange them in your cart the way they'll appear in the container. Make changes as needed.

Scale is relative. A plant used as a filler in one pot may make a nice thriller for a smaller pot. Typically, to create a planting that's in scale, thriller height should not be taller than two times the height of the container.

Think texture. Mix leaf and flower textures in your container gardens to create the most beautiful designs.

Favorite combinations
Find inspiration for your container designs in these classic combinations. You don't need to exactly duplicate the container plantings shown. If you like the color scheme, feel free to use different plants to produce that look. Be creative and adaptive, selecting plants that inspire you.

SUN CONTAINER
Black-eyed Susan serves as a thriller, Dragon Wing begonia and 'Buddy' gomphrena as fillers, and silver thyme as spiller.

SHADE CONTAINER
Pink-and-green caladium is the thriller, Infinity Pink Frost New Guinea impatiens is the filler, and variegated ivy is the spiller.

TROPICAL CONTAINER
Elephant's-ear towers as the thriller over orange impatiens, which acts as both filler and spiller plant in this combination.

FOLIAGE CONTAINER
A low thriller, deer tongue fern, is surrounded by 'Dark Heart' coleus and alternanthera serving as fillers and spillers.

Hanging baskets

Lift quick color to eye level and beyond

with hanging baskets. Whether dangling from a porch, pool screen, or tree, these moveable feasts of color elevate gardening, literally and figuratively. Nothing compares to a hanging basket dripping with blooms.

Select basket style

Before you begin, consider container style. Several basket styles dominate the market. Typically you'll choose from traditional plastic pots and hangers or durable, powder-coated steel baskets with some type of liner, such as coir, sphagnum moss, or kenaf fiber blankets. Which basket you select depends in part upon your personal style and the ambience of the areas where the baskets will go.

The types of plants you grow also influence basket choice. Plants that require full sun locations or soil on the dry side do well with a metal basket and porous liner. Plants that don't dangle enough to cover the planter are also great choices for metal baskets because they allow the basket to be part of the design.

Above: **For a spot that's splashed with sun part of the day, fill a basket with orange and yellow strawflowers, orange New Guinea impatiens, and golden creeping jenny (*Lysimachia nummularia* 'Aurea').**

Plastic pots lack porosity, which keeps soil moister, and they're lighter in weight than metal containers. Soil temperatures nudge higher in plastic pots, a boon for heat-loving spiller plants but a death knell for cool-season beauties.

Basic care

Soil. Choose high-quality potting soil designed for containers. These bagged blends include a high percentage of peat moss, which increases the moisture-holding capacity. Avoid using topsoil from your garden. It's too heavy for containers, and it compacts, smothering roots.

Plants. Pick plants according to the growing conditions where the basket will be displayed. If you're creating your own basket design, select plants with similar growth requirements.

Water. Because hanging baskets are elevated, plants experience higher air temperature and greater wind exposure, both of which suck the moisture out of plants and soil. Early in the season, check soil daily to determine water needs. As plants fill in and summer sizzles, anticipate the need to water baskets at least daily, sometimes twice daily if temperatures soar. An easy way to detect if a hanging basket is dry is to place your hand directly beneath the basket and lift up

slightly to feel the weight of the basket. Do this right after watering, when the soil is saturated, to learn what a wet basket feels like. When the soil is dry, the basket feels much lighter. Count on the lift test when plants fill in and it's impossible to shove a finger into the soil to check for moisture.

Fertilize. Most soils used in hanging baskets already contain a slow-release fertilizer. Begin feeding plants only when that fertilizer is scheduled to run out. Feed flowering baskets with a product (the middle number should be the highest). Feed leafy plants with a balanced 10-10-10 or similar fertilizer at the frequency recommended on the fertilizer label. Avoid fertilizing plants when the soil is dry or you risk burning roots. It's also unwise to fertilize baskets when heavy rain is forecast. The rain washes fertilizer from soil.

Trim. Remove dead blooms faithfully to encourage more flower buds to form. Trim leggy growth in midsummer, cutting plants back by one-third to one-half.

Turn. Hang baskets using swivel hooks for freewheeling color that spins in the breeze. Swivel hooks make it a cinch to turn baskets to encourage even growth. This is key for baskets in locations where only one side receives direct sun.

TEST GARDEN TIP

Best basket plants

Some plants thrive in hanging baskets. Check out these beauties by turning to the encyclopedia starting on page 124 to learn more:

BIDENS
CALIBRACHOA
LANTANA
LOBELIA (*above*)
PETUNIA
SCAEVOLA
TRAILING VERBENA

Hanging basket how-to
You'll spend more time selecting and shopping for plants than you will planting a coir-lined basket. Plan on completing the task in an hour or less.

1 FILL
Fill your planter, adding soil until it's level with the first row of planting holes. This wire planter and precut coir liner hold up to 18 side plants and 12 top-edging plants, all from 4-inch nursery pots, plus 1 centerpiece plant.

2 PLANT
Plant in layers. Slip a plant out of its nursery pot, immerse the root ball in a bucket of water, gently squeeze it to release excess water, and tuck the root ball into a planting hole. Repeat to plant each lower side hole, completing one layer of plants.

3 COVER
Cover root balls with potting mix. Plant the second layer of side plantings, followed by the centerpiece and edging, adding soil between root balls after each layer. Sprinkle the soil with water to moisten the container. Water thoroughly after a day or two.

Planting a
basket

If you are enamored of the balls of bloom displayed in public gardens

and theme parks, bring that look home to your yard. Instead of using a plastic hanging basket, where it takes all summer for the plants to inch their way around the pot to cover it, begin with a metal basket frame and liner.

A custom basket kit becomes a sphere of color with little effort. Best of all, you don't need to be an experienced gardener to succeed. Use the same principles of care as you do for hanging baskets.

How it works

If you start with a basket kit, slip a precut liner into the metal basket. Align holes in the liner with openings in the basket frame. Or, you can craft your own liner by purchasing liner material in bulk and cutting it to fit your basket. Cut holes in the liner to form planting pockets, and start planting.

Display options

You can showcase your finished basket by dangling it from a swivel hook or mount it on a column. Some basket kits provide hardware to attach the metal basket to a wooden or metal post. That's the easiest, quickest approach.

Some baskets are designed to perch atop narrow metal rods. These fit into a larger base pot that you also fill with quick color plants. The result is a double-decker garden sure to earn compliments. Some baskets fit into specialized stands in a freestanding planter on a patio or deck.

No matter which display option you choose, when you plant the top and sides of a hanging basket, you create a container with incredible flower power. It results in a quick color display that's tough to beat.

Opposite: **Choose 3- to 4-foot-tall columns to spherical display planters overflowing with lush trailing plants.**

Above: **A ball planter mounted on a post that's inserted into a container, creates a striking two-tier garden.**

Plant a sphere of bloom
For a look that's tough to beat, dress your yard with beautiful globes overflowing with flowers. Start with a ball-shape hanging basket and coir liner.

1 FILL
Fit the coir liner into both baskets, and fill with a quality potting mix designed for container use. Add moisture-retentive crystals if your mix doesn't contain them, along with slow-release fertilizer. Use a marker to dot the liner where you'll add plants. Space planting holes evenly, 2 to 3 inches apart.

2 ASSEMBLE
Place a piece of heavy cardboard over the soil of the basket that will form the top of the globe. Invert the basket, and place it over the base basket. Slip out the cardboard, and snap the baskets together. Use a sharp knife to cut planting holes in the coir.

3 PLANT
Before planting, soak the root balls in a bucket of water. Squeeze the soil gently to release excess water. Tuck each root ball through a planting hole. Use a spoon, if necessary, to loosen the soil. Firm soil around the plant until it's held snugly in place. Hang the basket, then water thoroughly.

Window boxes

Stuff a window box with
a blend of blooming and edible
plants. Cherry tomatoes and
dill add color and texture to
dark-leaf coleus and Dragon
Wing begonias.

For instant impact, few things beguile like a window box.

Displayed to dress your home's exterior with welcoming botanical charm, these wall-hanging containers suit any style dwelling, from cozy cottage to lavish estate or studio apartment. Not only do these classic planters give the exterior a colorful lift, they also provide views from indoors, giving you the sense of living in a garden.

Window boxes don't discriminate. They grace buildings with flowery ease whether or not you have a large yard, garden experience, or an eye for design. It's easy to succeed with a window box.

Getting started

Once you decide on a window box, choose a type. Wooden boxes made of rot-resistant wood such as cedar and cypress stand up to moisture. A pine box offers a cheaper price point, and coating it with exterior waterproofing sealant improves durability.

Fiberglass and plastic window boxes prove long lasting and lightweight. Metal hayrack-type planters fitted with a coir or similar liner lend the look of an English cottage.

No matter what type of container you choose, make sure it has drainage holes. If none are present, drill them. Use a spade bit to drill holes in wood or plastic boxes or a step bit for metal boxes.

Explore the different options with an eye to your home's architectural style and features. Some materials blend more harmoniously with home designs and exterior surfaces than others. Color-match your window box to your home, or select a neutral tone.

Placement matters

To position a window box for maximum visual appeal, follow a few simple rules. Where you place a window box determines the size you purchase. Choose a box equal to the window width or slightly wider. If wider, center the box on the window. For a window with shutters, purchase a box equal to the width of the space from the center of one shutter to the center of the other.

Position window boxes so they're readily accessible for maintenance. When adding boxes to second-floor windows, make sure you can easily irrigate and tend plants.

TEST GARDEN TIP

Luring butterflies

Window boxes can bring butterflies and hummingbirds right up to windows for closeup viewing. Plants such as lantana, Texas sage (*Salvia texana*), and pentas are nectar lures for these winged wonders.

How to attach a window box
A fully planted window box, especially when wet, is heavy and needs solid support to remain in position. Attachment isn't difficult.

Brackets. Use wood or metal brackets to support a window box against vinyl, shake, stucco, or wood lap siding or bricks. Place brackets so the top of the box rests at or below the window ledge. Inset brackets 6 to 8 inches from each end of the box, no farther apart than 2 feet. Attach brackets using deck screws or toggle bolts for siding; use expanding sleeve anchors for bricks. Always slip two or three washers over screws to create an air space between bracket and siding.

Screws. To attach a box to a deck rail, use 3-inch wood screws driven through the box into the rail. Insert a spacer block between the rear base of the box and the deck baluster so the box hangs level from front to back. You can also purchase window box kits that include hooks that wrap over deck rails to support the box.

J-hooks. To attach a hayrack to a deck rail, hang it on J-hooks attached to the surface with 3-inch wood screws.

1 window box 4 ways

Create a window box that's big on color and short on effort. These fuss-free designs blaze a trail with coordinated colors sure to give your house an inviting facade. Use these box designs as is, or mix and match plants from monochromatic gardens to create a kaleidoscope of quick color.

THINK PINK

THIS WINDOW BOX FEATURES FLORAL CUTIES WITH PINK PETALS.

The plants blend cool-season bloomers (dianthus, diascia, ivy geranium) with heat lovers (zinnia, pentas, flowering tobacco). Every flower has a rich nectar content that pleases butterflies and bees. Give this window box a spot with morning sun and afternoon shade to extend the bloom time of cool-weather flowers, and deadhead plants faithfully so more flowers form.

PLANT LIST

A. 4 Zinnia (*Zinnia elegans*)

B. 2 Dwarf pentas
(*Pentas lanceolata* 'Butterfly Blush')

C. 1 Gerbera daisy (*Gerbera jamesonii*)

D. 1 Ivy geranium (*Pelargonium peltatum*)

E. 1 Flowering tobacco (*Nicotiana alata*)

F. 2 Diascia (*Diascia barbarae*)

G. 2 Dwarf pentas
(*Pentas lanceolata* 'Butterfly Deep Pink'

H. 2 Dianthus (*Dianthus* 'Little Jock')

A PURPLE-BLUE NOTE

TRUE BLUE IS HARD TO COME BY IN THE GARDEN.

Purple and lavender shades often work in spaces where gardeners crave blue. This box dazzles with blue- and purple-tone bloomers that beckon butterflies and hummingbirds. These plants thrive in evenly moist soil and stage the strongest show in full sun. Snip spent flower spikes on Brazilian sage to encourage more blooms. The other plants don't require deadheading.

PLANT LIST

A. 3 Petunia (*Petunia* Suncatcher Sapphire)

B. 2 Blue anise sage
(*Salvia guaranitica* 'Black and Blue')

C. 1 Angelonia (*Angelonia* Angelmist Lavender)

D. 3 Nierembergia (*Nierembergia* 'Royal Robe')

E. 1 Nemesia (*Nemesia* Poetry Blue)

EASY GREEN

FOLIAGE MAKES A COOL FIRST IMPRESSION WITH LEAFY BEAUTIES.

This color scheme features a backdrop of fresh spring green that shines all summer long. If the coleus grows too large compared to the other plantings, snip the stems just above a pair of leaves. By summer's end, the Mexican feather grass sprouts airy seed heads. Place this box in full sun.

PLANT LIST

A. 2 Licorice plant
   (*Helichrysum petiolare* 'Limelight')
B. 2 Coleus
   (*Solenostemon scutellarioides* 'Kong Rose')
C. 1 Dichondra
   (*Dichondra repens* 'Emerald Falls')
D. 1 Plectranthus
   (*Plectranthus forsteri* 'Marginatus')
E. 1 Mexican feather grass (*Stipa tenuissima*)

MELLOW YELLOW

GET A POSITIVE OUTLOOK FROM A WINDOW BOX OVERFLOWING WITH HORTICULTURAL SUNSHINE. These joyous bloomers spread good cheer all season long, brightening overcast days and glowing at dusk. Several of these plants demand deadheading for continued flower power: marigold, shrimp plant, black-eyed Susan, and chrysanthemum. Pollinators mob this boxed garden, so enjoy the flitting, buzzing show. Provide full sun and consistent soil moisture for the strongest performance.

PLANT LIST

A. 2 Marigold (*Tagetes* 'Inca Yellow')
B. 1 Shrimp plant (*Pachystachys lutea*)
C. 3 Black-eyed Susan (*Rudbeckia hirta* 'Irish Eyes')
D. 2 Calibrachoa (*Calibrachoa* 'Yellow')
E. 1 Black-eyed Susan vine (*Thunbergia alata*)
F. 1 Chrysanthemum (*Chrysanthemum* 'Fortune')
G. 2 Lantana (*Lantana camara* 'New Gold')
H. 1 Creeping zinnia
   (*Sanvitalia procumbens* 'Golden Aztec')

Care tips Keep window boxes looking their best by following these simple steps:

Start by purchasing or making a high-quality potting mix containing peat moss, perlite, and/or vermiculite.

Water frequently because the small soil volume in a window box dries quickly, especially in boxes sited in full sun. Water when the soil is dry to the touch. In high summer, expect to water at least once daily.

Blend moisture-retentive crystals in the soil to reduce water needs, keeping them beneath the surface so they don't wick water out of the soil.

Deadhead plants faithfully to foster a strong, nonstop flower show.

Fertilize all flowering plants with a bloom-booster fertilizer, but use a balanced formula for foliage plants.

Other containers

A strawberry or pocket jar welcomes many quick color annuals, especially trailing ones like dazzling blue lobelia. Pocket jars also work well when planted with succulents or herbs.

Classic containers like hanging baskets and terra-cotta pots are workhorses in the garden. Although most of your containers may be conventional, consider punctuating outdoor spaces with a few unusual vessels. Uncommon containers underscore a gardener's personality, provide ambience, or inject a fun, unexpected touch.

Pots with purpose

Some unusual planters have distinctive forms that reflect their functions.

Wall planters feature one flat side to allow gardening on vertical surfaces. Nestle the flat edge snugly against a garden wall or fence and fill the rounded planting pouch with quick color. For wall planters mounted several feet off the ground, use strong spiller plants such as Silver Falls dichondra or trailing petunias in the Wave or Supertunia series.

A strawberry jar, with its chubby belly sprouting pockets on all sides, is a well-loved container. Fill the tops and pockets with strawberries or other trailing plants that tumble over the edges of the pot. Or fill the jar with succulents that easily thrive in the confines of the tiny pockets.

The rectangular shape and shallow depth of a trough offer ideal digs for shallow-rooted plants, such as succulents, alpines, thyme, or sword fern.

Victorian-era long tom pots are one type of extra-deep container, providing perfect growing conditions for plants that require a little extra room for roots to stretch such as ornamental sweet corn.

Containers can be fun

While some pots are purely functional, other containers are just plain fun. Look for pots shaped to mimic everyday objects, and add playful plants to provoke a smile. A pot resembling a head with a planting hole on top begs for a tuft of grassy hair.

A spherical container looks fabulous when sprouting the swordlike foliage of New Zealand flax. Colorful Mexican pottery rooster planters wow when the openings brim with the bright blooms of moss rose.

You can also plant in cast-off objects you have on hand—maybe stashed in a garage, basement, or attic. Natural containers, like a wooden box, bucket, or claw foot tub, make an easy transition to hosting a garden.

Or craft unexpected containers from objects with the capacity to hold soil. Candidates might include a lunch box, wicker laundry basket, weathered pair of shoes, or a chair with the seat replaced with a pot.

The only limit is your own imagination.

Succeed with unconventional pots

Follow these simple tips to make your one-of-a-find containers flourish.

Every container needs drainage holes. If your pot doesn't come with them, drill holes using a spade bit for wood or plastic, a step bit for metal, or a masonry bit for concrete or clay.

Protect the interior of vessels by tucking plants into plastic pots that slip inside the container. Or line a makeshift pot with plastic—poked with drainage holes—before planting.

Apply a few coats of exterior waterproofing sealant to wood, wicker, or metallic planters to increase durability.

To allow a beautiful container to shine, avoid stuffing it with a strong spiller plant whose growth will completely hide the container.

TEST GARDEN TIP

Pick your spot

Place uncommon containers in focal point positions. If you want to showcase a smaller pot, placing it on a pedestal, old stump, or wall helps it stand out. Include eccentric pots in an entry garden to entertain guests and passersby.

Finding pots
Create unusual containers by recycling found objects. It's not hard to unearth potential pots—if you know where to look. Investigate some of these locations to uncover treasures perfect for planting.

- **ANTIQUE OR JUNK STORE**
- **GARAGE SALE**
- **ARMY SURPLUS STORE**
- **USED RESTAURANT-SUPPLY STORE**
- **AUCTION**
- **SURPLUS STORE**
- **SWAP MEET**
- **ARCHITECTURAL SALVAGE STORE**
- **CURB SHOPPING DURING CITYWIDE CLEANUP**
- **YOUR OWN ATTIC**

Accessorize a deck or patio

Hard surfaces are necessary

in outdoor living areas to provide firm, clean footing. But while these foot-worthy materials welcome and withstand heavy traffic and outdoor furniture, they're not the most accommodating for growing plants. That's where containers come in. Add a few well-placed, pretty pots of quick color, and any outdoor space becomes a destination.

Patio pleasures

Count on container gardens to fulfill several roles in a patio setting. First, they help integrate the hardscape of an outdoor living space with the surrounding landscape. Pots packed with foliage and flowers subtly echo nearby plantings. You can even select plants that complement the adjacent landscaping.

Potted quick color also serves as a strong design element in outdoor spaces. A large container filled with a striking plant combination can function as a focal point, drawing the eye through the space.

A series of containers spaced throughout an outdoor room moves the eye through the setting. The effect magnifies when pots sprout identical plantings, beating a cadence for the eye to follow. A single row of potted gardens handily defines the edge of an outdoor setting or forms a wall that encloses a room.

Deck delights

Whether your deck features traditional wood or newer wood-alternative products, potted quick color transforms the space into a garden. The same design aspects of other container gardens also apply to decks. Pots of colorful plants tie a deck to its surroundings and can serve as focal points.

Growing quick color in containers on a deck means contending with site-specific conditions. In decks elevated significantly above ground level and exposed to full sun, the soil temperature in pots rises to the same level as air temperature or even higher when sun shines directly on containers.

Above: **Finish an outdoor room with living accessories: containers brimming with colorful plantings. Mix different container styles—hanging baskets, stand-alone pots, and boxes—for the prettiest scene.**

Opposite left: **The soft green leaves and yellow blooms and fruits of summer squash contrast beautifully with the teal container, providing beauty and edibles.**

As a result, soil tends to dry out quickly. Mixing water-holding crystals into the soil prior to planting ensures roots have access to moisture between irrigations. Even so, once container plants fill in, plan to water pots daily if your deck experiences a few sunny hours each day.

Warm soil benefits tropical plants that thrive in heat. If you provide adequate soil moisture, you'll enjoy outstanding growth from tropicals displayed on a deck. One easy way to water tropical plants is to place saucers beneath the pots once the plants mature. Early in the day, irrigate the plants until water runs through the soil and fills the saucer. This allows the roots to continue sipping from the saucer throughout the afternoon, especially during high summer.

It's not wise to let most plants sit in water overnight, however, because under the right circumstances, that can cause root rot. Water sitting in saucers can also attract unsavory wildlife or provide a breeding ground for mosquitoes. Dump any full saucers before dusk.

Wind can be a challenge on elevated decks. Select pots large enough to provide a weighty counterbalance for top-heavy plants. Consider inserting a few stones or bricks in the base of any pots that house tall plants.

Outdoor living container tips

Built-in containers provide greater square footage for planting than individual containers. When adding fixed planters to a deck or patio, incorporate seating into the design to gain extra space for entertaining.

If a patio area doubles as a play area for small children, select quick color foliage plants to avoid attracting stinging pollinators.

Fill individual pots with one kind of plant. This approach allows you to switch out plants that are not in peak color when you entertain. Choose plants with fragrant blooms to delight your family and guests.

A pot or saucer sitting directly on decking can discolor wood and provide moisture for mold and mildew. Protect surfaces by elevating containers and their saucers. Pot feet—as simple as small blocks of wood or as elaborate as special purchased items—make quick work of this task.

Below: **A container of sedge, salvia, and variegated sage adds a cool note to the otherwise hot-color theme in the furniture cushions and other containers.**

Bottom: **A vintage barn cupola retrofitted as a chandelier pulls double duty as a planter. Billows of gold lantana, coleus, and tendrils of trailing ivy enhance the special find.**

Grouping containers

Gather multiple potted plants to create the splendor of an in-ground border in a spot where gardening is otherwise impossible. Using containers you can fill a space with beautiful color and texture that rivals earthbound planting beds.

Making adjustments

Artfully arranged container gardens soften hardscapes and add living beauty that's easily changed through the seasons. Pots are portable and flexible, and a garden composed of containers naturally evolves through the growing season as plants peak and ebb. Enhance the drama by shifting pots around as the plants grow. Shortly after planting, cluster containers closely to create a sense of fullness. As plants mature and fill in, spread pots apart.

Introduce more play into a container garden by moving plants in peak bloom to the forefront of the garden or elevating them above their neighbors. Likewise, slip plants that are past their prime into less prominent positions.

Pairing impossible partners

Containers can play matchmaker for plants that can't intermingle in the garden due to differences in height. Slip short plants into pots and

Above: **Individual pots of foliage plants form a beautiful garden tapestry when gathered together. Elevating small containers allows them to blend into the scene.**

elevate them to unnatural heights to create surprising, unexpected quick color combinations.

For instance, a burgundy cordyline, which typically grows 4 to 5 feet in a single season, looks stunning beside a 'Vancouver Centennial' geranium, with chartreuse leaves splashed with brick red. The geranium grows only 12 to 18 inches tall, but by elevating its pot a mere 6 inches, the cordyline and geranium pairing shifts into eye-pleasing scale.

Other plants assisted with height include a tall dahlia with a short coleus (match the dominant shade of the coleus leaves to the color of the dahlia bloom) and tall purple ornamental millet with short annual phlox (*P. drummondii*).

Give plants a boost

When using multiple containers, position pots at varying heights for a more natural-looking scene with height and vertical interest. Lifting pots accomplishes several things:

Elevate small pots or plants to eye level to embody them with star power. Instead of being lost as ground-hugging squatters, they are lifted into scale with the surrounding scenery, commanding attention.

Showcase easily overlooked blossoms, by raising plants as they come into bloom. You can also shine a spotlight on artful objects such as a saucer-style birdbath or tabletop fountain simply by changing their height.

Invert pots or saucers, 5-gallon buckets, bricks, concrete blocks, or logs cut to length to add height. Build your own pot elevators with treated lumber, or rely on pot feet or manufactured plant stands. Any object serving as a plant hoist must be sturdy. A well-watered container is heavy enough to crush a flimsy stand. Plant supports also need a wide enough base that they won't easily topple in summer winds.

Camouflage container elevators by placing shorter pots full of rounded mound-shape plants such as lantana, pentas, melampodium, Profusion zinnia, or geranium in front of the elevators. To screen taller plant lifts, position misty-shape plants like Diamond Frost euphorbia or Mexican feather grass in front of the supporting objects.

Above: **Stairsteps and deck railings are natural locations to elevate blooming beauties.**

Same colors, different plants

Present a cohesive container garden display by filling separate pots with plants that echo one another's colors. Repeating hues and shades gives you freedom to create distinctive container gardens that still relate to one another. Gather these containers into a display, and you have a garden masterpiece.

SEEING RED
A trio of foliage plants—'Redhead' coleus, 'Red Star' cordyline, and 'Siam Ruby' banana—serve varying shades of red that sparkle when teamed with a container filled with red geraniums and rose nicotiana.

CHEERY YELLOW
Plant two pots identically to create a goofproof container blend. The yellow plants shown here are 'Versa Green Halo' coleus, 'Twinny' snapdragon, and Superbells Yellow calibrachoa.

garden
plans

Easy-to-follow planting plans take the guesswork out of designing a quick color garden. You'll find plans for landscapes of all sizes, from containers to sweeping borders.

p.**84**
PROJECTS
Unleash your creativity with these plans perfect for family fun, a weekend lawn makeover, or a blooming solution for shade.

p.**92**
CLASSIC DESIGNS
Discover ways to dress common landscape features with glorious color. Learn how strongly tinted foliage adds punch.

p.**100**
CONTAINER PLANS
Quick color does more than look good in pots and planters. Count on container gardens to beckon butterflies, create a focal point, or keep pace with the seasons.

Mailbox in bloom

Beautify one of your yard's most functional

accoutrements: the mailbox. This pocket garden creates curb appeal, eliminates some string-trimming chores, and adapts easily to surround a lamppost or flagpole.

Consider your mail carrier as you select plants so none grow taller than the level of the mailbox. Avoid plants that attract butterflies because these also lure wasps, bees, and other stinging pollinators. Select plants in colors that appear elsewhere in your yard or add some in nearby pots or beds to unify the areas. If your summers are hot, plants that look scruffy by midseason,

such as sweet alyssum, Dahlberg daisy, and Chinese dianthus, may need to be replaced.

When incorporating a vine in your design, you may want to check with your local postmaster before planting. Typically it's best to grow it along a support that's mounted behind and separate from the mailbox.

This ensures that vining stems and blooms—and any accompanying critters—remain located well beyond the reach of the mail carrier. Prune vining growth so it won't obscure the house address or block entry to the mailbox.

Curb appeal

When designing a garden for a street-level mailbox, consider the special growing conditions of the curbside location.

LOWER WATER NEEDS
Unless your hose easily reaches the curb, you would need to carry water to the street to give plants a drink. Instead, choose drought-tolerant beauties to pull off a great display without a lot of pampering.

FOLIAGE COUNTS
Aim for a mix of plants with colorful leaves and flowers. Curb gardens need continuity, and attractive foliage fuels a constant color show.

THINK BIG
Arrange plants in blocks of color to give the garden strong curb appeal that's easily visible from passing cars. However, if the only viewers who will see the garden are the mail carrier, your family, and passing pedestrians, plant as intricate a design as you like.

LOWER SOIL
As you build your bed, avoid raising the soil level above the surrounding grade. If the planting bed is higher, you risk having mulch or soil wash onto nearby lawn or the street during downpours. As you amend the soil prior to planting, it rises above surrounding surfaces. Relocate some of the extra soil to another spot in the yard. You can also rely on a raised edge, like the bricks in this garden, to contain soil. But even with an edging, it's best for the soil to be level with the grade.

PLANT LIST

A.	1 **Verbena**	*(Verbena × hybrida)*
B.	2 **Purple Wave petunias**	*(Petunia 'Purple Wave')*
C.	1 **Dahlberg daisy**	*(Dyssodia tenuiloba)*
D.	2 **Impatiens**	*(Impatiens walleriana)*
E.	4 **Sweet alyssum**	*(Lobularia maritima)*
F.	3 **Dusty miller**	*(Senecio cineraria)*
G.	1 **Clematis**	*(Clematis spp.)*
H.	1 **Dahlia**	*(Dahlia × hybrida)*
I.	2 **China pinks**	*(Dianthus chinensis)*
J.	3 **Gomphrena**	*(Gomphrena globosa)*
K.	3 **Zonal geranium**	*(Pelargonium × hortorum)*

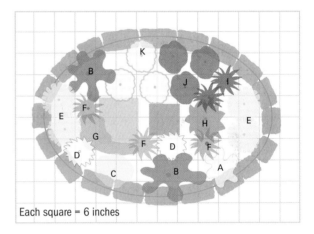

Each square = 6 inches

ASK THE GARDEN DOCTOR

Will road salt hurt my mailbox garden?

ANSWER: Many quick color plants make excellent choices for a streetside mailbox garden because of their short life span. Plants that live only for one full growing season are less affected by accumulated road salt. Salt could be an issue for the perennial clematis vine behind the box, however. To help with the problem, soak the soil with water in spring after the ground thaws. A deep watering helps move salts through soil and away from roots. For a deep soak, let water from a hose trickle very slowly onto the planting bed for an extended period. Make sure you don't wash soil away from clematis roots. Spring rains achieve the same effect, so water less if rainfall is abundant.

Cozy corner

Trade turf for blooms in a carefree corner cottage garden.

A mail-order picket fence section anchors the planting. The triangular planting bed nestles snugly into the yard's sidewalk-defined angle and adds more than curb appeal to the corner property. The quick color display also effectively deters pets and pedestrians from cutting the corner and wandering through the yard.

Packed with sun-loving bloomers, the garden features a mix of easy-growing annuals punctuated with just a few perennials. A tall butterfly bush fills the corner with deep purple flowers that butterflies can't resist. Hummingbirds also love to visit the petunia,

cosmos, zinnia, cleome, and penstemon (a perennial). At dusk, stroll by this garden for a whiff of sweet perfume from the flowering tobacco, butterfly bush, and petunia.

Most of this garden's color faces the street, so it enhances the street view. To add more color on the back side to improve views from indoors, simply duplicate some of the plant combinations in front of the cleome.

Stairstep the plant heights so the cleome isn't upstaged. Add a few stepping stones or pavers to allow easy access into the bed for planting and deadheading.

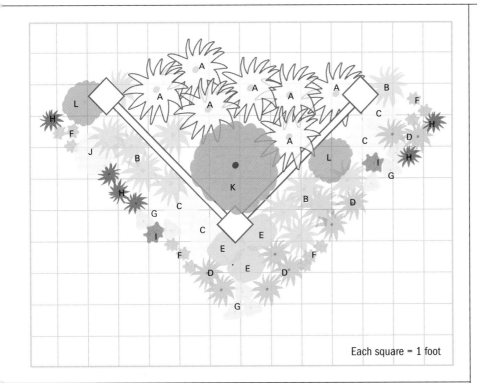

Each square = 1 foot

TEST GARDEN TIP

Snow removal

In wintry regions, this garden's sidewalk location makes it a repository for shoveled snow. Pile it carefully around the butterfly bush to avoid breaking the main stems. A layer of snow helps insulate perennials during winter's temperature extremes.

PLANT LIST

A. 7 **White cleome**
(Cleome hassleriana)
such as 'White Queen'

B. 12 **Cosmos**
(Cosmos bipinnatus)

C. 4 **Black-eyed Susan**
(Rudbeckia hirta)
such as 'Irish Eyes'

D. 9 **Narrowleaf zinnia**
(Zinnia angustifolia)
such as 'White Star'

E. 3 **Penstemon**
(Penstemon barbatus)

F. 12 **Dusty miller**
(Senecio cineraria)
such as 'Silver Dust'

G. 9 **Moss rose**
(Portulaca grandiflora)

H. 9 **Flowering tobacco**
(Nicotiana alata)

I. 2 **Petunia**
(Petunia × hybrida)

J. 1 **Speedwell**
(Veronica spp.) such as 'Fairytale';
perennial, Zones 4–8

K. 1 **Butterfly bush**
(Buddleia davidii)
such as 'Nanho Blue';
perennial, Zones 5–9

L. 2 **Feather reed grass**
(Calamagrostis × acutiflora);
perennial, Zones 4–9

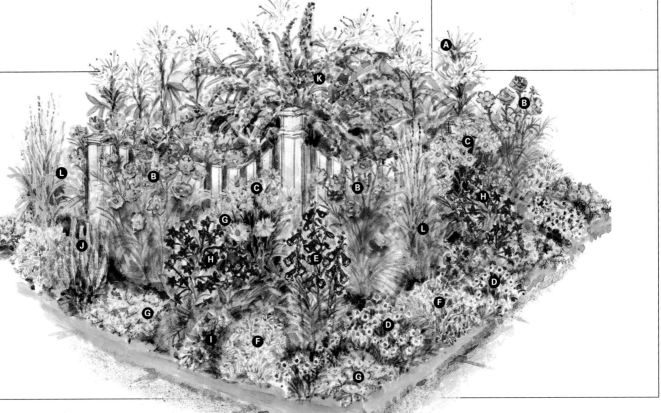

Made in the shade

PLANT LIST

A. **10 Impatiens**
(Impatiens walleriana)

B. **26 Tuberous begonia**
(Begonia × tuberhybrida)

C. **2 Boston fern**
(Nephrolepis exaltata)

Each square = 6 inches

Call on creative thinking to transform

Call on creative thinking to transform architectural elements such as a wall, alcove, or deck into a thriving garden. Container gardens provide the necessary sleight of hand to plant blooming beauty that thrives even in this shady location.

A double-decker row of containers complements the angular lines of the window, shake siding, and deck. The grouped pots resemble a window box when placed on a bench parked beneath the window. Fill in the empty space below the bench with more containers. Instead of a bench, a shelf atop brackets attached to the house, or stacked bricks or concrete blocks could be used to accommodate the pots.

The containers are the perfect height for growing shallow-rooted tuberous begonias. Their waxy blooms open in a mix of hues. Dark red petals seem to disappear quickly at dusk in a low-light setting like this, while yellow and salmon-tinted blossoms glow brightly.

Begonias grow with broad leaves that contrast with fine-textured ferns. The ferns overwinter indoors as houseplants. Hanging baskets of impatiens lift color to eye level, adding vertical interest to the otherwise horizontal scene. This planting pulls double duty, dressing exterior living spaces with vibrant color and framing the view from indoors with flowery beauty.

Quick color favorites for shade

It's always best to use shade-loving beauties for low-light areas. These colorful characters produce flowers or foliage in tints that brighten dark corners. For the lowest light settings, choose lighter colors, such as yellow, pink, or white.

BROWALLIA
Star-shape 2-inch flowers cover this plant all season long. Design plantings with blooms in three colors: white, blue, and purple. The dark tones have a white eye that glows in shady nooks. Plants grow 1 to 2 feet tall, 6 to 12 inches wide.

CALADIUM
Prized for its colorful foliage, caladium opens strappy or heartshape leaves painted with red, white, pink, green, or chartreuse. Leaf coloring may be speckled or solid. Veins often display contrasting shades. Plants reach 8 to 20 inches tall.

DRAGON WING BEGONIA
Stems that arch gracefully bear shiny, dark green 5-inch leaves and dangling red, white, or pink flower clusters. This bold plant tolerates heat and quickly grows 2 to 3 feet tall. Use three plants per 14-inch pot. Frost is the only thing that stops the blooming.

COLEUS
Coleus boasts immense variation. The leaves, splashed with shades from deep burgundy to neon green, carry the color. Plant size varies depending on the variety, or pinch to keep plants confined to certain heights. Choose brighter hues in shady spots.

FIBER-OPTIC GRASS
Clump-forming grass offers fine, bright green stems tipped with tiny white flowers that resemble fiber-optic lights. It's perfect for adding a fine texture to containers. Plants require consistent moisture to thrive. They grow about 1 foot tall and wide.

Goldfish garden

A fish out of water never looked prettier.
Gardeners of any age—but especially children—can craft this clever planting bed using scalloped concrete edging pieces. This fishy flowerbed introduces a sense of playfulness to a sunny yard. Each child may want to craft his or her own, making a small school of goldfish to dot the yard.

Flowers in shades of orange, gold, yellow, and red fill in the fish body. This large swath of bright bloomers attracts butterflies, adding another joyful element to the scene. If you're creating a new bed over existing lawn, use a spade to remove sod. Blend composted manure, peat moss, and perlite into the soil.

Children will enjoy helping with painting and planting. Show them how to water and, if they're old enough to handle a pair of small scissors, invite them to help remove spent blooms.

Deadheading is vital to this garden's continued flower show. But if you stop deadheading to allow marigold blossoms to set seed late in the season, you can teach kids about saving seeds. Start seeds indoors next spring, or let little fingers scatter them throughout the yard for cheery flowers next year. Marigolds are easy-growing beauties that are generally rabbit- and slug-resistant.

PLANT LIST

A.	**1 African daisy** (*Osteospermum* hybrid)
B.	**6 Plume celosia** (*Celosia argentea* var. *cristata*)
C.	**18 French marigold** (*Tagetes patula*)
D.	**1 Gazania** (*Gazania rigens*)

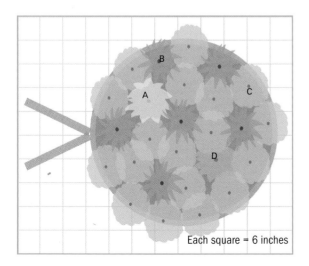

Each square = 6 inches

Make the fish

MATERIALS LIST

4 curved, scalloped concrete edging pieces
2 straight, scalloped concrete edging pieces
Stiff brush (optional)
Spray primer
Trim brush
5 bottles Anita's Yard & Garden Durable Outdoor Paint: #11811 Marigold Garden (yellow)
Small plastic bucket

5 bottles Anita's Yard & Garden Durable Outdoor Paint: #11823 Ladybug Red
Old plastic lid
Red colored pencil
Small round artist's brush
1 bottle each Anita's Yard & Garden Durable Outdoor Paint: #11802 Wrought Iron, #11801 Garden Gate White
Spray sealer

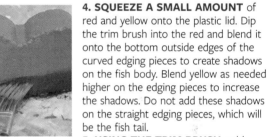

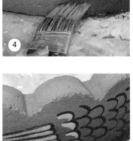

1. CLEAN THE EDGING PIECES with a stiff brush, if necessary. Prime each piece using a spray primer according to manufacturer's instructions. Let dry.

2. USE A TRIM BRUSH to paint the edging pieces yellow. Let dry.

3. IN A SMALL PLASTIC BUCKET, mix together three bottles of red paint and three bottles of yellow paint. Paint the orange mixture over the yellow base coat.

4. SQUEEZE A SMALL AMOUNT of red and yellow onto the plastic lid. Dip the trim brush into the red and blend it onto the bottom outside edges of the curved edging pieces to create shadows on the fish body. Blend yellow as needed higher on the edging pieces to increase the shadows. Do not add these shadows on the straight edging pieces, which will be the fish tail.

5. USING THE TRIM BRUSH, add yellow highlights to the scalloped edges of the fish body. Remember to paint the top edges of the pieces.

6. WITH THE RED COLORED PENCIL, draw eyes, a mouth, scales, and fins where desired. With the small round artist's brush, paint over the features with red paint.

7. ADD YELLOW HIGHLIGHTS to fins and scales, above and below the mouth, and around the eyes.

8. PAINT A BLACK OUTLINE around the eyes, black pupils, and white highlights.

9. USING THE SMALL ROUND BRUSH, paint red wavy lines on the straight edging pieces. Make the lines closer together in the center and farther apart toward the ends. Paint yellow lines between the red ones. Let dry.

10. FOR EXTRA PROTECTION from weather, seal the pieces with two coats of spray sealer in satin or gloss finish. Let dry.

11. SET PIECES IN PLACE, add soil appropriate for containers, and fill with colorful flowers.

Summer classics

This garden's flowery good looks just get better as the season goes along. These quick color performers have a reputation for flower power and continue opening blooms until frost arrives. Achieve maximum color by working a slow-release fertilizer into the soil prior to planting and keeping roots consistently moist as summer heat builds. Snip spent flowers to keep the blossoms coming.

With its ribbons of color, this bed beckons butterflies and hummingbirds. The design features a blue-and-pink palette with flowers in shades of lavender, silver, pink, and purple. You could easily substitute a darker ageratum (deep purple) and paler salvia (white or blue-and-white bicolors) to create an entirely different effect. Using a trailing Profusion Series zinnia to fill the edging role means using fewer plants to create the bold, colorful edge.

The yellow black-eyed Susan stands out in the pastel scheme. If you swap out other hues, explore the range of color available in black-eyed Susans, from dark mahogany to bronze to lemon yellow tones and bicolors.

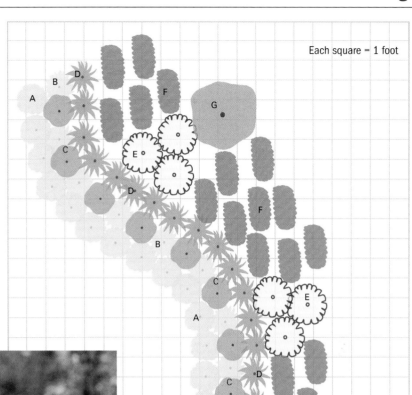

Each square = 1 foot

PLANT LIST

A. **25 Ageratum**
(*Ageratum houstonianum*)

B. **14 Dusty miller**
(*Senecio cineraria*)

C. **13 Vinca**
(*Catharanthus roseus*)

D. **25 Salvia**
(*Salvia farinacea*
'Victoria Blue')

E. **9 Black-eyed Susan**
(*Rudbeckia hirta*
'Indian Summer')

F. **21 Delphinium**
(*Delphinium* hybrids),
Zones 3–7

G. **1 Garden phlox**
(*Phlox paniculata*);
perennial, Zones 4–8

TEST
GARDEN
TIP

Annual advice

When purchasing annuals to plant a bed of this size, buy entire flats of the same type of plant to get the best price. If you're buying from a local independent garden center, talk with the owner to see if you can get a price break on a volume purchase. Check flats to ensure that plants along the edges aren't too short or that middle plants aren't too tall. Choose flats where plants demonstrate fairly even growth. If you're buying plants for this design, double-check ageratum labels to make sure you're buying a short variety. Some ageratum types grow as tall as the salvia.

Larger than life

Jungle-size tropicals lend a planting area an exotic look. This garden shines with a blend of nine plants grown primarily for their foliage and three bloomers. It showcases how gorgeous the display can be when it's designed using colorful leaves. The plant roster features the three key players of the quick color world: razzle-dazzle tropicals, tender perennials, and annuals.

The largest plants thrive in heat. When the soil warms, these easy-growing giants leap skyward, gaining inches every day at summer's peak. Adequate moisture and fertilizer enhances over-the-top growth of plants such as elephant's ear, canna, and castor bean. You'll get impressive results with soil that's amended liberally with compost and daily watering after plants gain some size.

A simple stone edging corrals the planting, which mostly melts away when frost arrives. This type of planting works well in regions with mild winters where you can replace summer performers with cool-season beauties. In snow-prone zones, it's the perfect garden-free location for heaping snow removed from sidewalks and driveways.

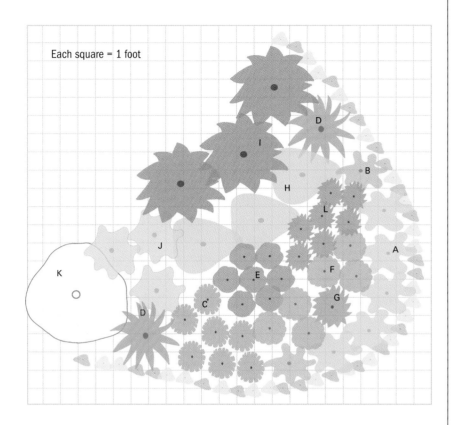

Each square = 1 foot

	PLANT LIST
A.	**5 Sweet potato vine** (*Ipomoea batatas* 'Margarita')
B.	**2 Sweet potato vine** (*Ipomoea batatas* 'Sweet Caroline Bronze')
C.	**7 Sweet William** (*Dianthus barbatus*)
D.	**2 Cardoon** (*Cynara cardunculus*)
E.	**7 Wax begonia** (*Begonia* × *semperflorens-cultorum*)
F.	**6 Coleus** (*Solenostemon scutellarioides*)
G.	**1 Persian shield** (*Strobilanthes dyerianus*)
H.	**3 Elephant's ear** (*Colocasia esculenta*)
I.	**3 Castor bean** (*Ricinus communis*)
J.	**3 Canna** (*Canna* × *generalis* 'Tropicanna')
K.	**1 Moonflower** (*Ipomoea alba*)
L.	**7 Dahlia** (*Dahlia* hybrids)

TEST GARDEN TIP

Shoot the moon

Moonflower vine offers a huge return on investment. For the price of a few seeds, you can enjoy weeks of amazing flowers that swirl open at dusk and close with the dawn. White blooms cast a pervasive fragrance that's wonderfully sweet. Soak the seeds overnight before planting them. Some gardeners also nick the hard seed coat using a file or sandpaper prior to soaking. If starting indoors, wait to transplant to the garden until after the threat of frost passes and the vines have two sets of true leaves. For a 24-hour show, intermingle moonflower and morning glory vines on a trellis.

Butterfly bonanza

Set a table for butterflies by creating

a planting bed packed with nectar-rich bloomers. Drifts of quick color beckon butterflies with upward-facing flowers that offer easy landing pads. Other blossoms open along spikes, providing multiple sips just millimeters apart—no flying required.

Some of the flowers are classic butterfly favorites: zinnia, mealycup sage, Mexican sunflower, and pentas. Many bear petals in bright colors, which lure butterflies. All of these plants prefer a sunny location, flowering strongest when they receive a minimum of six hours of sun daily.

To create this garden where grass currently resides, strip sod and amend the soil by mixing in compost, perlite, and peat moss. Blend in a slow-release fertilizer, then top the soil with some type of compost. Keep the soil moist until the new plants establish. Snip spent blooms to encourage a strong, ongoing flower show.

PLANT LIST

A. **3 Pentas** (*Pentas lanceolata*)

B. **5 Creeping zinnia**
(*Sanvitalia procumbens*)

C. **5 Mealycup sage** (*Salvia farinacea*),
such as 'Victoria Blue'

D. **8 Cosmos** (*Cosmos* spp.) such as yellow
Cosmos sulfureus 'Little Ladybird'

E. **2 Cleome** (*Cleome hassleriana*),
such as 'Rose Queen'

F. **3 Mexican sunflower**
(*Tithonia rotundifolia*)

G. **11 Zinnia** (*Zinnia elegans*), tall varieties
such as 'Cut and Come Again'

H. **6 Compact zinnia** (*Zinna* spp.),
such as the Profusion series

I. **7 French marigold** (*Tagetes patula*),
such as 'Yellow Boy'

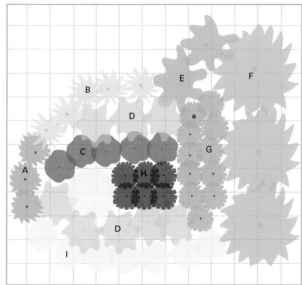

Each square = 1 foot

ASK THE
GARDEN
DOCTOR

What encourages butterflies to lay eggs?

ANSWER: Adult butterflies sip nectar from blooms. To host caterpillars, you need to grow the plants they eat. Identify the butterflies visiting your garden, research what their offspring eat, and add those plants to your garden. Herbs such as parsley, dill, fennel, and milkweed are a few host plants for common butterflies. Grow several of each type of host plant because caterpillars have big appetites. Host plants will be chewed. Consider locating them in a less prominent spot in the garden to avoid showcasing leafless stems.

Welcome
friends

Each square = 6 inches

Roll out a flowery carpet to greet family

and friends with this pleasing porchside bed. A blend of quick color annuals, perennials, and shrub roses give this area a steady procession of bud and bloom as the season unfolds. Some of the bloomers cast a sweet perfume that makes evening porch sitting a fragrant event.

In beds with high-frequency viewing, grow plants with sturdy constitutions that aren't diminished by heat or slight drought on days when you forget to water. This mix of plants offers a strong performance that stays on a colorful course all season long.

Brick edging separates ornamentals from surrounding lawn and makes mowing easy. Simply roll one wheel along the bricks for a neat clipping that doesn't disturb the flowers.

Keep plants looking their best with a ready supply of nutrients. Gently rake slow-release fertilizer into the soil around perennials in early spring. For the annual areas, hoe fertilizer and plenty of compost into the soil prior to planting. Snip spent blooms, stake rangy stems, and pull weeds when you see them. Keep a pair of pruners and a bucket tucked into a hidden spot near the planting bed to make tending plants easy.

ASK THE GARDEN DOCTOR

How do I avoid disturbing perennial roots when planting annuals?

ANSWER: At planting time, space annuals so their growth won't interfere with—or be overwhelmed by—mature perennial growth. This helps you avoid digging too close to perennial crowns. At the end of the growing season after a killing frost, gently pull spent annuals and add them to your compost pile. Heap some type of organic mulch, such as chopped autumn leaves or grass clippings, over bare soil and around perennial crowns. In the coldest Zones, once the ground freezes you can add a thicker mulch layer, if desired.

PLANT LIST

A.	**5 Hairy alum root** (*Heuchera villosa*)
B.	**10 Vinca** (*Catharanthus roseus*)
C.	**10 Ageratum** (*Ageratum houstonianum*)
D.	**5 Flowering tobacco** (*Nicotiana alata*)
E.	**7 Sweet alyssum** (*Lobularia maritima*)
F.	**3 Impatiens** (*Impatiens walleriana*)
G.	**3 Wax begonia** (*Begonia × semperflorens-cultorum*)
H.	**3 Catmint** (*Nepeta × faassenii*)
I.	**1 Magilla perilla** (*Perilla* Magilla)
J.	**5 Vista Bubblegum petunia** (*Petunia* Vista Bubblegum)
K.	**2 Knock Out rose** (*Rosa* Knock Out)
L.	**3 Black-eyed Susan** (*Rudbeckia hirta* 'Indian Summer')

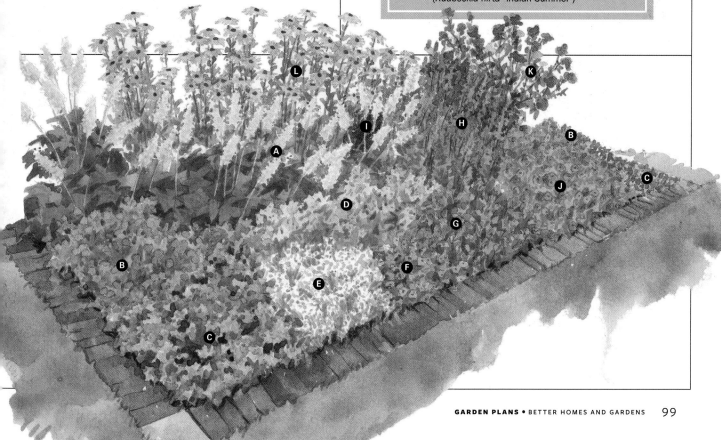

Seasonal changeouts

Plant a container that changes with the seasons. Start with a core group of slow-growing, long-lasting foliage plants that stay put from spring through fall. These plants provide the backbone color that remains steady through every season.

Complement the foliage favorites with bloomers that stage a pretty single-season display. Remove these seasonal flowers when they're spent, replacing them with fresh plants better suited to the following time of year.

CORE PLANTS

A. **3 Ruby grass**
(*Melinus nerviglumis* 'Pink Champagne')

B. **3 Alternanthera**
(*Alternanthera dentata* 'Purple Knight')

C. **3 Chartreuse licorice plant**
(*Helichrysum petiolare* 'Limelight')

D. **3 Coral bells**
(*Heuchera* Dolce Creme Brûlée)

SPRING CONTAINER (left)

3 Purple salvia
6 Purple viola
6 Purple pansy

SUMMER CONTAINER

3 Variegated orange-green-white coleus
3 Wax begonia ('Cocktail Rum')
6 Purple pansy

FALL CONTAINER

3 Flowering kale
3 Bronze chrysanthemum
('Blushing Emily')
6 Purple pansy

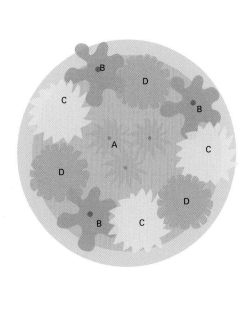

TEST GARDEN TIP

Primp and pamper

When a container garden is on center stage like this one, tending plants every few days keeps the show going strong. Trim dead leaves, snip spent blooms, and pinch rangy plants to promote bushiness. Follow strong prunings with liquid fertilizer to promote new growth. Use a bloom-booster fertilizer to encourage flowering.

Three-season show

Create a container garden that keeps pace with the seasons. Anchor the planting with a core group of slow-growing foliage plants that will keep their good looks from spring through fall. For a pop of color, add seasonal flowers for spring, summer, and fall color. Seasonal color shines for a time, but as temperatures shift, plants can lose their charms. When you swap plants, toss has-been beauties in the compost or tuck them into a partly shaded garden area. Here's how:

1 REMOVE PLANTS EASILY
The trickiest part of seasonal swap-outs is removing a plant without disturbing its neighbors. Using a sharp trowel, cut a circle around the plant you're removing, slicing neatly through roots. Pry the plant loose with a trowel. You may have to tug the plant free. Tuck the new plant into place, covering its root ball with fresh soil.

2 STAGE A SUMMER SHOW
As spring segues to summer, replace cool-weather bloomers with heat-tolerant varieties. You can create any color scheme you like. A palette of purple, orange, chartreuse, and pink holds its own in summer sun.

3 MAKE WAY FOR FALL FINERY
Remove plants swooning from summer heat. Replace with cool-season color. In colder regions, purchase the largest plants you can find for the fall show, since low temperatures won't promote lush growth. As nights chill, what you plant is all you'll get.

TEST
GARDEN
TIP

Roll out the barrel

To showcase big plants you need a big container, one that gives roots plenty of elbow room and handily anchors top-heavy plants. Half barrels work well for this task. Drill drainage holes, since these containers were designed to hold liquids. Elevate the barrel on small wood blocks attached to the bottom to increase airflow to roots and improve drainage.

PLANT LIST	
A.	**2 Canna** (*Canna* 'Tropicanna')
B.	**1 Firebush** (*Hamelia patens*)
C.	**3 Orange narrowleaf zinnia** (*Zinnia* hybrids), such as Profusion Orange
D.	**2 Yellow lantana** (*Lantana camara*')
E.	**1 Purple fountain grass** (*Pennisetum setaceum* 'Rubrum')

Colorful canna

Larger-than-life plants fill containers with riveting botanical drama. Design touches abound in this striking combination, which pairs the textural opposites of broad canna leaves with strappy purple fountain grass blades. Canna variegation patterns echo in the lantana leaves that are splashed with gold and green, and the firebush blooms reflect hues found in grass blades. The combination's sophisticated look intensifies as summer slips into fall.

A secret to growing large plants successfully in containers is enriching standard potting mix with compost and rotted manure. These materials supply slow nutrition and improve the soil's ability to hold water. Fertilize monthly. Remove spent canna blooms; the other plants typically don't require deadheading.

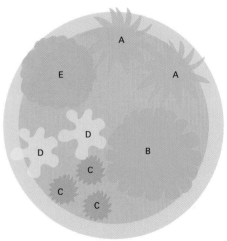

The recipe for pedestals

When elevating a pot on a pedestal, select a container with eye-catching details to capture attention before plantings fill out. Choose trailing plants that cascade to cover at least two-thirds of the container height. This waterfall of bud and bloom provides balance to the strong upright lines of pedestal and pot.

PLANT LIST

A.	**2 Canna** (*Canna* spp.)
B.	**1 Coleus** (*Solenostemon scutellarioides*)
C.	**3 Red ivy geranium** (*Pelargonium peltatum*)
D.	**3 Pink New Guinea impatiens** (*Impatiens hawkeri*)
E.	**2 Purple heart** (*Setcreasea pallida*)

Foliage on display

Introduce height to a planting bed using a pot-topped pedestal. The effect becomes even more compelling with a solid backdrop of shrubbery foliage.

Pack the container with a blend of foliage standouts in complementary hues such as purple and yellow, or red and green. Fill the pot with plants that reflect colors that are shown in nearby bed plantings to spark a harmonious conversation among plants.

The pedestal commands attention, then directs the eye upward to the container garden. Select a pedestal in proportion to the size and shape of pot you intend to showcase on it. In turn, choose a tall plant, like canna, that has the necessary height to counterbalance the pedestal.

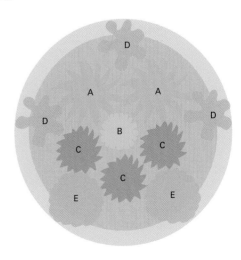

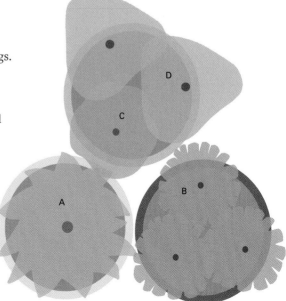

**Group pots for
a big effect**

Clustering pots of
individual plants makes
staging a picture-perfect
scene a snap. You can
always replace problem
or faded plants. Using
individual pots also works
better in a setting like this,
where a low step provides
an ideal lift for containers.

Pots in plural

A trio of 18-inch-tall glazed ceramic crocks
brightens patio corner when filled with simple quick color plantings.
These plantings sizzle with vibrant red and yellow pairings.

    A thread of red or pink weaves through the separate pots,
unifying the plantings. Plants in individual plastic pots that are
slipped into large ornamental containers offer the easiest seasonal
change. You can pot up and prepare color in another part of the
garden, then swap pots quickly when plants pass their peak.

PLANT LIST

A.   **1 Coleus** (*Solenostemon scutellarioides*
     'Oscar')

B.   **3 Geranium** (*Pelargonium* 'Caliente Fire')

C.   **1 Browallia** (*Browallia* 'Endless Illumination')

D.   **2 Caladium** (*Caladium bicolor*)

TEST GARDEN TIP
Keep a wood box new

To preserve a wood window box, plant into a plastic window box liner that fits inside the box, or line the box with plastic that's punctured with a few drainage holes. Treat a new wood window box with exterior waterproofing sealant prior to planting.

Pretty as a picture

Customize your view of the great outdoors with

a living window treatment. A sunny exposure combines with a season-long parade of blooms to ensure this window garden beckons butterflies. Encourage a strong flower show with a one-two punch of TLC.

First, faithfully remove spent blossoms. Second, use a bloom-booster fertilizer. When planting this window box, you'll have to pack in the plants. Feel free to knock excess soil off root balls to diminish the size. In some instances, you may have to shoehorn plants into place. Don't fret that you're damaging roots beyond repair. The plants will perk up once they're receiving consistent watering.

PLANT LIST	
A.	**3 Golden creeping jenny** (*Lysimachia nummularia* 'Aurea')
B.	**2 Marguerite daisy** (*Argyranthemum* 'Dress Up Primrose Path')
C.	**5 Geranium** (*Pelargonium* 'Caliente Deep Red')
D.	**2 Verbena** (*Verbena* 'Lanai Upright Violet')
E.	**2 Angelonia** (*Angelonia* Angelface Blue)
F.	**1 Serena Blue angelonia** (*Angelonia* Serena Blue)
G.	**5 Lantana** (*Lantana camara* Landmark White)

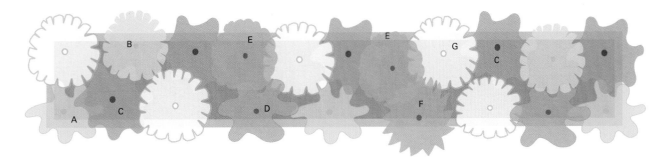

growing the plants

Healthy plants and practically perfect growing conditions are the keys to head-turning quick color. Learn how to coax the most from your plantings.

Consider light conditions

Designing quick color plantings offers

Designing quick color plantings offers endless opportunities for creative expression. You can establish a formal mood, celebrate unusual and quirky plant forms, or go for classic color combinations as you mix and match plants.

Unlimited design options can prove to be overwhelming when you visit the garden center. How do you select plants that will perform best in your garden? Winnow the number of choices by considering the amount of available light in your various planting areas.

Sun vs. shade

Some plants thrive in full sun; others need dark, shadowy corners to strut their stuff. Before you buy any plants, study how sunlight interacts with the areas where you plan to place quick color plantings. You might have a deck that's bathed in all-day sun, or maybe you're dealing with a bed on the east side of a garage. In that setting, morning sun will fade to afternoon shade, creating part shade.

Above: **Marigold and calamint (*Calamintha nepeta*) grow best when planted in a spot that receives at least six hours of direct sun daily. More sun is better, yielding stronger growth.**

Can a plant that needs full sun grow with part shade?

ANSWER: Plant tags specify what light level results in maximum growth. When you place a sun-loving plant in a shadier spot, the plant won't necessarily die, but growth will be affected. Flower number may decrease, stems may stretch and become gangly, or variegation patterns may diminish.

Light shifts with the seasons. A planting area beneath a deciduous tree such as a maple receives full sun in spring, but once leaves appear, full shade shrouds the space. A southwest-facing deck may receive intense sun in summer that fades to a daily splash in fall or spring as the sun drops lower in the sky.

Where you garden also influences a plant's light requirements. A plant that grows best in full sun in New England most likely requires afternoon shade in the intense afternoon sun of the South. In the Pacific Northwest, less sun, more clouds, and lower temperatures may cause sun lovers to languish while shade-loving plants flourish in a sunny location that would kill them in Southern California.

Light needs

As you research and shop for plants, you'll encounter light descriptions such as full sun, part sun, part shade, and full shade. These terms refer to the sunlight a plant needs to yield a top-notch performance. Unsure what these terms mean? You're not alone. Here's the lowdown on light requirement lingo.

Full sun plants should receive at least six hours of sun per day.

Part sun plants should receive three to six hours of sun per day, preferably in morning or early afternoon, not during the hottest parts of the day.

Part shade plants thrive with three to six hours of sun per day, but require shade during the afternoon when the sun is hottest. This condition describes the area on the east side of a building or beneath a tree, where the sun shines during the morning. Dappled shade is dotted with brief spots of sunlight.

Full shade plants need fewer than three hours of direct sun per day. Filtered sunlight or light shade is necessary for the rest of the day. This describes a location on the north side of a building or under a spreading tree where sunlight briefly penetrates the canopy at some point during the day.

Great color for sun and shade Try some of these favorites for a quick color show that's easy to grow in sun or shade.

SUN

ANGELONIA
Spikes covered with snapdragonlike blossoms in blue, purple, pink, or white shades make long-lasting cut flowers.

PHLOX
This underused annual with self-cleaning blooms comes in hues of white, blue, pink, and salmon, as well as star patterns and tricolor blends.

STRAWFLOWER
Savor bronze, gold, russet, red, pink, purple, or orange blends on daisylike flowers with papery petals.

MARIGOLD
Sturdy stems are topped with critter-resistant blooms in shades of gold, orange, russet, yellow, or blends.

CELOSIA
Diverse flower types offer colors from palest pink to fiery red, to lemon yellow, and many hues in between.

SHADE

BROWALLIA
Star-shape flowers in purple, white, or blue; darker shades frequently have a white eye.

DRAGON WING BEGONIA
Waxy, deep green, elongated leaves are punctuated by dangling blossom clusters in pink or red.

POLKA-DOT PLANT
Eye-catching heartshape foliage layers a green background with pink, white, or red flecks.

WISHBONE FLOWER
Snapdragon-like blooms come in purple, yellow, white, or pink with white throats that contrast with darker shades.

NEW GUINEA IMPATIENS
Flowers in red, pink, white, salmon, orange, or other shades adorn plants that can tolerate part sun.

Dig in

It doesn't matter whether you're raising your colorful charmers in pots or planting beds, good soil is the key to outstanding growth. Soil needs to provide a place for roots to sink in and anchor the plant, plus offer water, nutrients, and air.

The ideal soil should be light and fluffy, full of pockets for air, water, and roots. In a container, you can easily engineer soil to perfection. In a bed, amending soil may prove a little trickier, is possibly costlier, and definitely requires more elbow grease.

Soil for containers

In the confined environment of a planting container, it's essential to maintain a good balance between moisture-holding ability, drainage, and air spaces in the soil. Because of this, avoid using soil from your yard to fill containers. Garden soil is too heavy, compacts too easily, and typically drains too slowly to work well in pots and other containers.

Commercial bagged mixes provide the right blend of components for plants to thrive. Typically these mixes contain ingredients such

Above: **When preparing a new bed for quick color plantings, start by amending the soil. Mix in materials such as well-aged manure, perlite, and compost to give plants an ideal footing.**

as peat moss, coir/coconut fiber, vermiculite, perlite, sand, and ground bark. The label states if it is a soilless or soil-based mix.

A soilless mix is very lightweight and dries out quickly. Its primary component is peat moss, coir/coconut husk fiber, sawdust, or wood chips. A soil-based mix is heavier and retains moisture and nutrients longer than its soilless cousin.

Soil-based mixes contain sterilized garden loam in addition to soilless components.

Both types of mixes work well in containers. You might want to experiment with each to see which is ideal for your conditions and plants. In general, mixes designed for container use work well in traditional plastic pots 10 to 16 inches in diameter. These mixes often include a slow-release fertilizer and water-retention crystals, which enhance plant growth while whittling away your garden to-do list.

In larger containers like a half-barrel planter, blend soil-based and soilless mixes with compost for good results. For most quick color plants, a ratio of one-half soil-based mix with one-fourth soilless mix plus one-fourth compost yields strong growth. Topdress the container annually with well-rotted compost, and fertilize regularly with a liquid fertilizer.

For small containers that dry out easily, such as window boxes and hanging baskets, blend compost and water-retention cyrstals into a soilless mix. These additional components enable the mix to hold water better, a boon in small growing spaces.

Soil for planting beds

For in-ground growing, amend the soil to improve its drainage, water-holding ability, and nutrition. Mixing compost or a potting mix labeled for garden use into most existing soils gives an extra edge to grow gorgeous plants. These mixes are frequently sold as "garden soil" and include a blend of peat moss, composted manure, and other natural materials such as composted rice hulls, fine forest mulch, or composted pine bark.

If you have sandy soil, adding compost and water-retention crystals to the soil improves water-holding ability. With hard clay soil, compost is a key ingredient for loosening soil and reducing compaction.

Always take time to expend the effort to improve your soil. You'll wind up with healthier plants that grow better and look fantastic.

ASK THE GARDEN DOCTOR

How do I keep pests out of my compost pile?

ANSWER: Avoid adding meat, bones, and fatty foods (cheese, salad dressing, oils) to your compost. These materials ferment as they compost, creating odors that beckon critters. If your pile draws local deer to feast on kitchen scraps, use a trowel to bury those items in the pile. Remember that insects populate a compost pile in large numbers—that's a good thing. They help break down materials.

DIY compost It's easy to start a compost pile. Spread a 3-inch-thick layer of brown material on top of soil or lawn. Top the brown material with a 3-inch-thick layer of green material. Continue layering as materials become available. Aim for a pile that's at least 9 cubic feet to achieve good breakdown. As the pile increases in height, support it with some type of fencing held in place with stakes. Some gardeners use discarded wooden pallets as a compost bin.

1 BROWN MATERIAL
Chopped dried leaves, dried grass, small wood chips, twigs, soil, and shredded newspaper contribute valuable carbon and microorganisms to the pile.

2 GREEN MATERIAL
Fresh grass clippings, kitchen scraps from fruits and vegetables, and garden waste (but nothing diseased) provide valuable nitrogen to the pile. Add corncobs to create air pockets.

3 WATER
Water is crucial for bacteria to grow and decomposition to occur. Keep the pile as moist as a wrung-out sponge. Covering the pile with a tarp helps retain moisture. For the fastest breakdown, turn the pile every two weeks.

Shopping for plants

You'll get the best results

with quick color efforts when you start with healthy plants. In spring, many retailers that don't normally specialize in gardening sell plants. To get the healthiest plants from home improvement stores, groceries, and mass merchants, shop the day the plants arrive. At this point, they shouldn't be swooning from inadequate care.

You'll always find healthy plants at dedicated garden centers. These businesses make their living from plants, so they provide consistently better care over the long haul. But if you know

how to spot a healthy plant, you can shop anywhere and make a good choice.

As you peruse annual seedlings at the garden center, look for plants that are short, stocky, and covered with flower buds.

To make the best choice, avoid purchasing cell packs filled with blooming plants, except in cases where you want to make sure you're buying plants of a particular color. Blooming container annuals often have inadequate root systems, and have used up some of their bloom time so they won't bloom as long.

Above: **Plant price varies with pot size. If you sort plants by container size to help the clerks, you'll get a faster check-out and avoid getting charged a 5-inch price for a 3-inch pot.**

Packs vs. pots
No rules determine when you should plunk down extra cash for a bigger container. Use these guidelines to boost your confidence—and save money—when shopping.

Flower Packs (Cells)

PAY ATTENTION Small three-cell packs may cost as much as four- or six-cell packs. Don't buy pricey nine-cell packs unless you truly need nine plants. Annuals in branded pots often command the highest price but deliver on performance.

CHECK THE EDGES Plants in cells near the edges of flats of annuals are likely to be drier and rangier than ones crowded in the center. Water them before loading them in your warm car.

REASONS TO BUY CELLS Cells offer volume at a lower price than pots, making it more affordable to plant in groups of three or more, which makes annuals look their best. You can get extra plants to tuck into pots. In warm climates, they are ideal for planting cool-season annuals in autumn for color all winter.

DRAWBACKS Cells take longer to fill out in the garden but ultimately provide the same results as potted plants.

Flower Pots

BEST FOR TROPICALS Quick color tropicals and ornamental grasses usually come in quart or gallon pots because they're larger plants and simply won't fit in smaller pots. The good news is that you may not need multiples. They command such attention that one or two create the desired impact.

REASONS TO BUY POTS Buying plants in larger pots creates a bigger, quicker impact in the garden. Pots of annuals provide color-ready, cool-season punch when air and soil temperatures are too low to permit growth. When spring wanes in warm zones, pots are better choices to get a good display before summer heat.

DRAWBACKS Pots cost more per plant than packs. Examine sizes carefully. Quick color annuals are frequently sold in 3-, 4-, and 5-inch pots, each larger size costing more.

Avoid these plants
Gorgeous gardens start with healthy plants. Learn how to select plants that show the most promise—and even more important, which plants to avoid.

DISEASE
If you spot disease in a cell pack, don't buy any seedlings from that flat. If your choice is limited, choose packs located the farthest away from the diseased plants.

ROOT-BOUND
Slip seedlings out of their cells to examine roots. A large mass of roots with little soil signals a seedling that has been in the pack or pot too long. Look for a balance of healthy white roots and soil. Unhealthy roots are brown and often have a sour odor.

LEGGY PLANTS
Leave stretched-out, leggy plants behind. Tall seedlings have likely been in cell packs or pots too long. If stems are stocky and have healthy foliage from top to bottom, they're a safe bet. Look for healthy, sturdy plants with flower buds that aren't open yet.

Planting time

Transfer plants into containers and

planting beds as soon as the soil is warm enough. It's not ideal for plants to remain in their store-bought pots, especially small cell packs. Plants may become root-bound and start to suffer from malnutrition. But don't plant too soon. Damp, cold soil can cause plants to stall and even rot.

If you can't tackle planting right away, store plants in a spot somewhat sheltered from direct sun to slow down soil drying and reduce watering chores. Where plant supplies are limited, you may end up purchasing plants too early for planting. In this case, locate plants where you can protect them from a late frost—and where nibbling bunnies or deer won't find them an easy feast.

Tips for successful planting

Soak terra-cotta or other porous containers in water before planting. Otherwise, the dry pots will wick moisture out of the soil and away from plant roots.

Block drainage holes with a piece of screen, coffee filter, or newspaper to keep soil from spilling out.

Above: **Try to plant on a cloudy or overcast day or in the early evening. In those conditions, plants lose less water to heat stress and recover more quickly from transplant shock.**

Cover the bottom of containers 12 inches and larger with a few inverted plastic 4-inch pots. Don't fill more than one-third of the total container volume with empty pots. This technique reduces the pot's weight and the amount of soil you need. It also increases airflow around plant roots. Skip this step if you're filling the pot with permanent plantings that will remain in the pot for years.

Fill a container half- to three-quarters full with potting mix. Blend in slow-release fertilizer and water-retention crystals. Top with more mix.

Arrange plants, in their pots, on top of the planting bed. Finesse the arrangement until you're happy with it. With containers, first arrange the plants on a nearby surface, then duplicate that configuration in the pot.

Moisten the root balls before planting, especially if they're dry.

Remove one plant at a time from its pot. With small pots, gently squeeze the pot and turn it over, cradling the plant's stem with your hand. The plant should slip out of the pot. With larger pots, lay the pot on the ground and press on it on several sides. Invert it, and the plant should slip out. Never pull a plant out of its pot by the stem; you risk breaking it.

Dig a shallow hole in the soil to accommodate the plant's root ball. For plants with small rootballs, speed up the process with the stab-and-plant method. Grab a trowel with the blade facing down and the concave side toward you. Stick it into the soil and pull gently forward, forming a hole. Slip the plant into the hole.

Add and firm the soil around the young plant. In containers, add soil around plants, gently tamping but not packing. Leave 2 inches between the soil surface and the top of containers to provide room for mulch and water.

Water plants once they're in the soil. Soak the soil thoroughly with a gentle shower. Irrigate containers until water flows freely from the drainage hole.

Mulch

Add a layer of mulch to plantings in beds and pots. Mulch slows water evaporation from soil, reduces soil temperature, and helps suppress weeds. Gritty mulches discourage slugs. Rocky mulch can deter digging rodents. In planting beds, add a 2-inch layer of mulch, but make it 3 inches in the hottest regions. In containers, add 1 inch of mulch, leaving 1 inch of space between the mulch and the lip of the pot.

Keep plant tags

Save your plant tags as a reference tool for future plantings. In containers, tuck the tags along the edge of the pot. If the planting proves especially pleasing, save those tags for next year's shopping list. With in-ground plantings, stash tags in a labeled envelope and keep the tags of plants that you want to repeat in future.

How many plants It's easy to overbuy when confronted with beautiful blooms and foliage hues en masse at the garden center. Determine beforehand how many annuals you'll need for your planting beds.

1 RESEARCH
Research the plants you want to determine plant spread or spacing. At the garden center, that information appears on plant tags. To determine how many plants to buy, divide the length of your bed area by the plant spacing. Repeat with the bed width, and multiply those two numbers together. That's how many plants you need to fill your bed.

2 SPACE
Spacing varies. If you have a long growing season, space plants farther apart. Gardeners in northern areas can space closer for the best show. Some annuals, such as Supertunia petunias, grow so vigorously they need ample spacing: one plant every 10 to 15 inches. You can safely space most annuals at a distance equal to half their mature height.

3 AVOID CROWDING
Avoid planting shoulder to shoulder. It yields instant impact, but plants become overcrowded and require more frequent watering and more fertilizer. Crowded plants also prove more susceptible to disease.

4 BUY MORE
Buy about 10 percent more plants than you need so you have extras to fill curving bed edges and to replace any plants that die early in the season. Tuck extra annuals into garden beds or into pots on a deck or patio to unify garden and outdoor living areas.

Watering

Provide consistent moisture to quick color plants

and you'll savor stunning displays throughout the growing season. As plants grow, their water needs change. Young plants use less moisture; mature plants require much more.

Irrigation frequency also varies based on the season. In cooler weather, plants need less water. During summer's dog days, it may seem like you can't water enough, especially small containers or pots jam-packed with plants.

Irrigation frequency

Eyeballing your plants to decide whether they need watering is risky, because the same symptoms result from under- and overwatering. The most foolproof method to determine whether a plant needs water is by checking the soil. In containers, gently push a finger into the soil to your second knuckle. If the soil is dry to the touch, water. In planting beds, check the soil at a depth of 3 to 4 inches. Slip a trowel into the soil and gently pull it forward to check moisture levels.

Irrigate containers until you see water flowing freely from drainage holes. As plants mature and temperatures soar with summer's arrival, place saucers beneath pots to catch runoff so plants can sip throughout the day. If a soilless mix dries out completely, stand the pot in a large container filled with water. It may require an overnight soak to rewet the soil completely.

When you water planting beds, soak the soil about 8 inches deep. This won't happen with a quick dribble from the hose. For large planting

Above: **Simple actions conserve much water in the garden. Install a soaker hose on an automatic timer with a rain shutoff valve to apply water efficiently when plants need it.**

areas, rely on some type of automatic irrigation such as a sprinkler, drip system, or soaker hose to make watering a breezy, hands-free affair.

Water wisely

Make the most of your irrigation efforts by adopting conservative watering practices.

Reduce runoff. Soaker hoses and drip irrigation systems apply water directly to soil, eliminating runoff and evaporation that can occur with overhead sprinkling.

Slow evaporation. Water early in the day when temperatures are low to reduce evaporation losses.

Use crystals. Water-retention crystals absorb moisture and then slowly release it to plant roots. Mix them into the soil in pots and planting beds.

Avoid wind. Overhead watering and windy conditions don't mix. The water gets blown off target and wind wicks water from plants via leaves. Wait until air is calm to water. Set automatic systems to deliver water during the least windy times of the day.

Apply mulch. Maintain a 2- to 3-inch-deep mulch layer to reduce water evaporation from the soil in planting beds.

Maximize assets. Add planting areas that take advantage of your yard's natural attributes. For instance, water-loving plants thrive in low spots that collect water and near downspouts where runoff douses soil.

Inspect lines. Check automated irrigation systems seasonally to ensure lines aren't clogged or ruptured. This is vital in areas with hard water, where accumulated deposits frequently block irrigation heads.

Reset timers. Seasonally, reset automated irrigation timers to ensure water is being delivered according to moisture needs. If you don't have one, add an automatic rain shutoff valve.

Stop watering. Install a hose-end watering wand with a shutoff valve that allows you to stop the water flow as you drag the hose. This is key when watering container plants that are scattered throughout outdoor living areas.

TEST GARDEN TIP

Capture rain

Celebrate rainy days by adding rain barrels to downspouts, especially in locations close to your gardens. Make sure the barrel overflow drains away from your home to avoid swamping your foundation (and maybe your basement).

Drought-tolerant color

Many quick color plants, once established in a planting bed, survive on only a small amount of water. In containers where soil dries out rapidly these same plants require more frequent watering. Try a few of these outstanding annuals for dry spots in your garden.

AGERATUM Fringed blooms in shades of blue, purple, pink, and white are butterfly favorites. Look for tall or short types.

BLACK-EYED SUSAN Diverse colors dress petals in traditional gold, russet, and hues in between, plus bicolors. Snip stems for bouquets.

BLANKET FLOWER Blossoms sizzle in orange, red, yellow, or blends. The blooms of this heat-loving plant lure many pollinators.

GAZANIA Flowers open and close with the sun, revealing petals in gold, white, pink, red, orange, raspberry, or bicolors.

GOMPHRENA Lollipoplike blooms stand atop stems. Petals have a papery texture. Look for purple, white, red, and pink shades.

LANTANA This butterfly favorite opens rounded flowers that stage a multicolor show. Blossoms typically change color as they age.

MOSS ROSE Thick succulent leaves form along ground-hugging stems. Blooms open in a rainbow of shades. Plants self-sow.

SUNFLOWER Classic sun-loving bloomer offers petals in hues from gold to bronze to bicolor blends. Look for shorter types for small gardens.

VINCA Flat-faced flowers unfurl in hues of red, white, pink, purple, burgundy, or coral shades. Plants are exceptionally heat-tolerant.

NARROWLEAF ZINNIA This rambling groundcover opens daisylike blooms in yellow, orange, or white. Plants resist mildew.

Fertilizing

Quick color plants are high-performance beauties that

require a steady supply of nutrients to maintain their intense displays. Despite their big appetites, most quick color plants aren't picky eaters and respond to simple all-purpose fertilizers with strong growth.

A few quick color performers boast more of a diva personality and demand specific nutrients to fuel their flowers or foliage. Hibiscus plants, for example, don't respond with heavy flowering to traditional bloom-booster fertilizers containing extra phosphorus. These tropicals need more potassium to reach their full potential. Bananas also grow best when they're lapping up a little extra potassium.

Elephant's ear thrives with ample nitrogen, and begonias crank out flowers when they're given bloom-booster fertilizer. Some plants, such

Above: **A small dose of water-soluble fertilizer quickly produces visible results. Use it to replenish nutrients when frequent rains have washed away slow-release fertilizers.**

as morning glory, won't produce blooms when they have too much nitrogen. It's best to do quick research to ensure you're providing the ideal diet for your quick color plants.

Fertilizer labels specify the percentage of nitrogen (N), phosphorus (P), and potassium (K) in the product. That percentage is listed as a series of numbers, such as 15-30-15 (N-P-K). In this formulation, 15 percent of the fertilizer is nitrogen, 30 percent is phosphorus, and the final 15 percent is potassium.

You can use those numbers to gauge if the product is a high-nitrogen fertilizer, which promotes leaf growth, or a high-phosphorus type, which increases flowering. Potassium helps overall plant health.

Slow-release fertilizer

Slow- or gradual-release fertilizers are excellent for quick color plants. These products feature special coatings that gradually release nutrients, usually over a period of three to nine months. The fertilizer label will clearly specify the time frame. Slow-release products frequently are already blended into bagged potting mixes, both soilless and soil-based types.

If you purchase mixes that don't contain fertilizer, add it prior to planting. Midway through the growing season, if needed, you can work more slow-release fertilizer into the soil.

Soluble fertilizer

Dissolved in water, soluble fertilizers deliver a quick nutrient burst. They're easy to handle and store and contain a high percentage of nutrients per weight. In soil with organic matter, nutrients from a soluble fertilizer are retained. But in sandy soil or soilless mixes, nutrients move out of root zones quickly when more water washes through the soil. Most liquid fertilizers are poured onto soil. Some are sprayed onto the leaves, which absorb nutrients.

Organic fertilizer

Organic fertilizers include compost and manure, which provide slow-release nitrogen. These fertilizers typically are used with planting beds or large containers like half-barrel planters. They improve soil structure, encourage soil microbes and earthworms, and contain a high level of micronutrients that plants need to grow.

Some organic fertilizers, such as bonemeal, blood meal, or cottonseed meal, are concentrated. A small amount of these materials offers a large nutrient boost, which explains their often higher price. Although meal fertilizers are a good organic choice, they require microbes to break them down. That means they can't provide readily available nutrients during colder seasons when microbes are inactive.

Too little nutrition

Most plants give clues when available nutrients are insufficient to fuel growth. Watch foliage carefully. When nitrogen is scarce, leaves turn yellow. Too little phosphorus causes leaves to turn reddish or purple. Older leaves burn and drop when potassium is in short supply. Other symptoms of nutrient deficiency include weak or slow growth and smaller leaves and flowers.

ASK THE GARDEN DOCTOR

How can I fertilize every time I water?

ANSWER: You can apply liquid fertilizer to plants directly through your garden hose by adding a siphon attachment to your hose. It attaches to the faucet end of the hose. This device siphons a solution of fertilizer concentrate you mix in a bucket. The concentrate dilutes with the water flowing through the hose.

Fertilizer and pots

Container materials influence how much you have to water, which has a direct impact on fertilizer retention in soil. When plants are watered more frequently—from rain or irrigation—nutrients tend to wash from the soil more quickly. Plants watered less usually retain nutrients longer.

TERRA-COTTA
Unglazed terra-cotta allows air and water to move through the container. They are good for plants that prefer dry soil. Clay pots need more frequent irrigation, which washes away nutrients quicker. Fertilize plants in these pots more often.

PLASTIC
Plastic containers aren't porous and tend to retain water longer. This is good for plants that prefer consistent moisture around their roots. Soil in plastic pots won't dry out as fast or need water as often, so nutrients stay in the soil longer.

Grooming your garden

Removing spent blooms on plants encourages more flower buds to form. Hand pruners make quick work of this task. Toss faded blossoms onto the compost pile.

Basic plant maintenance
includes a variety of activities: deadheading, pruning, staking, and scouting for pests and diseases. Tackle many of these tasks while you water, as part of a daily care routine, to maintain your garden with little effort.

Deadheading
Snipping or pinching blooms when they fade keeps a garden looking good. It also stops seed formation, which shifts most annual plants into a death march. During summer heat and humidity,

spent flowers may also develop a fungus that spreads to other plant parts.

Removing faded flowers encourages more blossoms to form. For annuals that send up a flower spike, such as 'Victoria Blue' or 'Coral Nymph' salvia, clip the entire spike near its base. Remove dead flowers before seedpods mature. Keep clippers handy and deadhead daily.

Some plants are self-cleaning, meaning that spent blooms drop of their own accord. These include begonia, impatiens, and vinca.

Pruning

You should prune quick color plants at several points during their lives.

At planting. Prune flowers so the plant directs energy into root formation. Pinch off growing tips to promote branching and blooms.

Throughout the growing season. If stems become bare, trim back to just above where a leaf attaches. Fertilize with a liquid product. New growth should emerge. Any time plants grow out of bounds or out of proportion with surrounding plantings, clip to bring growth into balance. Remove faded leaves and flower stalks that form on foliage plants such as coleus and polka-dot plant.

Midseason. Prune by one-third to one-half any plants that are blooming only at the far ends of ever-lengthening, ungainly stems. Fertilize after to encourage fresh growth. Plants that benefit from this treatment include petunia, Swan River daisy, sweet alyssum, and verbena.

Staking

Many tall quick color plants grow sturdy stems that resist flopping. But some, such as cleome, 'Flamingo Feather' celosia, heliotrope, and tall varieties of flowering tobacco and zinnia, have a tendency to sprawl or fall over. Others, like Dragon Wing and tuberous begonias, have arching growth habits and succulent stems that sometimes snap beneath the weight of leaves and flowers.

Stake plants as needed throughout the growing season. Hoop and half-hoop stakes work well with many quick color plants, as do sturdy sticks from tree or shrub trimmings. Both of these materials tend to disappear among foliage.

Scouting

Whenever you water, inspect plants for signs of insects or diseases. Clues might be discolored or misshapen leaves. Insect pests may be easy to spot. Identify the problem before treating it. Check with a local garden center or your county extension office to learn treatment options.

ASK THE GARDEN DOCTOR

Do I need to deadhead petunias?

ANSWER: A garden center can't risk unsightly faded blooms dangling from plants. The newer spreading petunias self-clean, meaning the old blooms eventually drop off. But if you dislike the look, remove them.

Refresh a container
Keep quick color containers looking top-notch by replacing straggly, overgrown plants with fresh performers that are rarin' to grow.

1 BEFORE
Tropical foliage plants such as spiky New Zealand flax maintain their great looks year-round. Annuals like petunia can become leggy as the season wears on. To refresh, remove plants that are no longer attractive.

2 DURING
Salvage plants that still look healthy, like this Sweet Caroline Raven sweet potato vine and Euphoric White euphorbia. Trim plants as needed to spur new growth. Replace loose soil with fresh potting mix.

3 AFTER
Add new plants that complement the ones you saved. 'Vancouver Centennial' geranium, 'Artist Purple' ageratum, and 'Orange Marmalade' crossandra dazzle against the existing dark foliage tones and white euphorbia.

Fall and winter

When cold weather signals the time to shift plants into winter quarters, use a hand truck or dolly to move large containers.

As summer turns to fall, quick color plants shift gears. Some slide into a cool-weather-induced slump where growth slows and flowers fail to open. Some quick color plants, such as calibrachoa, nemesia, Swan River daisy, and verbena can withstand a hard freeze. Others, such as impatiens, sweet potato vine, and zinnia, turn into mush when temperatures slip near freezing.

Truly tropical plants swoon the moment temperatures dip below 45°F. Others have somewhat more stalwart personalities and withstand autumn's brisk mornings without missing a blooming beat.

It's worth doing a little research so you can protect tender plants in the case of a brief, unexpected cold snap that's followed by temperatures plants can survive.

Once you know which plants fade soonest in fall, plan to replace them with cool-weather choices or, in colder zones, with lively winter decor, such as evergreen boughs and berried branches.

Winter storage

In cold climates where quick color tropicals and tender perennials won't survive winter outdoors, consider storing plants indoors or in conditions that induce winter dormancy.

The best plants to overwinter are ones that stage a stronger show with age. For instance, the older an angel's trumpet (*Brugmansia*) or a vegetatively propagated geranium gets, the more blooms it will have. Or, you may want to overwinter big plants for budgetary reasons.

It's easy to dig canna rhizomes and caladium tubers after a freeze and pack them into peat moss for winter storage. They don't require much room and survive without rigorous care. You can pack them into a box to store.

Other plants can overwinter in a sunny window or sunroom. They may lose leaves when they're first brought indoors and most likely won't flower much, if at all. Through winter, water only when the soil is dry to the touch. If your only storage location offers minimal light, consider supplementing with grow lights.

It's easy to store tropicals in containers. If you place the pots in a location where temperatures hover just above 60°F, the plants will enter dormancy and won't grow through winter. Give them only enough water to keep roots alive and stems from shriveling. In this situation, plants drop most of their leaves, but they'll awaken from their dormant state when longer days and warmer temperatures return. There's no need to give dormant plants bright or supplemental light; you can store them in a dark, cool, dry part of the basement.

Choose which plants to overwinter based on available storage space. Avoid crowding plants. That's an invitation for pests and diseases to develop. Remember that plants probably won't grace your indoor settings with the same stature and color they provide outdoors, where sunlight is abundant and temperatures are optimal for over-the-top growth.

Above: **To overwinter elephant's ear, dig up the roots, and allow them to dry. Brush off soil and store in a cool, dark place. Packing roots in peat moss is optional.**

Cold-weather container savvy

As Jack Frost starts to tiptoe around the garden, take steps to protect pots from winter's intense cold.

Purchase coldproof pots when possible. These containers feature fiberglass, resin, and other high-priced plastic materials that withstand cold temperatures. Cast-iron containers also may stay outside.

Avoid pot materials such as terra cotta, ceramic, and concrete which absorb moisture. When soil freezes, any moisture also freezes and expands, which usually results in chipping, cracking, or shattering of the pot. If you must leave these containers outdoors for winter, it's best to empty them, turn them upside down, and elevate them above the surrounding surface. Slipping a board beneath the pot provides sufficient separation from the ground and reduces the chances of the container absorbing moisture from nearby surfaces.

plant encyclopedia

Dream up a quick color garden and find the plants to bring it to life. Look for flowers that display favorite colors, boldly dramatic tropical plants, and blooming plants that glow with continuous color.

OLD FRIENDS
Tried-and-true plants grace the garden like cherished friends who drop in for an annual visit. Look for favorite plants, including some bred with new twists.

SOMETHING NEW
Celebrate the adventure of gardening by adding new flowers and foliage to your roster. Untried plants open a world of possibilities to experiment with every year.

HOW TO SUCCEED
Check out the details you need to succeed with each plant. From soil to fertilizer to pruning tricks, discover secrets from the pros and use them in your garden.

Abutilon
(*Abutilon × hybridum*)

A cousin to hibiscus, abutilon features bell-shape blossoms that dangle in shades of pink, yellow, white, and red. Abutilon holds its own in landscape and container plantings, where flowers beckon hummingbirds and butterflies. The leaf shape provides its common name: flowering maple.

Best site

Abutilon craves consistently moist soil. In containers, use a soilless mix containing coir. In northern zones, site plants in sun. In southern and western regions, provide shade during the hottest part of the day. Zones 9–11.

Growing

Pinch growing tips of branches to promote shorter, compact plants with stronger stems. During peak flowering, fertilize container plants weekly with a half-strength solution. Plants grow 12 to 48 inches tall and up to 24 inches wide.

Design ideas

Allow dangling flowers to shine by displaying plants on a pedestal or in a hanging basket. In mixed containers, abutilon plays a filler or spiller role. Use in butterfly or hummingbird gardens.

varieties:

❶ **'FAIRY CORAL RED'** Salmon pink blooms blanket plants from spring to fall. 1 to 2 feet tall, 2 feet wide. Zones 7–11.
'LUCKY LANTERN WHITE' A genetic dwarf that opens creamy white, full-size bells. 1 foot tall and wide. Zones 8–11.

Acalypha
(*Acalypha wilkesiana*)

Give your garden a touch of the tropics by incorporating this Fiji native, also called copperleaf, into planting beds and pots. A tender perennial that thrives in heat and humidity, it unfolds leaves mottled with shades of green, red, pink, bronze, and yellow. Look for wide- to narrow-leaf types.

Best site

Plant in full sun to part shade in rich, moist, fast-draining soil. Best leaf color develops in full sun. Zones 8–11.

Growing

During the growing season, consistent moisture fuels growth. In winter, excessively wet soil can rot plants. Stems can snap in strong winds; tuck acalypha into sheltered locations.

Design ideas

Use as an upright thriller plant in containers. Pair with orange flowers, a lemony coleus, and a chartreuse alternanthera or sweet potato vine for summer-long sizzle. Plant in beds as a "madras skirt" for 'Pretoria' canna or elephant's ears. The colorful foliage also holds its own in beds.

varieties:

❶ **'BOURBON STREET'** Narrow dark green leaves edged with glowing pink and orange. Up to 3 feet tall and 2 feet wide. Zones 10–11.
'COPPER HEAD' Green to copper leaves splashed with pink. Up to 3 feet tall and 2 feet wide. Zones 8–11.

African Daisy
(*Osteospermum* hybrids)

If you dote on daisies, try this true sun lover in your garden. African daisy brightens the scene all season. Its cold-tolerant blooms come in many shapes and sizes, and the wide range of hues includes orange, bronze, yellow, purple, and pink.

Best site

Plant in full to part sun in well-drained soil. The foliage is somewhat succulent, hinting that plants don't need an abundance of water. Overwatering is the surest way to kill them, especially in containers. Hybrids with dark blue or purple-tinted centers tend to have greater frost tolerance. Zones 9–11.

Growing

Flowers open at sunrise and close each day at sunset. Petal forms vary from traditional smooth to spoon shape. Remove spent blooms to encourage continuous flowering. Strongest flowering occurs when night temperatures are cool. During the heat of summer, blooming may wane, but the flower-bud count recovers with cooler weather. Pinching the stem tips promotes branching and increased blossom numbers.

Average plant size is 12 to 14 inches tall by 8 to 14 inches wide. Compact types grow 6 to 12 inches tall and wide.

Design ideas

Grow in pots with plants that sport complementary flower or foliage color. Gold and orange selections go well with purple fountain grass as a thriller with a plant in a darker hue, such as 'Blackie' sweet potato vine or purple calibrachoa, as a spiller. Place purple African daisies next to brightly hued sun-loving coleus varieties and toffee-tone sedges. African daisy boasts a strong landscape presence when planted en masse.

varieties:

❶ **'3D BERRY WHITE'** Double flower with white petals and upright berry-tinted center. Flowers stay open even in low light. 12 to 16 inches tall and 18 to 24 inches wide.

❷ **'ASTI WHITE'** White petals around a purple center. 12 to 18 inches tall, 2 feet wide.

❸ **'ASTRA PURPLE SPOON'** Spoon-shape purple petals, dark purple center. 8 to 12 inches tall and wide.

❹ **'ORANGE SPARK SYMPHONY'** Purple-dusted tangerine petals, purple center. 8 to 14 inches tall, 12 to 14 inches wide.

❺ **'ZION APRICOT PINK'** Butter yellow petals with pink center. 10 to 16 inches tall, 14 to 20 inches wide.

Ageratum
(*Ageratum houstonianum*)

Fringed buttonlike blooms top plants with deep green, crinkly leaves. Plant sizes range from ankle- to knee-high, offering landscape options as edging or in cutting gardens. The flowers open in a variety of hues, including blue, purple, pink, and white, and are butterfly favorites.

Best site
Grow plants in bright sun to light shade in rich, well-drained soil. In southern regions, protect plants from harsh afternoon sun. Ageratum has moderate drought tolerance but should be watered when rain is scarce. Zones 9–11.

Growing
This underused plant presents a strong color display from summer heat to frost. Ageratum is generally untroubled by neglect, insects, or even overattentiveness. Most types require deadheading to look their best. In landscape plantings, make deadheading easy by lightly shearing the plants. Some varieties self-sow freely, so deadheading keeps volunteer seedlings to a minimum.

Ageratum benefits from regular feeding. Use an all-purpose or bloom-booster fertilizer. Plants collapse quickly following frost.

Design ideas
Ageratum often counts as a source of blue in the garden, providing abundant blooms that open all season long. The compact, uniform, tidy growth habit of short varieties works well as an edging plant and in formal or knot gardens. You can find short and tall varieties, too. Tall varieties present loose, open forms that add charm to cottage and cutting gardens. All sizes perform well in containers. Use the smaller types as edging or rounded mound fillers, and taller ones as fillers or thrillers, depending on the planting partners.

varieties:

1. **'ARTIST PURPLE'** Deep purple blooms. 8 to 12 inches tall, 10 to 12 inches wide.
2. **'EVEREST BLUE'** True blue flowers. 26 inches tall, 8 to 12 inches wide.
3. **'HAWAII SHELL PINK'** Uniform midsize plant with pinkish button flowers. 6 to 12 inches tall and wide.
4. **'HAWAII BLUE'** Heavy-flowering, uniform plant. 6 to 8 inches tall and wide.
5. **'PATINA DELFT'** Unusual blossoms with a white center and purple fringe. No deadheading needed. 6 to 12 inches tall, 9 to 16 inches wide.

Alternanthera
(Alternanthera spp.)

In sun-drenched spaces where other plants wilt, try alternanthera. Heat tolerance makes this colorful foliage plant a boon for areas where summer sizzles. In most varieties, leaf hues intensify as sunlight increases. Alternanthera embodies easy-growing, low-maintenance beauty at its best.

Best site

Plant in well-drained, moist soil containing some organic matter. Alternanthera's colorful foliage isn't succulent and requires evenly moist soil to thrive. Leaves develop the most intense, eye-catching hues when placed in full sun. The exception is the variety 'Partytime', which colors nicely in shade or sun. Zones 8–11.

Growing

Pinch at planting time and again when new shoots are 2 inches long to produce a bushy, well-branched habit. Throughout the growing season, snip growth as needed to maintain plant shape or height. Flowers are dainty but easily overlooked since they form at joints where leaves attach to stems. Leaves are the showstoppers on this plant.

Alternanthera requires consistently moist soil. Plants wilt dramatically when the soil moisture is inadequate. For plants in pots, if the soil dries and heavy wilting occurs, move the pot into shade and dunk it into a large container of water until the soil is moist and the leaves revive. Feed plants with a liquid or slow-release all-purpose fertilizer.

Design ideas

Alternanthera supplies reliable color echoes or contrast in plantings. This foliage plant works well in containers as either a thriller or filler. Plant it en masse in the landscape as a striking groundcover. Thin-leaved types pair well with taller, coarse-textured foliage and can fill out a knot garden design.

Snip stems of taller varieties to use in bouquets. Pair with gomphrena, zinnia, or celosia, or create a mixed foliage arrangement using perennial foliage such as ribbon grass stems, coralbell leaves, and baptisia stems.

varieties:

1 **'LITTLE RUBY'** (*A. dentata*) Dark burgundy leaves on compact plants. 9 inches tall, 1 foot wide. Zones 10–11.

2 **'PURPLE KNIGHT'** (*A. dentata*) Dark purple leaves develop best color in full sun. 18 to 36 inches tall, 2 to 3 feet wide. Zones 10–11.

3 **'PARTYTIME'** (*A. ficoidea*) Bright green leaves splashed with hot pink; for shade or sun. 15 to 24 inches tall and wide. Zones 8–11.

4 **'RED THREADS'** (*A. ficoidea*) Fine-textured burgundy leaves. 8 inches tall, 14 inches wide. Zone 11.

5 **'BRAZILIAN RED HOTS'** (*Alternanthera* hybrid) Best color of pink-and-green leaves in full sun . 18 to 36 inches tall, 18 to 24 inches wide. Zones 10–11.

Angelonia
(*Angelonia angustifolia*)

Watering restrictions and deer don't curtail the flower power of this heat- and humidity-tolerant tender perennial. Its orchidlike blooms form spikes along upright stems. Flowers decorate the garden in shades of blue, purple, pink, and white, contrasting with narrow, dark green leaves.

Best site

Plant in full to part sun in well-drained soil. In planting beds, mix slow-release fertilizer into soil. Use soilless mixes in containers. Angelonia is evergreen in frost-free areas. With mulch, plant roots may overwinter where temperatures stay above the mid-20s. Zones 9–11.

Growing

Deadheading isn't required, but you can prune stems lightly to promote bushiness, which results in more flowers. Established plants show good drought tolerance but need deep watering during the hottest parts of summer. If you don't mix slow-release fertilizer into soil at planting time, feed regularly with a balanced or bloom-booster fertilizer.

Design ideas

Angelonia provides hard-to-find blue-purple tones and is often called summer snapdragon. Plants come in tall, upright, trailing, or spreading forms. In beds, select the Serena or Serenita Series, which are less costly because they're seed grown. Cut stems for bouquets when the lower flowers along a spike are open and the upper buds show color. Blooms open along the spike after picking, lasting 10 days in a vase.

varieties:

1. **ADESSA PURPLE** Large, orchidlike deep purple blooms. 1 to 2 feet tall, 1 foot wide.
2. **ANGELMIST SPREADING BLUE** Use this blue trailing type in baskets or as a spiller. 4 to 10 inches tall, 12 to 20 inches wide.
3. **APPLIQUE PINK** Deep pink blooms on tall plants. 18 inches tall and wide.
4. **SERENITA PURPLE** One in a series of shortest angelonia varieties. Does well in humidity. 12 to 14 inches tall and wide.
5. **ANGELMIST PURPLE STRIPE** White flowers boast purple stripes. 12 to 18 inches tall, 9 to 12 inches wide. Zones 9-11.
6. **CARITA CASCADE LAVENDER** Semitrailing growth habit ideal for hanging baskets or as spillers. 8 to 12 inches tall, 20 to 26 inches wide.
7. **SERENA WHITE** 16 to 20 inches tall, 12 to 14 wide. May grow 50 percent taller in the South.

Angel's Trumpet
(*Datura metel*, *Brugmansia* spp.)

Exotic beauty and haunting fragrance combine in two plants both given the common name angel's trumpet. Brugmansia opens flowers that dangle beneath leaves. Datura, sometimes also called devil's trumpet, bears flowers that face upward.

Best site

Both plants thrive in full sun to part shade in rich, well-drained soil. Datura grows in leaner soil, but best growth occurs in richer soils. In containers, use a standard soilless potting mix. Both are tender perennials. Datura is hardy in Zones 9 to 11; brugmansia, Zones 10 and 11.

Growing

Provide consistent moisture for best growth, but avoid overwatering. In containers, increase watering frequency as plants grow larger throughout the growing season. If the soil dries, leaves wilt. Plants are deer- and rabbit-resistant.

Datura sprawls. Space plants 3 feet apart unless you're staking them. In Zones 5 to 7, allow some seedpods to ripen and scatter seeds. In protected locations of Zones 7 and 8, plants may return from the root after winter.

Brugmansia grows upright and responds to pruning by producing side branches that yield flowers. Pinching growing tips reduces overall plant size. Plants flower year-round in frost-free areas. The greatest flower numbers typically occur in summer, although some varieties stop blooming during intense summer heat.

In regions where plants aren't winter-hardy, overwinter container specimens indoors near a sunny window. All parts of both plants are toxic if eaten.

Design ideas

Brugmansia and datura grow well in containers and add fragrance to patios and outdoor seating areas. Allow the sweet fragrance to waft indoors by placing plants near windows often opened.

varieties:

❶ **BRUGMANSIA** (*B.* × *candida*) Blooms up to 10-inches long in shades of pink, gold, and white. 8 to 10 feet tall, 6 to 8 feet wide, usually smaller in containers.

❷ **BRUGMANSIA 'ECUADOR PINK'** (*B. hybrid*) Up to 10-inch-long blooms in shades of pink, gold, and white. 8 to 10 feet tall, 6 to 8 feet wide, usually smaller in containers.

❸ **DATURA 'BALLERINA'** (*D. metel*) Double, 6- to 8-inch blooms with a whorled inner trumpet. Purple and white, yellow, or solid white. 3 feet tall and wide.

❹ **DATURA** (*D. inoxia*) White, 6- to 8-inch trumpets unfurl after the sun sets or on cloudy days. 2 to 6 feet tall, 2 to 6 feet wide; smaller in containers.

Baby's Breath
(*Gypsophila muralis*)

Clouds of tiny pink blooms float above the bright green leaves of baby's breath. This airy beauty offers fine texture to any quick color combination and looks gorgeous planted solo in containers. A low-maintenance plant, it thrives without pampering and self-sows.

Best site

Plant in full sun in cool-summer areas and in part sun in regions with hot summers. Baby's breath requires excellent drainage. Mix perlite or coarse builder's sand into the soil. Annual.

Growing

Baby's breath forms a compact mound. A bloom-booster fertilizer promotes flowering. Deadheading isn't necessary, but you can shear it lightly if spent blooms become unsightly. Temperatures above 86°F reduce flowering.

Design ideas

Count on baby's breath as a spiller plant to soften container edges. It makes a great replacement for lobelia or sweet alyssum or a partner for bacopa. Plant solo in hanging baskets, or tuck into rock gardens or between paving stones.

Bacopa
(*Sutera cordata*)

Bacopa adds a punch of flowering might to containers or beds. Starry flowers in shades of white, lavender-blue, or pink blanket trailing stems that can reach up to 3 feet long. The flowers may bloom so profusely they obscure leaves.

Best site

Plant in full to part sun in well-drained, slightly acidic soil. Zones 9–11.

Growing

Keep the soil consistently moist though not waterlogged. Plants that dry out drop flowers and buds before they wilt. Pair with a wilt-prone plant, such as coleus, petunia, or alternanthera, so you get a signal when the soil is too dry. After dropping buds, plants require two weeks to renew blooming. Prune to maintain shape or curtail trailing stems. Remove any dead stems that accumulate beneath living growth. Feed with an all-purpose fertilizer.

Design ideas

Use as a spiller plant in container combinations, plant solo in hanging baskets, or tuck into planting beds as a groundcover.

varieties:

❶ **'GYPSY DEEP ROSE'** Dark rose semidouble and fully double tiny flowers. 8 to 10 inches tall, 12 to 14 inches wide.
   'GARDEN BRIDE' Single pink-and-white bicolor blossoms. 6 to 12 inches tall, 9 to 12 inches wide.

varieties:

❶ **BETTY BLUE** Large lavender-blue blossoms bloom even in hot weather. 4 to 8 inches tall, 8 to 10 inches wide.
   BIG PEARL FALLS Lavender-pink blooms. 8 to 12 inches tall and wide.

Banana
(*Musa* spp.)

Accent your garden with exotic flair, courtesy of easy-to-grow banana plants. Leafy statures soar to 6 feet or more in a single growing season, filling even the most mundane setting with drama. Leaves feature solid green, wine red, or blends of the two colors.

Best site

Plant in well-drained soil enriched with organic matter. In planting beds, add 6 to 12 inches of compost or organic matter. For containers, choose a well-drained potting mix with moisture-retentive material, such as coir or water-retentive crystals. The minimum container size should be 15 gallons.

Full sun is best in northern regions; in southern areas, provide light shade at midday. Give variegated types part shade to prevent leaf scorch. Select a site sheltered from strong winds to prevent leaf shredding. Zones 7–11.

Growing

Wait to plant bananas until temperatures are reliably in the 60°F range. Lower temperatures slow growth. Fastest growth occurs between 80°F and 95°F. Provide consistently moist but not overly wet soil. Spread a 3-inch-thick layer of mulch around plants to retain soil moisture. Feed plants regularly during the growing season with an all-purpose or high-potassium fertilizer.

Older leaves yellow and fall from the plant as new growth appears. If you dislike the look of yellowing foliage, cut it from the stem, then chop it into chunks and add it to the mulch at the base of the plant to add potassium to the soil.

Design ideas

Bananas serve as shrubs or small trees in the landscape in regions where they're hardy. Plant several in a row for a leafy privacy hedge.

In colder regions, bananas work best planted in containers. They fill the thriller role in pots when skirted with frilly choices such as asparagus fern or variegated lantana.

varieties:

❶ RED ABYSSINIAN (*Ensete ventricosum* 'Maurelii') A cousin of a true banana, with maroon-red stems and leaf undersides. 8 to 10 feet tall, 6 to 8 feet wide. Zones 10–11.

❷ PINK-FRUITING BANANA (*M. velutina*) Bright pink fruits are inedible. 4 to 6 feet tall, 3 to 4 feet wide. Zones 7–10.

❸ 'SIAM RUBY' (*M. acuminata*) Ruby-red leaves speckled with chartreuse green. Color intensifies with sun. 6 to 8 feet tall and wide. Zones 9–11.

❹ 'DWARF RED' (*Musa* sp.) Red stems and red-skinned fruit. 6 to 8 feet tall, 3 to 4 feet wide. Zones 8–11.

BLUE JAVA (*M.* 'Ice Cream') Fruit that tastes like vanilla ice cream. 8 to 15 feet tall, 6 to 8 feet wide. Zones 8–11.

Begonia (*Begonia* spp.)

For a summer-long floral display that doesn't flag or falter, turn to begonias. This diverse plant group boasts ideal traits: variety, versatility, reliability, and durability. Flower forms range from simple open-face flowers to intricate blooms resembling fringed carnations or ruffled roses. Some blossoms grow as large as 6 inches across; others dangle daintily with strappy petals. Flower color runs from red to white to yellow and many shades in between.

Best site

You can find various types of begonias that thrive in every level of light, from full sun to full shade. All begonias require rich soil that's well-aerated and well-drained. In planting beds, adding compost or other organic matter achieves both requirements. In containers, use a high-quality soilless mix. Many begonias are susceptible to root rot, so it's vital to create a rooting environment that drains well. Hardiness varies by species.

Growing

Sizes range from 6-inch mounds to 2-foot-tall plants. All thrive with high humidity and mild temperatures above 65°F. Fertilize flowering types regularly using a bloom booster. For the foliage-only begonia 'Gryphon', use an all-purpose slow-release or liquid fertilizer.

You can easily overwinter many begonias. Fibrous types grown in pots, including 'Gryphon', overwinter easily indoors near a bright, sunny window. Plants may drop their outdoor leaves as they adjust to interior conditions. Once new leaves emerge, the plant should display slow winter growth. Keep the soil moist, but don't overwater. Set plants on a pebble tray to increase humidity.

To store tuberous begonias, act before frost kills the top of the plant. A light frost can nip a few leaves, but be sure to dig tubers before the whole plant is killed. Clip stems as close to the soil as possible. Gently dig the tubers and allow them to dry on screens for a few days. Store in peat moss, shredded paper, or newspaper in a cool (35°F to 45°F), dark place.

Design ideas

Begonias hold their own in planting beds or containers. Some types—'Gryphon', Bolivian, and tuberous—create a strong show in pots. Grow trailing types of begonias in hanging baskets or in pots on pedestals to allow the stems to dangle freely. In landscape beds, begonias provide large swaths of color.

wax begonia varieties:

❶ BIG ROSE WITH BRONZE LEAF
(*B. × benariensis*) Blooms larger than golf balls grow on a part Dragon Wing, part fibrous-rooted begonia. No deadheading is needed. Site in any light level from full sun to full shade. Red flowers with green or bronze leaves. 1 to 2 feet tall, 10 to 24 inches wide. Zones 10–11.

❷ BRAVEHEART ROSE BICOLOR
(*B. semperflorens-cultorum*) Single pink-and-white blossoms and dark green leaves. Site in any light level from full sun to full shade. Use as landscape bedding, for edging, or in containers as a filler or thriller. 14 to 16 inches tall, 10 to 15 inches wide. Zones 9–11.

tuberous begonia varieties:

3 PIN-UP FLAME (*B. × tuberhybrida*) Glowing yellow blooms edged in scarlet and orange. In cool northern regions, plants withstand full sun. Ideal for containers as an upright thriller or filler. 10 to 12 inches tall and wide. Zones 9–11.

4 NONSTOP YELLOW WITH RED BACK (*B. × tuberhybrida*) Yellow fully double blossoms open to 4 inches across. Use in containers in part to full shade. 8 to 12 inches tall, 12 to 16 inches wide. Zones 9–11.

5 NONSTOP MOCCA PINK (*B. × tuberhybrida*) Chocolate bronze leaves contrast with deep rose pink flowers up to 4 inches across. For part to full shade; heat-tolerant. 10 inches tall, 12 to 15 inches high. Zones 9–11.

other begonia varieties:

6 BONFIRE ORANGE (*B. boliviensis*) Fiery 2-inch-long blooms often obscure up to half of the foliage. Best in full sun to part shade. In heavy shade, flowers are fewer but larger; plants may spread and grow shorter. Use in containers, especially pots on pedestals, to showcase the cascading growth, or in low-maintenance planting beds. Stands up to summer rains and drought. Temperatures higher than 72°F reduce flower size and color intensity; higher than 79°F increase plant size and reduce flower size. Up to 20 inches tall and wide. Zones 9–11.

7 CHARISMA SCARLET RIEGER (*B. × hiemalis*) Roselike, double, 2½ -inch-diameter flowers in rich red contrasting with clear green leaves. Deadhead for more blooms. For filtered sun or part shade in beds or as a spiller in containers and hanging baskets. 10 to 14 inches tall, 12 to 14 inches wide Zones 9–10.

8 DRAGON WING PINK (*B. hybrida*) Pink or red blooms, shiny green leaves. For full to part sun. Plant solo in containers, in mixed plantings as a thriller, or in the garden. Combine in shade with impatiens or browallia; in sun with trailing Profusion zinnias or melampodium. 15 to 18 inches tall and wide. Zones 9–11.

9 'GRYPHON' (*B. hybrida*) Dark green leaves marked with silver. Low-water-use begonia that combines with other shade-loving plants or goes solo in containers. 10 to 24 inches tall, 16 to 18 inches wide. Zones 10–11.

Bidens

(*Bidens ferulifolia*)

Fill your garden with living sunshine by adding bidens. With its golden flowers, this heat- and drought-tolerant dazzler fits easily into landscape or container designs. Growth is strong and vigorous. The ferny foliage is frequently obscured by a profusion of flowers.

Best site

Plant in full sun in light, free-draining soil. Sandy soil mixed with organic matter or loam is ideal because it mimics bidens' native soil in Central and South America. You can tuck plants into a location with part shade, but expect fewer flowers to open. Zones 9–11.

Growing

Plants require consistently moist soil, but avoid overwatering. No deadheading is needed with most varieties. These nonstop bloomers typically offer bushy to semitrailing growth.

By late summer, growth may become rangy and lanky. If this occurs, cut plants back by one-third to renew growth and flowering.

Design ideas

Bidens fills many roles in the garden. In a rock garden, it forms trailing mounds of starry gold flowers. In a mixed landscape border, use it as a colorful edging or groundcover. Include it in wildlife or butterfly gardens, too.

In pots or window boxes, low-fuss bidens operates as a spiller to soften container edges. It forms a groundcover in pots when paired with plants trained as single-stem standards. Bidens plays a filler role in mixed containers; its stems with golden blooms weave between plants to fill empty spaces. It's a good partner for dark broadleaf plants such as purple millet, burgundy coleus, and alternanthera. In a hanging basket, bidens remains tidy, with no dropped blossoms.

varieties:

❶ **GOLDILOCKS ROCKS** Golden blooms on a mounded, trailing plant. 12 to 14 inches tall, 10 to 14 inches wide.

❷ **'GIANT SUN COMPACT'** Large bright yellow flowers on compact plants. 4 to 7 inches tall, 8 to 10 inches wide.

❸ **'NAMID COMPACT YELLOW'** Brilliant gold blooms. 4 to 6 inches tall, 8 to 10 inches wide.

❹ **'YELLOW CHARM'** Lemon yellow blossoms. 8 to 12 inches tall, 1 to 2 feet wide.

Black-eyed Susan
(Rudbeckia hirta)

Light a fuse of sturdy-stemmed color with black-eyed Susan. Also known as gloriosa daisy, this familiar bloomer boasts outstanding heat tolerance, durability to withstand extreme weather variations, and intense flower power. Drought-tolerant and deer-resistant blossoms lure butterflies and bees.

Best site

Plant black-eyed Susan in soil with average fertility and moisture. Full sun yields the best flowering. This stalwart tolerates poor, clay, and rocky soils, but wet, poorly drained soil kills it. Zones 5–8.

Growing

Technically a biennial or short-lived perennial, black-eyed Susan is often grown as an annual. In some situations it returns reliably from the root; in others, it readily reseeds. Deadhead blooms to encourage more flowers and to limit self-seeding.

In the landscape, water new plants until they're established and become drought-tolerant. Plants are susceptible to powdery mildew. During wet, rainy summers, plants in containers especially can develop powdery mildew. In general, plants grow 2 to 3 feet tall and 1 to 2 feet wide, but size depends on variety.

Design ideas

Black-eyed Susan punctuates a summer border with strong, sturdy-stemmed color. Its coarse texture pairs well with fine-textured plants such as ornamental grasses, Mexican petunia, and mealycup sage (*Salvia farinacea*). Use smaller varieties in pots. When growing larger varieties in containers, choose a pot at least 14 inches wide and water frequently.

Design a low-maintenance, low-water-use garden by filling a planting bed with black-eyed Susan, blanket flower, angelonia, Mexican feather grass, and verbena. These bloomers create a flowery, colorful scene from early summer to hard freeze. Black-eyed Susan is a wonderful cut flower; plant extra to fill vases.

Black-eyed Susan is a natural for prairie and wildflower gardens, where it is favored by butterflies and hummingbirds. Seed heads add winter interest and attract foraging birds.

varieties:

❶ 'CAPPUCINO' Bicolor 4-inch blooms in shades of bronze, mahogany, gold, and auburn atop sturdy stems. 24 to 30 inches tall, 12 to 18 inches wide.
❷ 'INDIAN SUMMER' Large, clear gold flowers 6 to 9 inches across. 18 to 24 inches tall, 1 foot wide.
❸ 'MAYA' Double golden 4-inch flowers. Good for containers. 18 inches tall, 1 foot wide.
❹ 'PRAIRIE SUN' Large yellow petals with a gold eye and green center. 30 to 36 inches tall, 18 to 24 inches wide.
❺ 'TIGER EYE GOLD' Semidouble blooms the size of tennis balls bloom with orange-and-yellow petals and a dark brown eye ringed with gold. 2 feet tall and wide.

Blanket Flower
(*Gaillardia* spp.)

Cheery color sizzles and sparks in blanket flower. This tough, deer-resistant bloomer interjects bright color into plantings from early summer to fall. Flowers with boldly tinted petals of red, yellow, orange, and gold attract butterflies.

Best site

Blanket flower grows in a variety of soils, from sandy, well-drained soil high in organic matter to poor soil, which the plant prefers. When growing blanket flower in containers, use a commercial potting mix designed for pots.

Full sun yields the best flower show. This tender or short-lived perennial exhibits differing degrees of hardiness even in the same yard, depending on microclimates. Most types are hardy in Zones 5 to 10.

Growing

Heat- and drought-tolerant blanket flower is carefree except in soggy soil, where crown rot can develop. Remove spent blooms to keep plants looking neat. Some plants self-sow, but seedlings won't come true to named cultivars. Cut back plants in fall.

Design ideas

This native bloomer gets its name from the way the plants used to blanket the North American prairies in a patchwork of bright colors. In the garden, newer varieties don't spread as freely as the wildflower types. Blanket flower is a natural companion for other drought- and heat-tolerant plants including ornamental grasses, angelonia, lantana, Mexican petunia, and salvia.

Use this plant in cottage or wildflower gardens and low-water-use landscapes. It makes an ideal addition to a butterfly or wildlife garden. Because blanket flower thrives with good drainage, it's a good choice for raised beds, terraced gardens, and hillside areas.

varieties:

❶ **'MESA'** (*G. × grandiflora*) Single yellow flowers; blooms from seed its first year. 12 to 18 inches tall, 15 to 18 inches wide. Zones 5–10.

❷ **GALYA RED SPARK** (*G. × grandiflora*) Red double blooms. 12 to 16 inches tall, 10 to 12 inches wide. Zones 8–10.

❸ **'ARIZONA APRICOT'** (*G. aristata*) Golden petals with an apricot ring surrounding the center. Ruffled, multipetaled blooms 3 to 3½ inches across. 1 foot tall and wide. Zones 3–10.

❹ **'ORANGES AND LEMONS'** (*G. aristata*) Peach-orange petals burnished gold at the tips surrounding a gold center. 22 to 26 inches tall, 12 to 18 inches wide. Zones 6–10.

❺ **'ARIZONA RED SHADES'** (*G. aristata*) Some of the crimson flowers are tipped with yellow. 10 to 12 inches tall, 1 foot wide. Zones 3–10.

Browallia
(*Browallia* spp.)

If you've always used impatiens in your shade garden, try something different: browallia. This underused shade-loving bloomer craves warm, dappled shade. Plants open dainty blooms in blue, purple, white, lavender, or pink from summer until frost. White blossoms brighten shadowy corners.

Best site

Plant in fertile soil that's consistently moist yet well drained. Adding humus or organic matter such as compost creates ideal footing for browallia. Keep the soil consistently moist without overwatering.

Plants can grow in sun or shade, depending on where you garden. In northern latitudes and cool-summer areas, this tender plant can withstand a sunny location. In more southern locations, grow it in dappled sun and provide protection from harsh afternoon sun. Plants typically grow 1 to 2 feet tall and 9 to 12 inches wide. Zones 9–11.

Growing

Browallia requires warm soil and air to grow. Temperatures below 40°F cause damage, so don't set plants out in spring until all danger of frost is past. At planting time, pinch the growing tips to encourage branching. If plants are already branched, pinch the tips of branches. As the season wears on, plants may need staking.

Too much fertilizer spurs lush leaf growth but few flowers. In planting beds, mix compost and a bloom-booster slow-release fertilizer into the soil. In containers, use a bloom-booster fertilizer.

Deadhead as needed to prevent browallia from setting seed. In the warmest regions, plants may self-sow, but volunteers typically don't emerge soon enough to flower before frost.

Design ideas

This shade lover forms a large, airy mass of sparkling blooms. Plant it en masse to fill shady spaces with arresting color. Capitalize on browallia's trailing ability by planting it atop a wall or in hanging baskets. In baskets or other containers, water plants frequently to keep the soil consistently moist.

Use browallia to grace a shaded cottage or wildlife garden. Hummingbirds and butterflies love this bloomer and seek it out in planting beds and containers.

YOU SHOULD KNOW Pinch plants before the first fall frost, dig, and tuck them into pots for winter color indoors. Plants won't bloom as well inside, but if they're kept in bright, indirect light with moist soil (don't overwater), you'll be rewarded with flowers.

varieties:

1. **BROWALLIA** (*B. speciosa*) Purple-blue blooms with white centers. 1 to 2 feet tall, 9 to 12 inches wide. Zones 9–10.
2. **ENDLESS FLIRTATION** Star-shape white blooms; use as a spiller in containers. No need to deadhead. 10 to 14 inches tall, 8 to 10 inches wide. Zones 10–11.
3. **ENDLESS ILLUMINATION** Profuse lavender flowers. 10 to 14 inches tall, 8 to 10 inches wide. Zones 10–11.

Caladium

(Caladium spp.)

You'll have it made in the shade with the lush, tropical foliage of caladium. Leaves, which are deer and rodent resistant, provide season-long color in shades of green, red, pink, white, and chartreuse. Midribs and margins also boast bright tints. Newer strapleaf or lanceleaf types withstand more sun.

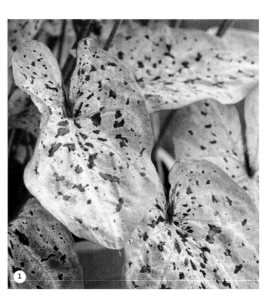
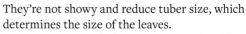

Best site

The ideal site is in part shade in warm, moist, well-drained soil. Caladium colors best in dappled shade. It grows in deep shade but may show subdued leaf color. Newer varieties tolerate part-day sun. Zones 9–11.

Growing

The soil must be warm at planting time—at least 70°F—or caladium rots. Many gardeners start tubers indoors in small pots.

Mix a slow-release all-purpose fertilizer into the soil prior to planting. Use a 5-10-10 fertilizer every four to six weeks. Apply 1 tablespoon per plant in beds and 1 teaspoon per container. High-nitrogen fertilizers cause faded leaf color. Fertilizer on the foliage will burn leaves.

Soil temperatures higher than 85°F reduce leaf color. Mulch the soil to help lower the temperature. Pull or cut blooms as they appear.

They're not showy and reduce tuber size, which determines the size of the leaves.

You can treat caladium as an annual and let frost kill it, or dig tubers you want to save. To save, dry tubers for a week away from full sun. When leaves are dry, snip them. Store tubers in mesh bags or pack in sphagnum peat moss where temperatures won't drop below 60°F.

Design ideas

Use caladium tubers solo in containers or mingle them. The broad leaves contrast with ferny or grasslike foliage of Boston and asparagus fern, sedge, and small-leaf coleus. It blends well with begonia, impatiens, and browallia.

In the landscape, use white and light-tone leaves to brighten shady spots. Caladium provides color as intense as flowering annuals for a fraction of the price.

varieties:

❶ **'MISS MUFFET'** (*C. bicolor*) A dwarf caladium with medium sun tolerance. Leaf color varies with sun exposure: pale yellow in sun, chartreuse in shade. Leaves spotted with blush and burgundy. 6 to 12 inches tall, 6 to 9 inches wide.

❷ **'YELLOW BLOSSOM'** (*C. bicolor*) Yellow leaves with magenta veins and pink spots. 6 to 12 inches tall, 9 to 12 inches wide.

❸ **'ROSE GLOW'** (*C. bicolor*) Dark rose leaf centers. 8 to 16 inches tall, 6 to 9 inches wide.

❹ **'FLORIDA RED RUFFLES'** (*C. bicolor*) Dark red lanceleaf type with a green border; sun-tolerant. 6 to 12 inches tall, 6 to 9 inches wide.

❺ *CALADIUM HUMBOLDTII* Small tubers with petite leaves; from Thailand. 12 inches tall, 6 to 9 inches wide.

Calibrachoa
(*Calibrachoa* hybrids)

Resembling a mini petunia, calibrachoa possesses abundant blooms. Sometimes called million bells, this mounded, trailing plant opens 1-inch-wide flowers in shades including purple, red, white, yellow, and orange. Contrasting colors frequently show along petal veins or painted flower throats.

Best site

Plant in rich, well-drained soil. Calibrachoa benefits from soil amended with organic matter, such as compost, fine forest mulch, or other locally available materials. Plants are sensitive to soil moisture and easily killed by overwatering. Established plants tolerate moderate drought. Site calibrachoa in full sun for strongest bloom. Plants grow and tolerate light shade, but flower number decreases as the amount of shade increases. Zones 9–11.

Growing

Typically, calibrachoa mounds 3 to 9 inches tall and trails 6 to 24 inches wide, although individual varieties vary. Deadheading isn't required, but plants benefit from shearing, which promotes branching and increases flower number. Prune plants lightly at planting time and again in midsummer, especially if they look straggly. Give plants an overall trim at this point, removing up to one-third of the growth. Fertilize afterward to jumpstart fresh growth, which flowers strongly right up to frost.

Plants benefit from monthly fertilizer applications of a soluble product with a 20-10-20 (N-P-K) formulation.

Water only when the soil is dry to the touch. Calibrachoa performs best in containers because its roots are sensitive to overly moist soil and rot easily. For in-ground growing, it's best to use raised beds to provide adequate drainage. If plants wilt and the soil is wet, the diagnosis is probably root rot.

Design ideas

With its high flower count, calibrachoa creates luxurious hanging baskets. Plant a mix of complementary hued varieties in a moss basket and savor the beauty that steadily unfolds all summer long. The brightly tinted blooms beckon hummingbirds and butterflies. Display the hanging baskets near windows so you can watch the air show.

In containers, count on calibrachoa to fill a spiller role, softening pot edges as it cascades gracefully. With its wide range of bloom colors, calibrachoa provides a contrast with or complement to any combination of plants. Select these bloomers with the care of an artist to create color echoes in container plantings.

Because of its small stature, calibrachoa is easily lost in a large landscape setting. As long as soil drainage is adequate, this bloomer functions well in a small planting bed as an edging plant or in spots where it can form tidy mounds of color.

YOU SHOULD KNOW

Petchoa is a new plant that combines the best of petunia ("pet") and calibrachoa ("choa"). Plants boast strong roots, large, vibrant flowers, and non-sticky leaves. Petchoa withstands weather extremes: heat, summer storms, and cold, including temperatures that dip below 30°F.

varieties:

1 **'CABARET DEEP BLUE'** Rich purple-blue flowers from early in the season till frost. Leaves stay green even in high soil pH. 6 to 10 inches tall, 10 to 12 inches wide.

2 **'CAN CAN ORANGE'** Bright orange blossoms; use a high-iron fertilizer. 15 inches tall and wide.

3 **'MINIFAMOUS DOUBLE YELLOW'** Large clear yellow double blooms. 7 to 10 inches tall, 20 inches wide.

Canna
(*Canna* × *generalis*)

Splash some calypso color into your garden with exotic, easy-care canna. Newer varieties offer dazzling leaf hues that demand attention. Look for tall types to anchor the back of borders, and add dwarf selections as patio plantings. Canna blooms boast tropical character in vibrant shades.

Best site

Plant in full sun in deep, rich soil. Work organic matter into planting beds. For containers, use a commercial potting mix. Canna tolerates part shade and poorly drained soil. Tuck cannas along the edges of water gardens with their pots or roots partially submerged. Avoid windy locations because high winds can shred leaves, break stems, and topple plants. Zones 7–11.

Growing

In spring, growth starts when temperatures rise above 50°F. Striped or dark-leaf varieties don't achieve full pigmentation until temperatures consistently remain above 60°F. As canna grows and attains size, it benefits from more frequent watering. In containers, plants require consistently moist soil to maintain leaf colors.

Feed plants with an all-purpose fertilizer, either a slow-release type mixed into the soil or a liquid form. Too much nitrogen causes plants to elongate and become susceptible to wind damage. When growing cannas in containers, select a pot at least 15 to 18 inches wide.

In Zones where canna isn't winter hardy, dig and store the rhizomes to replant the following spring. When foliage dies after frost in fall, cut plants to 4 inches. Dig the rhizomes and store them in a protected spot until dry. Pack in peat moss or shredded paper for winter storage in a cool, dry place.

In areas where canna is winter hardy, cut plants to soil level when leaves start to die.

Design ideas

Canna's bold presence begs for finer-textured companions, such as ornamental grasses, ferns, and lantanas. Even tall zinnias look fine textured when planted next to chunky canna stems and leaves. Tall canna varieties, especially dark-leaf ones, create a backdrop in a planting bed or serve as a thriller in containers. Dwarf types work well in pots and beds, or along paths. Cannas with colorful leaves function as focal points in a landscape. They look beautiful partnered with quick color annuals or perennials. Flowers attract hummingbirds and butterflies.

varieties:

❶ **'PRETORIA'** Also called 'Bengal Tiger'. Green-and-yellow-striped leaves, maroon leaf edges, orange flowers. 6 feet tall, 18 to 24 inches wide.

❷ **'TROPICAL BRONZE SCARLET'** Dwarf plant with 3- to 4-inch red blooms above bronze-purple leaves. 30 inches tall, 15 to 18 inches wide.

❸ **'TROPICANNA'** Also sold as 'Phasion'. Bold stripes of chartreuse, red, pink, gold, and green. Tangerine-orange flowers. 4 to 6 feet tall, 18 inches wide.

Cardoon
(*Cynara cardunculus*)

Plant cardoon—sometimes called artichoke thistle—for its strong sculptural presence and deer resistance. Jagged, thorny silver leaves extend to 20 inches long, and in late summer a flower stem appears. Blooms resemble thistles, with 1½- to 3-inch-wide purple tufts that draw all kinds of insects.

Best site
The ideal site has rich, well-drained, moist soil in full sun, but this plant can grow anywhere. Too much shade prevents flowering. Zones 7–9.

Growing
Water regularly, but allow the soil to dry out between waterings. Work compost or slow-release fertilizer into the soil prior to planting, then topdress with more in midseason.

Plants produce flower stalks late in the growing season. Cardoon may self-sow to the point of being invasive, so remove spent flowers before they set seed.

Design ideas
Cardoon is best as a solo accent or focal point plant. It partners well with other bold quick color plants, such as castor bean, canna, elephant's ear, and banana. Flowers attract butterflies.

varieties:

1 CARDOON Taprooted plant with architectural appeal. Due to size, cardoon doesn't grow well in containers. 6 to 9 feet tall, 4 to 6 feet wide.

Castor Bean
(*Ricinus communis*)

Castor bean seems like a fairy-tale beanstalk. From a single bean, a plant can soar up to 15 feet in a single growing season, bearing tropical-looking leaves as wide as 3 feet across. The striking seedpods are colorful and prickly. All parts of a castor bean are poisonous.

Best site
Plant in full sun in rich, moisture-retentive soil that drains well. Castor bean tolerates light shade but may not flower or grow as large. Because of its height, avoid windy sites. Zones 9–11.

Growing
In warmer zones, plants may be invasive. Stems are hollow and benefit from an 8- to 10-foot stake to prevent stalks from toppling in storms.

All parts of the plant contain ricin, a poison. To prevent mild illness, avoid contact with the sap. Remove flowers before they form seeds. One chewed seed can kill a child or pet.

Design ideas
Castor bean serves as an architectural focal point. Use it as a support for annual vines. Growing it in a large container curtails the size. Avoid placing containers in outdoor living areas.

varieties:

1 'CARMENCITA' Bronze-red leaves accented with brilliant red seedpods. 3 to 10 feet tall, 3 to 4 feet wide.

Celosia
(*Celosia* spp.)

Variety is the hallmark of the celosia family. Distinctive flower forms resemble foxtails, feathery wheatlike plumes, a human brain, or a rooster's comb. For all of these blossom types, colors include purple, pink, red, white, orange, and yellow. Leaves vary from green to purple-red and bronze.

Best site

Plant in full sun in average to rich, well-drained soil. In containers, use a commercial potting mix. Established plants are drought tolerant. After planting, water whenever the soil is dry to help celosia seedlings establish. Celosia is cold sensitive. Wait to plant until temperatures are reliably above 40°F. Hardiness varies by type.

Growing

Avoid watering in the evening to prevent fungus. Remove spent blooms at the base of the blossom stem. Celosia thrives in heat and humidity and likes its roots warm.

Plume and cockscomb (brain) types work well in pots. Fertilize by blending slow-release fertilizer into container soils. Mix compost or slow-release fertilizer into planting beds. Granular fertilizers may cause the blooms of cockscomb types to split, so use liquid fertilizer.

Design ideas

Celosia is a heat-tolerant bloomer that adds color where sun blasts out other plants. It performs well in containers on a full-sun raised deck. Avoid growing the wheat types in containers; they perform better in planting beds.

Every celosia dries well but also performs well in fresh bouquets. Touchable blooms are perfect for children's gardens, and they beckon hummingbirds and butterflies. Allow a few stems to mature and set seed in fall to feed birds.

Cockscomb celosias serve well as edging plants in small beds. Their peculiar "brain" form makes it challenging to blend them artfully with other plants in a large-scale planting.

Plume celosia, however, forms eye-pleasing swaths of color when planted en masse. Wheat celosia adds a strong vertical element to plantings and mixes well with perennials.

varieties:

❶ **'AMIGO YELLOW'** (*C. argentea* var. *cristata*) Cockscomb-type celosia with yellow blooms. 6 to 8 inches tall, 8 to 10 inches wide.

❷ **'GLOW PINK'** (*C. argentea* var. *plumosa*) Chubby, pyramidal pink plumes, green foliage. 10 to 12 inches tall, 8 to 10 inches wide.

❸ **'SMART LOOK RED'** (*C. argentea* var. *plumosa*) Heat-tolerant with bronze-tone leaves and 10- to 12-inch deep-red plumes. 10 to 24 inches tall, 6 to 8 inches wide.

❹ **'FLAMINGO FEATHER'** (*C. spicata*) Pink foxtail flowers that fade to white. 3 to 4 feet tall, 18 to 24 inches wide.

'KOSMO' (*C. spicata*) The first dwarf wheat celosia, in white, red, yellow, and pink. 8 inches tall and wide.

Cleome
(*Cleome hassleriana*)

Cleome belongs in every garden. Its heat and drought tolerance comes in in a pretty, deer-resistant package. Plants demand attention with whiskery two-tone blooms and beanlike seedpods. Count on cleome for large pools of dramatic color in summer gardens.

Best site
Plant in full sun in fertile, well-drained soil. Cleome grows in poor soil, but best growth occurs with a rich footing. Part shade is okay; too much shade diminishes the flower show. Avoid windy locations. Zones 10–11.

Growing
Set plants out or sow directly after all danger of frost has passed. In warmer regions, water new plants until they're established. Add a layer of mulch around plants after they've grown 6 to 8 inches tall. Keep mulch from resting against stems; cover the soil only enough to retain moisture. Cleome is drought-tolerant once established, so cut back on watering as plants gain height.

Once plants are in the ground, fertilize every six to eight weeks. Alternatively, mix a slow-release fertilizer or compost into the soil at planting time. In containers, fertilize more frequently (weekly with half-strength water-soluble food) unless you blend a slow-release fertilizer into the mix.

In the garden, plants look most natural planted in odd-numbered clumps of five or more. Space plants to accommodate mature size—as much as 24 to 30 inches apart. Older varieties have thorns on stems and may give off an unpleasant odor, so use caution working around mature plants.

Design ideas
Older varieties of cleome that grow 4 feet or taller are a natural choice for back-of-the-border plantings or forming an annual flowery hedge. Newer varieties offer shorter stature perfect for pots or planting along paths or patios. Check plant tags to be sure you're purchasing the height you want.

Cleome is a classic cottage garden plant. It's a favorite for cutting and wildlife gardens. Butterflies and hummingbirds mob the blooms, as do bumblebees and other pollinators. Ripening seedpods grow 4 to 5 inches long and add interest to the scene.

Older varieties self-sow. Deadhead plants if you don't want to contend with volunteer seedlings. Some taller varieties develop bare stems at the base as the season progresses. To disguise lanky stems, add shorter bloomers in front of them, such as annual phlox, Profusion zinnia, geranium, and angelonia.

YOU SHOULD KNOW Cleome first appeared in seed catalogs in the 1830s. Spidery flowers come in shades of pink, purple, and white. Blooms start opening low on the stem about midsummer and steadily open up the stem. It takes weeks for the entire flower spike to burst into bloom. The result is that each stem has flowers in several shades, from newly opened, deeply tinted petals to faded pastel ones. Flower buds at the top of the stem feature the darkest hue.

varieties:

❶ 'SPARKLER WHITE' Snow-white flowers. Plants self-sow freely. 36 to 48 inches tall, 16 to 18 inches wide.

❷ SENORITA ROSALITA Odorless, non-reseeding plants with lavender-pink blooms and darker green leaves. 24 to 48 inches tall, 20 to 24 inches wide.

❸ 'VIOLET QUEEN' Purple blooms age to light pink and self-sow freely. 36 to 48 inches tall, 18 to 24 inches wide.

Coleus (*Solenostemon scutellarioides*)

This versatile plant, grown for its stunning foliage, presents nonstop color all season long. Leaves present a kaleidoscope of hues, patterns, and textures. Shades of electric lime, bright gold, deep maroon, hot pink, and many more colors pair well with many other plants. Newer varieties of this traditional shade-favorite even partner beautifully with sun lovers.

Best site

Plant in full sun to full shade, depending on variety. Read the plant tag carefully to provide the ideal light level to coax maximum color from leaves. Coleus isn't picky about soil; it can be rich or poor, high in organic matter, or sandy. Coleus cannot grow in poorly drained soil. That leads to root rot and quickly kills plants. In containers, use a soilless mix that drains well. Zones 10–11.

Growing

Easy growing and practically goofproof, coleus dishes out big rewards for little effort. To savor a striking foliage show, give plants enough water to keep leaves from wilting and fertilize on a regular basis. The more you feed, the more coleus grows, yielding larger, lush plants.

Flower spikes form on some varieties starting about midsummer. Blossoms are small and unattractive. Snip stem tips with blooms along with a set or two of leaves below them. This simple pruning process promotes branching and fuller growth.

Plants collapse quickly after temperatures hit 32°F. Plant size depends on variety. Look for plants that grow from 1 to 3 feet tall by 9 to 24 inches wide.

Design ideas

Because of its exquisitely patterned foliage, coleus fills many roles in the garden. Group plants in garden beds to form a ribbon of color. When designs feature other plants with bold foliage hues, count on coleus in subdued shades to bridge the gap between sizzling tones.

Brightly tinted coleus varieties also hold their own as focal points in planting beds and containers. The vast variety of foliage hues allows coleus to strike up conversations with many plant combinations. Use coleus as a go-to plant when creating quick color designs.

shade-loving coleus varieties:

1 **'FISHNET STOCKINGS'** Bright green leaves with burgundy veins and edges. Part to full shade. 2 to 3 feet tall by 16 inches wide.

2 **KONG SCARLET** Huge leaves up to 9 inches wide with scarlet centers skirted with maroon and edged in neon green. Best color in shade. 18 to 20 inches tall, 15 to 18 inches wide.

3 **'INDIA FRILLS'** Leaves in chartreuse with pink to maroon centers; ruffled edges; welcome as a trailer in combinations. Part to full shade. 6 to 12 inches tall by 18 to 24 inches wide.

4 **'BLACK DRAGON'** Velvety black-purple leaves with ruffled edges and ruby centers on a well-branched plant. Part to full shade. 1 foot tall and wide.

(5)

sun-tolerant coleus varieties:

⑤ **UNDER THE SEA BONEFISH** Burgundy-maroon leaves with lime-green edges; deeply scalloped. Best color in sun to part shade. 15 to 18 inches tall, 10 to 12 inches wide.

⑥ **'RELIGIOUS RADISH'** Deep pink-and-burgundy leaves. Heat-tolerant; grows in full sun to full shade. 24 to 42 inches tall, 12 to 18 inches wide.

⑦ **'WASABI'** Chartreuse color that doesn't fade. Part sun. 18 to 30 inches tall, 16 to 28 inches wide.

⑧ **'HENNA'** Uniform leaves in chartreuse to copper with burgundy undersides. Heat tolerant; grows in part sun to shade. 22 to 28 inches tall, 14 to 16 inches wide.

⑨ **'GNASH RAMBLER'** Whorled, curly leaves in blends of purple, hot pink, and red. Heat-tolerant; best color in part to full sun. Up to 18 inches tall by 1 foot wide.

⑩ **COLORBLAZE VELVET MOCHA** Narrow burgundy leaves. Sun or shade. 2 to 3 feet tall, 18 to 24 inches wide.

⑪ **'COPPER GLOW'** Bright orange leaves in part sun; deep, glowing copper in full sun with a narrow band of gold-edged leaves. 10 to 24 inches tall, 18 to 24 inches wide.

Cordyline
(*Cordyline* spp.)

Give your yard a touch of the tropics with cordyline's colorful foliage. The strong upright form of this plant, native to Australia and the Western Pacific, commands attention in the garden and graces any container or bed. Cordyline boasts water-wise, low-maintenance beauty.

Best site

Plants thrive in a variety of soils, from those rich in organic matter to poor sandy soils. Cordyline tolerates poor drainage but yields best growth in well-drained soil. Most cordyline varieties withstand full sun to full shade but leaf colors develop differently in response to light. In general, the best leaf color occurs with exposure to increased sunlight.

Cordyline is a good choice for seaside gardens, because plants tolerate salty conditions. It's a good idea to provide some protection from salt-laden winds. Zones 8–11.

Growing

Cordyline is a rugged performer that rewards minimal care with steady growth. Most types offer excellent drought tolerance once established, although container specimens benefit from regular irrigation. Fertilize both established landscape plants and containers early in the growing season with slow-release fertilizer mixed into the soil at planting time. High fluoride levels may burn leaf tips.

Plants are hardy to about 15°F. At about 10°F, the foliage burns but roots remain alive as long as the soil doesn't stay frozen. In spring, new growth emerges from the roots. In colder zones, move plants indoors near a bright window for winter. Water when the soil is dry to the touch.

Design ideas

Count on cordyline for steady color. In planting beds in warmer zones, it is a low-maintenance choice for mass planting on slopes or as part of a foundation planting. The upright form adds an exclamation point and serves as a focal point in garden beds. The eye-catching foliage works well as a thriller plant in container combinations.

varieties:

❶ **'KIWI'** (*C. fruticosa*) Leaves with splashes of green, pink, red, white, and purple; best color in part shade. 6 to 15 feet tall, 3 to 8 feet wide.

❷ **FESTIVAL GRASS** (*C. hybrida* 'JURred') Shiny burgundy leaves are redder in full sun, darker purple in full shade. Stems branch at the base. Usually 2 to 3 feet tall and wide; may grow to 4 to 8 feet tall, 3 to 6 feet wide

❸ **ELECTRIC PINK** (*C. banksii*) Dark maroon leaves edged with bright pink. Part shade to full sun. 4 to 8 feet tall, 2 to 4 feet wide.

❹ **'RED STAR'** (*C. australis*) Dark red to burgundy foliage with stiff upright habit. Full to part sun. 3 to 6 feet tall by 3 feet wide.

Cosmos
(*Cosmos* spp.)

Although the flowers may appear delicate, this bloomer brings strong, heat-proof color, growing best during the sunny, sizzling days of summer. Two cosmos types feature vastly different flower colors: bright yellow, orange, and red shades; or pastel pinks, white, and deep magenta.

Best site

Place in full sun in well-drained soil that's rocky, sandy, peaty, or loamy. If the soil fertility is too high, cosmos flowers less, stems become lanky, and the plant is susceptible to disease. Cosmos withstands drought conditions. Zones 9–11.

Growing

Cosmos is easy to grow. Snip spent blooms after they fade until frost is near. Taller types may need staking. Direct-sow seeds in late spring for midsummer blooms; make a second sowing in early summer for late-summer flowers.

To create a dense stand, allow spring-sown plants to set seed, then clip to 12 to 18 inches tall, allowing seed heads to fall to the ground. Warm summer soil sprouts seeds quickly.

Near the end of the growing season, allow flowers to set seed to encourage self-sowing. Self-sown cosmos flower later than those raised by a garden center. Use both types to ensure a continuous supply of cosmos flowers.

C. sulphureus plants range in height from 3 to 6 feet. Most cultivated types sold for quick color mature at 12 to 15 inches. Blossoms typically open 2 to 3 inches wide above green leaves that are lobed, but not ferny. *C. bipinnatus* has fine, feathery foliage. It grows 1 to 6 feet tall with flowers that measure 2 to 4 inches across, depending on the variety.

Design ideas

If your garden has harsh sun, turn to cosmos. It creates striking drifts in beds. Taller varieties form backdrops for shorter annuals. Include cosmos in a cutting garden. Cut stems last up to 10 days. Flowers provide a nectar source that lures butterflies. Cosmos grows easily from seed, perfect for children or beginning gardeners.

varieties:

❶ **'SONATA WHITE'** (*C. bipinnatus*) Dwarf with white blooms. Sonata series includes carmine red, pink, and white. Compact size fits in the front of borders. 6 to 12 inches tall and wide.

❷ **'DOUBLE CLICK'** (*C. bipinnatus*) Semidouble to double flowers in a mix of carmine red, white, and pink. 2 to 3 feet tall, 18 to 24 inches wide.

❸ **'SEASHELLS'** (*C. bipinnatus*) Hollow, tube-shape blooms in carmine red, rose, pink, and white with a two-tone appearance. 3 to 6 feet tall, 6 to 12 inches wide.

❹ **'COSMIC ORANGE'** (*C. sulphureus*) Semidouble, 2-inch-wide orange blooms. 12 to 18 inches tall, 9 to 12 inches wide.

Creeping Zinnia
(*Sanvitalia* spp.)

Cover the ground with a living blanket of miniature sunflower-like blooms. This tough and underused beauty opens single or double blossoms without pause from midsummer to frost. Plants stand up to heat, humidity, and drought.

Best site

Plant in well-drained soil in full sun. The soil can offer light to rich fertility, but the most important aspect is that it drains well. You can grow creeping zinnia in part shade but plants will open fewer blooms. Use a lightweight peat-based soil mix in containers. Zones 9–11.

Growing

Avoid planting too early; this Central American native craves warm soil. Set plants out after danger of frost has passed. To create a thick carpet of leaves and flowers, space plants about 4 to 6 inches apart.

Plants are drought tolerant once established. Avoid overwatering. Plants withstand summer heat and humidity without succumbing to diseases. Don't worry about deadheading. Creeping zinnia flowers so profusely that new blooms overtake and obscure old ones. Plants grow 6 to 12 inches tall and 15 to 18 inches wide.

Design ideas

The creeping nature of this perky bloomer makes it a perfect choice for edging planting beds and skirting paths or sidewalks. Plants don't survive foot traffic, so space them far enough from paths to permit full spread while avoiding accidental crushing. The plant's free-flowering habit readily suits the carefree abandon of a cottage garden.

Blossoms make a great addition to a wildlife or butterfly garden. The plant has a small enough stature and the right temperament to thrive in a rock garden.

Creeping zinnia serves as a spiller plant in container gardens. It shines in hanging baskets and pouch planters, where stems freely cascade.

varieties:

❶ **'ORANGE SPRITE'** (*S. procumbens*) Ruffled semidouble flowers with green centers; trailing habit good for containers. 4 inches tall, 10 to 14 inches wide.

❷ **'TSAVO DOUBLE GOLD'** (*S. speciosa*) Fully double blooms with brown-toned centers and bright gold petals; mounded habit. 8 to 12 inches tall, 10 to 14 inches wide.

❸ **'MILLION SUNS'** (*S. speciosa*) Gold flowers; compact plants; longer flowering period than other creeping zinnias. 8 inches tall, 12 inches wide.

Dianthus
(*Dianthus* spp.)

Dianthus bears lovely, old-fashioned blooms of white, pink, burgundy, purple, and similar hues in single colors and bicolor combinations. Look for two major types: sweet William (*D. barbatus*) and China pinks (*D. chinensis*). Cold tolerant and deer resistant, they attract butterflies and other pollinators.

Best site
Both types of dianthus prefer full sun and well-drained soil. Drainage is vital to plant survival. Poorly drained soil is the most frequent reason dianthus fails. In containers, use a light peat-based potting mix. In hottest regions, provide light shade during the hottest parts of the day.

Although both dianthus types are short-lived perennials, they're grown as annuals or self-sowing biennials. See variety information below for hardiness.

Growing
Set out these cold-tolerant plants in early spring up to two weeks prior to the last frost date for your region. Mix a slow-release fertilizer into the soil at planting time. When growing plants in containers, feed according to label instructions with water-soluble liquid fertilizer once plants start showing signs of growth.

Dianthus is susceptible to fungal diseases, so avoid mulching with wood products or organic materials. Gravel mulch works well.

Remove individual faded blossoms to encourage more flower buds. Prune plants hard after flowering to promote their perennial nature, especially sweet William types. Relocate self-sown seedlings in early spring or fall.

Design ideas
With its self-sowing tendencies, this old-fashioned flower fits well into a traditional cottage garden. In other landscape settings, mass dianthus along the edges of planting beds or use in small clusters in rock gardens. Plants provide deer-resistant color; some varieties offer fragrance. Dianthus grows well in containers as a filler plant. It also attracts butterflies and is a good early-season bloomer to attract pollinators.

varieties:

❶ **'IDEAL CRIMSON'** (*D. chinensis*) Bright red blooms with white centers; fringed petal edges. 1 to 3 feet tall by 6 to 12 inches wide. Zones 9–10.

❷ **NIGRESCENS** (*D. barbatus nigrescens*) Bronze-green leaves topped with fragrant maroon-to-black blooms. Suitable for cutting. 20 to 24 inches tall, 8 to 12 inches wide Zones 5–10.

❸ **DIABUNDA PURPLE PICOTEE** (*D. barbatus*) Fragrant flowers with purple petals edged in white with white centers. 10 inches tall, 8 to 10 inches wide. Zones 5–10.

❹ **'PARFAIT RASPBERRY'** (*D. chinensis*) Light pink with raspberry center; fragrant blooms from late spring to midsummer. 6 to 10 inches tall, 8 to 10 inches wide. Zones 6–10.

Diascia
(*Diascia barberae*)

A relative of the snapdragon, diascia thrives in cool seasons and withstands several frosts. Flowers sparkle in a wide array of colors, including pink, coral, white, and lavender. With an upright or trailing habit, diascia's usefulness in the garden abounds. Blossoms lure butterflies and early pollinators.

Best site

Plant diascia in compost-rich, well-drained soil. For containers, use a soil-based mix. Choose a spot that offers full sun in spring and light shade in the heat of summer, especially in warmer regions. Zone 9 to 11 hardiness is most common.

Growing

At planting time, blend a slow-release fertilizer into garden beds or container soil. With in-ground plantings, fertilize once more in late summer, before the fall flush of growth. Avoid overfertilizing plants, which leads to lush foliage growth at the expense of flowers. Keep plants well watered for best growth and flowering. Although plants are drought-tolerant, lack of water causes flower drop and scraggly growth. Diascia doesn't require deadheading.

When night temperatures hover above 75°F in the heat of summer, plants may stop flowering.

During this time, shear plants lightly, removing any scruffy growth and trimming stems back by one-fourth to one-third.

Design ideas

In early spring or fall, use upright varieties in containers or the landscape as you would pansies or snapdragons. In warm climates, plants bloom through winter. Choose mounded varieties as filler plants in containers and semitrailing types to spill over pot edges or at the tops of walls to create flowery cascades. Used as groundcovers, trailing types work well beneath roses. Upright diascia varieties are ideal in border, cottage garden, or meadow-style plantings, especially when mixed with penstemon, African daisy, and snapdragon. The colors of diascia blossoms work well with silver or gray foliage. Plants look wonderful with gravel mulch.

varieties:

❶ **DIVA RED** Larger flowers and improved heat tolerance; pair with dark pansies in spring and black coleus in summer. 8 inches tall and wide.

❷ **FLIRTATION ORANGE** Orange blooms on a plant with a mounded form. 8 to 12 inches tall and wide.

❸ **FLIRTATION PINK** Semitrailing plant good for hanging baskets or containers. 8 to 12 inches tall and wide.

❹ **PICCADILLY DENIM BLUE** Large, light violet-blue flowers; frost-hardy. 1 foot tall and wide. Zones 8–11.

❺ **SUN CHIMES RED** Large red blooms; some heat tolerance; mounding habit grows to trailing. 12 to 18 inches tall, 9 to 12 inches wide.

Dichondra
(*Dichondra* spp.)

A trailing foliage plant that cascades or spreads from 3 to 6 feet in a single season, dichondra forms lush falls of silver or green. The vine boasts heat and drought tolerance, and the dense, matlike growth is deer resistant.

Best site

Plant in full sun to light shade in soil that offers a low to medium moisture level. Dichondra thrives best in soil with an alkaline to neutral pH, but is adaptable to other soils. Plants used as groundcovers require well-drained soil to prevent the vines from rotting. Zones 9–11.

Growing

Keep plants well watered until established, then provide occasional irrigation during extended periods of drought. Plants wilt when soil dries out but recover quickly following irrigation.

When planted as a groundcover, dichondra forms a thick mat of foliage because the stems root along the soil's surface. The vine spreads by stems that creep above and below ground. When using dichondra as a groundcover, take care when planting near lawns because it can invade and be difficult to eradicate.

Design ideas

Dichondra shines when used in hanging baskets or in containers as a spiller plant. The green form works best; the silver type quickly blankets the pot and spreads across surrounding surfaces, so always elevate the pot.

To create a curtain of color, use this vine in window boxes or containers located along an elevated deck. Plants also work well situated atop a retaining wall and allowed to drape over it. Vines look attractive spilling among rocks surrounding a water garden.

As a groundcover, the dense growth provides effective erosion control. Dichondra can be a good lawn alternative in warm climates, especially in areas too shady for grass to grow well. It doesn't withstand heavy foot traffic. Use it in areas that are less heavily traveled.

varieties:

❶ **'SILVER FALLS'** (*D. argentea*) Silvery small leaves and stems; Native to desert areas of the Southwest and northern Mexico. 2 to 3 inches tall, 3 to 4 feet wide or long.

❷ **'EMERALD FALLS'** (*D. repens*) Deep green, 1-inch-wide, rounded leaves. Use as a groundcover or container plant. 2 to 4 inches tall, 3 feet wide or long.

Dusty Miller
(*Senecio* spp.)

Celebrate heat-tolerant, low-maintenance beauty with the lacy leaves of dusty miller. This foliage favorite, with its cool, wool-felted leaves, provides a perfect foil for bright bloomers. Deer- and frost-resistant, the plant holds its own in beds, borders, and containers.

Best site

Plant this Mediterranean native in well-drained or sandy soil. In containers, dusty miller prefers evenly moist soil. Once it's established in beds, plants are drought tolerant. Site in full sun to part shade. Plants tolerate full shade, but the foliage color may fade somewhat.

Dusty miller is grown as a summer annual in northern climates In subtropical regions like Florida and the Gulf Coast, it's grown as a winter annual because plants can't survive summer rains and humidity. In Mediterranean-type regions, like California, dusty miller grows as a perennial shrub. Zones 7–11.

Growing

Water new plantings daily until roots develop. This is most important in sandy soils. Although established plants are fairly drought tolerant, they should be irrigated during extended dry periods. Prune as needed if growth becomes straggly. Feed dusty miller monthly in planting beds; twice monthly in containers.

Design ideas

Dusty miller's silver foliage creates a pleasing accent with colorful flowers. It forms a sophisticated effect paired with lavender, blue, or pink. For sizzle, blend it with red, orange, or yellow. The leaves make a nice addition to garden-fresh bouquets. Use plants in containers or planting beds. Smaller types make wonderful edging plants.

varieties:

❶ **'SILVER DUST'** (*S. cineraria*) Silver leaves with a lacy, cut pattern; remove flower buds as they appear. 8 to 18 inches tall, 6 to 16 inches wide. Zones 8–10.

❷ **'BLAZIN' GLORY'** (*S. cephalophorus*) Silvery, tongue-shape leaves in a rosette; slow grower, reaching mature size over several seasons. Red flowers. Requires well-drained soil. 12 to 18 inches tall and wide. Zones 9–11.

❸ **'COLCHESTER WHITE'** (*Centaurea gymnocarpa*) Not a true dusty miller but acts like one on steroids. Finely textured silvery foliage on arching branches; thrives in heat, drought, and dry shade. Prune for branching. 2 feet tall, 3 feet wide; smaller in containers. Zones 7–11.

Elephant's Ear
(*Colocasia esculenta*)

Tropical style thunders into the garden when elephant's ear is in the mix. This large-leaf, easy-growing personality commands attention. Plant size is a direct result of available moisture and fertilizer. Add summer heat, and you can almost watch leaves grow bigger by the hour.

Best site

Plant in slightly acidic soil rich in organic matter. Elephant's ear needs consistent moisture; plants reach maximum size in moist to wet soil. Plants can grow in containers submerged 6 to 12 inches deep or planted in soil along pond edges.

Site elephant's ear in full sun if you can provide enough moisture to prevent wilting. In drier and hotter regions, provide part shade. Zones 6–11, depending on the variety.

Growing

Provide consistent moisture in full sun situations. Use a soaker hose or drip irrigation for easiest watering. Elephant's ear requires heavy fertilizing to fuel growth. Enrich the soil with composted organic matter prior to planting. Use a water-soluble fertilizer every two to three weeks during the growing season, or mix slow-release fertilizer into the soil at planting time.

In areas where plants aren't hardy, dig tubers in fall after the first frost. Store them in a cool, dry place where temperatures stay above 45°F. Where plants are hardy, use caution when planting elephant's ear in pondside settings. If plants escape into natural waterways, they become invasive and displace native species.

Design ideas

Choose elephant's ear to grace water gardens with exotic splendor. This plant makes a big statement. The large leaves don't work well in tiny or formal gardens, but anywhere else they create a lush, junglelike ambience. This is a great plant for children to plant and tend, rewarding efforts with larger-than-life results. Site it near outdoor living areas to stir a tropical feel. In planting beds, it towers over flowering annuals for a dramatic scene.

varieties:

❶ **'BLACK MAGIC'** Leaves open green, then develop purplish-black colors in full sun. 3 to 6 feet tall and wide. Zones 8–11.

❷ **'TEACUP'** Green leaves with purple veins form a cup. Purple stems. 2 to 6 feet tall, 3 to 4 feet wide. Zones 7–11.

❸ **'MADEIRA'** Black-purple leaves; hybrid variety. Size is between a caladium and full-size elephant's ear, good for containers. 2 to 3 feet tall and wide. Zones 6–11.

❹ **'RED STEM RHUBARB'** Red stems and veins; bright green leaves. Needs well-drained soil. 2 to 5 feet tall, 18 to 24 inches wide. Zones 7–11.

❺ **'MOJITO'** Green leaves with splatters, splotches, and speckles of dark purple. 1 to 3 feet tall, 3 to 4 feet wide. Zones 7–11.

Euphorbia
(*Euphorbia* hybrids)

A blizzard in a container—that's what this bedding euphorbia resembles when in flower. Dainty white or pink-blushed blooms blanket foliage all season long. Nothing fazes this quick color plant. It flowers through record-breaking heat and drought conditions, and deer and rabbits leave it alone.

Best site

Plant in very well-drained, dry or moderately moist soil. Mix slow-release fertilizer or compost into planting beds. Use a soilless mix for containers. Grow in full sun to part shade. Zones 10–11.

Growing

Euphorbia doesn't require deadheading or pruning, although plants can be pruned at any time and they bounce back fine. It has a strong character but succumbs to overwatering. Make sure the soil dries out between irrigations. If plants wilt from lack of water, they revive quickly following watering. For even more flowers, fertilize plants in containers with a bloom-booster product.

Plants offer moderate salt tolerance. Use in seaside gardens or streetside plantings in areas where winter requires salt treatments on roads.

Euphorbia stems contain milky sap that can irritate sensitive skin or anyone allergic to latex. Use caution if you have had a skin reaction to poinsettia, which is a type of euphorbia.

Design ideas

Versatile and always beautiful, euphorbia can easily fill many roles in the garden. It's a standout planted solo in containers. In the landscape, plants flower continuously through rugged heat and drought, making them a good choice for sunny beds near paved areas or buildings, where reflected heat singes other annuals.

In containers, use euphorbia as a filler plant. The fine, airy texture pairs well with plants that have a coarser texture, such as petunia, African daisy, and geranium. It pairs beautifully with New Zealand flax, sedges, and caladium.

varieties:

❶ 'STARDUST PINK SHIMMER' Large blooms with a pink blush and dark leaves. Good for containers. To 8 inches tall and wide.

❷ 'STARDUST WHITE SPARKLE' Dark foliage and large white flowers. To 8 inches tall and wide.

❸ 'WHITE MANAUS' Exceptionally heat tolerant. 3 feet tall by 14 inches wide.

❹ BREATHLESS WHITE (*E. hypericifolia*) White blooms, medium green foliage. Ideal for containers. 8 to 12 inches tall, 10 to 12 inches wide.

❺ DIAMOND FROST (*E. graminea*) Airy white blooms all season long. 12 to 18 inches tall, 10 to 12 inches wide.

Flowering Cabbage & Kale
(*Brassica oleracea*)

Brighten the late fall and winter garden with foliage that stands up to frosts and light snow. Flowering cabbage produces a tight head, while its kale cousin forms a more open, flowerlike rosette. Plant centers flush in hues that include rose, pink, white, and creamy yellow.

Best site

Plant in full sun to part shade in well-drained soil. In containers, use a peat-based soilless mix. Shade is necessary in hot regions. Some types are true annuals; hardiness varies by variety.

Growing

Flowering cabbage and kale are low-maintenance plants. They require consistent moisture to fuel growth. Mulch them in southern zones to conserve soil moisture. In northern regions, water until the ground freezes. When outer leaves yellow, feed with an all-purpose fertilizer.

Keep an eye out for cabbage loopers, which feed on leaves. This is worse in the South but can be an issue in mild winters in northern zones. Treat caterpillars with *Bacillus thuringiensis* (*Bt*).

Cool air triggers pretty leaf pigments. Leaves remain green until temperatures fall below 50°F.

Design ideas

Create striking plantings by pairing flowering kale and cabbage with bold-petal bloomers. In containers, partner them with cool-weather annuals such as pansy, dianthus, snapdragon, or stock. Try purple-leaf kale with bright yellow pansies for an eye-popping display. In southern regions, fill a pot or flowerbed with ornamental kale backed by paperwhite narcissus.

Kale and cabbage blend with fall perennials such as asters, sedums, ornamental grasses, and garden mums. Mass plantings of ornamental cabbage and kale look fantastic planted against a backdrop of evergreen shrubs.

Flowering kale and cabbage are edible; harvest tender leaves from the centers of plants. Design a salad garden by planting flowering kale, mesclun, chives, snow pea, and parsley.

varieties:

❶ **'COLOR UP PURPLE'** Flowering cabbage. Leaves turn intense violet-purple as plants mature. 10 inches tall by 1 foot wide. Annual.

❷ **'OSAKA RED'** Flowering cabbage. Plant center blushes hot pink, white outer leaves remain pale green; purple veins. 6 to 12 inches tall, 12 to 18 inches wide. Annual.

❸ **'KALEIDOSCOPE'** Flowering kale. Ruffled purple-green leaves and magenta-pink veins. In the South, leaves may be lavender. 2 feet tall, 15 inches wide. Zones 6–11.

❹ **'PEACOCK RED'** Flowering kale. Deeply serrated, feathery dusty green leaves; bright reddish-purple leaf color in cold weather. 10 to 12 inches tall and wide. Annual.

Flowering Tobacco
(*Nicotiana* spp.)

Star-shape red, pink, white, chartreuse, or purple blooms with long tubular necks paint a gorgeous scene in planting beds and containers. Some types self-sow and naturalize to keep the show going. The shorter kinds add rich swaths of color when planted en masse.

Best site

Plant in consistently moist but well-drained soil high in organic matter. In containers, use a soilless mix. Site in full sun to part shade. Provide afternoon shade in hot regions. Hardiness varies.

Growing

Avoid overfertilizing in-ground plants, which results in bigger plants with few flowers. Fertilize potted plants regularly or mix slow-release fertilizer into the soil at planting time.

Taller varieties may require staking. Insert hoop stakes around plants when they're young. You can also insert half-hoop stakes as needed once plants reach mature size.

Shear shorter types after flowering and then fertilize; new flower buds should form in 14 to 18 days. With taller types, cut stems selectively.

Some flowering tobacco species self-sow. In Zones 6 and colder, these plants typically don't appear in the garden until early summer. Start seeds in late winter indoors or purchase plants.

Design ideas

The bedding varieties of flowering tobacco provide steady color. Light shades glow at dusk, so site plants near pathways or outdoor living areas. Enjoy the powerful perfume of fragrant varieties by locating them near outdoor seating areas. Types with chartreuse flowers combine well with bold red petunia, blue scaevola, and coleus in shades of red, burgundy, or pink.

Some flowering tobacco varieties attract hummingbirds. Nearly all beckon butterflies. The white, taller types attract hummingbird moths.

varieties:

❶ **NICOTIANA LANGSDORFFII** Clusters of fragrant 2-inch-long lime blooms. Self-sowing. 3 to 6 feet tall, 1 to 3 feet wide. Zones 10–11.

❷ **NICOTIANA ALATA** Nonfragrant flowers in shades of red, white, pink, and chartreuse. 3 to 5 feet tall, 1 to 2 feet wide. Zones 10–11.

❸ **NICOTIANA SYLVESTRIS** Basal leaves to 3 feet long. Flower stems up to 5 feet, with 3-inch-long fragrant white blooms. 3 to 5 feet tall, 1 to 2 feet wide. Zones 10–11.

❹ **'METRO LIME'** (*Nicotiana × sanderae*) Nonfragrant chartreuse flowers. Pair with red flowers. 12 to 15 inches tall, 8 to 10 inches wide. Annual.

❺ **'WHISPER'** (*Nicotiana* hybrid) Fragrant flowers open pure white, change to blush, then pink. Disease-resistant. 32 to 40 inches tall, 2 feet wide. Zones 10–11.

Gazania
(*Gazania* spp.)

Gardens sizzle all summer long with gazania. A native of South Africa, this annual offers heat, drought, frost, and salt tolerance. Flowers sparkle in a rainbow of hues, from pastel pinks to deep orange to bright gold—and many variations and bicolors in between.

Best site
An ideal site offers full sun with sandy, well-drained soil, but gazania tolerates drought-plagued and low-fertility soils. In containers, use a commercial soilless mix. Gazania is grown as an annual in most of the country but survives winters in Zones 10 and 11.

Growing
This bloomer requires little care to keep it looking good. Too much TLC in the form of water and fertilizer actually can harm plants. No fertilizer and little water are needed during the growing season. Plants in containers require more frequent irrigation; otherwise, water only when the soil is dry.

Most gazania plants require sunlight for blooms to remain open; they shut tightly on cloudy, overcast days and at night. The new Sunbathers hybrids have blooms that stay open in low light conditions, including nighttime.

Design ideas
Make gazania your go-to choice for hot, dry areas where most plants fizzle and die by midsummer. Gazania thrives in planting areas with reflected heat, such as along sidewalks, driveways, and buildings. Gazania is a good pick for containers on elevated decks, where soil temperatures soar.

In the garden, gazania works well as an edging plant. Its vibrant blooms pair beautifully with the strong, solid hues of alternanthera, purple heart, and New Zealand flax. The flowers are butterfly favorites so incorporate them into wildlife gardens.

varieties:

❶ **BIG KISS WHITE FLAME** (*G. rigens*) 4-inch-wide flowers with rose stripes on creamy-yellow petals that fade to white. 8 to 10 inches tall and wide.

❷ **'DAYBREAK TIGER MIX'** (*G. rigens*) Mixed flowers in creamy white with rose stripes, yellow-gold with red stripes, and variations. 8 to 10 inches tall, 6 to 8 inches wide.

❸ **'NEW DAY BRONZE SHADES'** (*G. rigens*) Large blooms in tones of orange and bronze. 8 to 10 inches tall, 6 to 8 inches wide.

❹ **SUNBATHERS SUNSET** (*G. hybrid*) Crested red-orange semidouble flowers open in low-light conditions and at night. 12 to 14 inches tall, 10 to 12 inches wide.

Geranium (*Pelargonium* spp.)

A garden favorite, geranium earns a well-deserved place in quick color designs. Versatile and tough, it produces loads of flowers all season long. Blossoms feature a variety of forms, including the well-known ball-shape flower clusters and less familiar dainty, open flowers. Leaves display bands or zones of color, along with colorful splotches, splashes, and edges.

Best site

Geranium is a full-sun plant. Tuck it in a spot that receives at least four hours of direct sun. Regal and ivy geraniums benefit from light shade during hot summer months.

Air circulation is important for healthy growth, but stems tend to be brittle. Protect plants from strong winds to prevent stems from snapping. Provide rich, well-drained soil high in organic matter. In containers, use a peat-based soilless mix. Zones 9–11.

Growing

Geraniums thrive in warm temperatures. Plant after all danger of frost has passed and the soil is warm. To help prevent disease outbreaks, water early in the day so leaves and flowers can dry before night arrives.

Geraniums are heavy feeders. Blend a slow-release fertilizer into the soil at planting time. Four to six weeks after planting, start fertilizing with a water-soluble food. Use a bloom-booster product for flowering geraniums and an all-purpose food for types grown for colorful foliage.

Mulch in-ground plantings to retain soil moisture. Remove spent flowers, snapping off the entire blossom stem at the base. If rain soaks blooms that aren't quite spent and petals start turning brown, remove the flowers before they mold, which can infect leaves.

In the South, flowering slows during the summer and refreshes as autumn arrives.

Watch for caterpillars on leaves. Handpick and dump them into soapy water or spray *Bacillus thuringiensis* (*Bt*). Geranium budworms, the larvae of hummingbird moths, burrow into flower buds and feed on developing petals, resulting in malformed, stunted blossoms. The best way to control budworms is to examine developing buds for worms and knock them into soapy water. You can also spray *Bt* on flower buds when you realize you have a problem. It won't affect caterpillars feeding inside buds but can stop worms that haven't yet burrowed in.

Look for varieties that are resistant to edema, a leaf blister that occurs when plants take up more water through their roots than they can use or release through their leaves.

Design ideas

Geraniums offer versatility in the garden and shine when grown in containers, hanging baskets, and window boxes. With the exception of ivy geraniums, all types also add strong swaths of color to planting beds. In general, geraniums boast deer resistance and moderate heat tolerance. The types with larger flowers attract hummingbirds and butterflies.

Names to watch for

GERANIUM VARIETIES (*Pelargonium*)

'Crystal Palace Gem' Heirloom from 1869.

Round, two-tone green leaves, salmon-red blooms. Pair with dark-tone sedge and white nierembergia. 1 to 3 feet tall and wide. Zones 9–11.

Caliente Deep Red Cross between an ivy and zonal geranium with pleated ivy geranium leaves

and zonal-style flower heads. Heat-tolerant. Resistant to edema. 12 to 18 inches tall, 12 to 14 inches wide. Zones 9–11.

ZONAL GERANIUM (*P. × hortorum*)

The most common type of geranium is easily identified by dark markings on leaves. A cluster of individual blooms stands above foliage on stout stems. Size is typically 1 to 2 feet tall. Dwarf types measure less than 10 inches; miniatures are less than 6 inches tall.

fancy-leaf & zonal geranium varieties:

1 **'GRAFFITI VIOLET'** Fancy leaf. Starlike hot pink flowers; narrow petals and pleated leaves. 1 foot tall, 10 to 12 inches wide. Zones 10–11.

2 **'INDIAN DUNES'** Fancy leaf. Pleated bright chartreuse leaves with a maroon-brown blotch. Narrow-petaled flowers in shades of scarlet-orange. Pair with dark red to burgundy coleus or alternanthera. 6 to 12 inches tall, 12 to 15 inches wide. Zones 10–11.

3 **'AVENIDA MOSAIC RED'** Zonal. Pink-blushed white petals with splatters and specks of deeper scarlet. Classic green leaves with a dark band of green. Use alone or with 'Black and Blue' salvia and lavender calibrachoa, or with purple fountain grass. 18 to 24 inches tall, 15 to 18 inches wide. Zones 10–11.

IVY GERANIUM (*P. peltatum*)

Also known as ivyleaf geranium, this group has ivylike leaves and grows in a trailing manner. Typically used in hanging baskets and window boxes as spillers, they usually bloom in pink, maroon, and red tones. Flower size is smaller, more open, and looser than a zonal geranium.

ivy geranium varieties:

4 **'ROYAL LAVENDER'** Lavender-blush flowers. Deep green leaves. Excellent edema resistance. Heat tolerant. 10 to 18 inches tall, 14 to 24 inches wide. Zones 10–11.

5 **'ROYAL CANDY PINK'** Pink-and-white bicolor blooms. Deep green leaves. Excellent edema resistance and heat tolerance. 10 to 18 inches tall, 14 to 24 inches wide. Zones 10–11.

6 **'ROYAL SCARLET RED'** Scarlet flowers contrast with deep green leaves. Strong edema resistance. 10 to 12 inches tall, 14 to 18 inches wide. Zones 10–11.

geranium

MARTHA WASHINGTON OR REGAL GERANIUM

This is a bushy, upright, cool-season geranium. Plants thrive when temperatures stay below 60°F. When summer sizzles above that mark, plants stall and stop blooming until cool fall air arrives. Large, 2- to 5-inch-wide blossoms may be single or double with petals typically painted pink, burgundy, white, lavender, or other hues. Many flowers are bicolors, featuring splashes or edges of another shade.

regal & hybrid regal geranium varieties:

7 **'ELEGANCE BURGUNDY'** (*P. × domesticum*) Solid green, toothed leaves. Deep burgundy-purple blooms. Flowers 2 to 5 inches across with pinkish background and dark burgundy eye. Shade during summer months. 2 to 3 feet tall, 12 to 18 inches wide. Zones 9–11.

8 **'GRANDIOSA CHERRY PICOTEE'** (*P. × domesticum × crispum*) Beautiful blooms and toughness combined. Better heat tolerance and disease resistance than most regal geraniums. 10 to 20 inches tall and wide. Zones 9–11.

9 **'ELEGANCE MAIDEN ICED WINE'** (*P. × domesticum*) Burgundy petals with a deep maroon center and white edging. Leaves offer a pretty contrast in bright green. Protect plants from hot afternoon sun. 12 to 18 inches tall and wide. Zones 9–11.

SCENTED GERANIUM

Many scented geraniums are true heirloom plants, passed down through gardening generations from cuttings. Plants produce scented oils in their leaves. You can release the scent by brushing or rubbing foliage. Fragrances include a host of delicious aromas, including peppermint, rose, lemon, nutmeg, chocolate, and apple. Plants flower less than other geranium types; blooms that appear are dainty and small compared to zonals. Scented geraniums grow more lushly than other types. Prune freely to control size and increase branching. Use leaves fresh or dried to flavor desserts, tea, jelly, herbal vinegar, fruit dishes, and baked goods. Dried leaves make a wonderful addition to potpourri.

scented geranium varieties:

10 **'MABEL GREY' LEMON** (*P. citronellum*) Sharply lobed leaves. Strongest lemon fragrance. Rare pink flowers with deep rose smudges on upper petals. Trainable as a single-stem topiary. 2 to 4 feet tall, 12 to 18 inches wide. Zones 8–11.

11 **NUTMEG** (*P. fragrans*) Frilly, gray-green leaves edged and splashed with chartreuse. Spicy nutmeg scent. Dainty white blooms blushed with rose-pink stripes. Use alone in containers or with other sun-loving bloomers. 8 to 12 inches tall, 18 to 24 inches wide. Zones 8–10.

12 **PEPPERMINT** (*P. tomentosum*) Green leaves covered with silky white hairs, creating an angoralike effect. Intense peppermint scent. Clusters of small white flowers open occasionally. 1 to 3 feet tall and wide. Zones 10–11.

Gomphrena
(*Gomphrena* spp.)

Heat- and drought-tolerant good looks grace the garden when you plant drifts of gomphrena, also known as globe amaranth. This globe-headed bloomer features papery flowers that open from summer until frost. Butterflies can't resist the blossoms in hues of purple, red, lavender, and white.

Best site

Plant in full sun in average, well-drained soil. Gomphrena tolerates a wide range of soil types, from infertile or sandy soils to clay or good loam. Avoid soils that don't drain well. Soggy soil spells a quick end to the blooming show. Tender perennial in Zones 9 to 11.

Growing

Low maintenance best describes gomphrena's care level. Mature plants offer strong drought resistance. Gomphrena stands up to Texas- and Deep South-style heat. In hot regions, apply mulch after planting to preserve soil moisture. Pinch young plants to promote bushiness, which increases flower number.

However, provide consistent and adequate moisture throughout the early part of the growing season. If possible, irrigate so plants achieve peak growth potential.

Two types display different growth patterns. G. globosa typically reaches 1 to 2 feet tall and 6 to 12 inches wide. G. haageana grows 24 to 30 inches tall and 12 to 18 inches wide.

Design ideas

Gomphrena is an excellent choice for planting beds or containers. Use smaller *G. globosa* types as edging plants in beds. Taller *G. haageana* varieties hold their own in the back of a border.

The cloverlike flowerheads add texture that's striking in mass plantings. Gomphrena pairs well with sweet potato vine, broadleaf coleus, castor bean, or banana. Include it in butterfly and cutting gardens. The papery blooms make long-lasting fresh flowers and retain their color when dried, so place them in areas where you can view them from indoors in cooler weather.

varieties:

❶ **'ALL AROUND PURPLE'** (*G. globosa*) Purple flowers. 1 to 3 feet tall, 6 to 12 inches wide.

❷ **'LAS VEGAS PINK'** (*G. globosa*) Bright pink blooms. Excellent heat tolerance, even in the South. 16 to 20 inches tall, 14 to 16 inches wide

❸ **'FIREWORKS'** (*Gomphrena* spp.) Hot pink petals tipped with gold. Best-flowering gomphrena. No deadheading required. 24 to 26 inches tall, 8 to 10 inches wide; can grow to 4 feet (or more) in Southern climates.

❹ **'QIS PURPLE'** (*G. globosa*) Large, 1½-inch-diameter purple flowers. 18 to 24 inches tall, 12 to 15 inches wide.

❺ **'STRAWBERRY FIELDS'** (*G. haageana*) Clear red blossoms on long stems ideal for cutting. 1 to 2 feet tall, 9 to 12 inches wide.

Grasses & Grasslike Plants

These plants imbue a landscape or container design with drama and architectural interest. Strong, upright types provide a vertical element, and small, arching forms add elegance and fine texture to combinations. Leaves contribute color, including shades of deep purple-black, toffee, hot pink, chartreuse, and variegated patterns. Seed heads linger on many plants beyond frost, increasing interest in winter garden scenes.

Best site

Most grasses and grasslike plants thrive in sun but tolerate part shade. Plants frequently develop strongest leaf colors in full sun. Average, well-drained soil is usually sufficient to fuel growth, but some plants, such as rushes, need or tolerate excess moisture. Others, such as fountain grasses, tolerate drought and sandy soil. In containers, use a peat-based soilless mix. See varieties lists for hardiness information.

Growing

Size varies greatly among grasslike plants, from a dainty 6 inches tall to a hard-to-miss 6 feet tall. Some plants form a tidy clump, while others tend to spread, especially in landscape settings with ideal growing conditions.

Irrigation is most important in beds and borders while plants are establishing. Once plants send up steady new growth, many have good drought tolerance. Water potted plants more frequently, whenever soil is dry to the touch. Larger grasses in containers use moisture at a fierce rate in summer heat. Mix water-retention crystals into the soil prior to planting to reduce watering. Research the water needs of the plants you grow and provide accordingly.

Mix an all-purpose slow-release fertilizer into the soil prior to planting. Supplement as needed during the growing season according to label instructions. Grasses are generally low maintenance, pest free, and deer resistant.

Design ideas

Grasses and grasslike plants add a strong textural element and a sense of movement to plantings. Narrowleaf and fountain types pair well with broadleaf plants such as canna, begonia, banana, or coleus, and chunky bloomers, such as zinnia, black-eyed Susan, and marigold. Grasses with broader leaves, like ornamental millet and corn, complement spreading plants such as Zahara or Profusion zinnia, sweet potato vine, and SunPatiens.

In containers, grasses are often used as thrillers or fillers. In the landscape, use shorter grasses as edging plants and taller types for screening purposes. Plant grasses in odd-numbered clumps for drama and attention.

Names to watch for

FIBER OPTIC GRASS (*Isolepis cernua*) Short, blousy mounds of light foliage. Upright leaves arch as they mature. Flower spikes resemble fiber optic strands. Full or part shade; in full sun with constant moisture. Needs moisture-retentive, well-drained soil. 6 to 8 inches tall, 18 to 20 inches wide. Zones 5–10.

MEXICAN FEATHER GRASS
(*Nassella tenuissima*, formerly *Stipa tenuissima*) Upright, fine needlelike foliage. Silky flowers with tufts of green turn blond in midsummer. Wispy seed heads add winter interest. Use solo or blend with other plants. Part to full sun. 2 feet tall and wide. Zones 7–10.
'**Pony Tails**' 16 to 24 inches tall, 24 inches wide. Zones 7–10.

RUBY GRASS (*Melinis nerviglumis*) Clumping grass native to South Africa. Blue-green foliage. Silky pink flowers in late spring on stems that extend 1 foot above foliage. Flowers mature to white. Full sun. Light, well-drained soils with consistent moisture. 10 to 12 inches tall, 8 to 10 inches wide Zones 9–10.
'**Pink Crystals**' 18 to 24 inches tall, 9 to 18 inches wide. Zones 8–10.
'**Savannah**' 6 to 12 inches tall, 9 to 12 inches wide. Zones 8–11.

SEDGE (*Carex buchananii*)
Narrow, upright, striking red-brown foliage. Also known as New Zealand hair sedge. Plant in moist, quick-draining soil in full sun to part shade. Use in containers as a filler or in landscape beds. For impact, plant in groups of three or more. 1 to 2 feet tall and wide. Zones 6–10.

sedge varieties:

1 **'FOX RED'** Bronze-red leaves with buff tone at the tips. 2 to 3 feet tall and wide. Zones 5–10.

2 **'RED ROOSTER'** Narrow copper-red to light bronze foliage curls on the ends. 24 inches tall by 12 inches wide. Zones 7–10.

3 **'GREEN TWIST'** (*C. buchananii* f. *viridis*) Narrow olive green leaves twist at the ends; strong upright clump. 16 inches tall, 18 to 24 inches wide. Zones 6–9.

RUSH (*Juncus*)
Distinctive upright or curly foliage. Full sun to shade. Tolerates wet growing conditions. Thrives in pots and moist, well-drained soil. Size varies with plant type. Zones 4–10.

rush varieties:

4 **'TWISTER' CORKSCREW RUSH** (*J. effusus spiralis*) Coiled leaves slowly unwind as they grow. Full sun to part shade; needs moisture-retentive soil. Grows in standing water up to 4 inches deep. Use in containers or in a bog or water garden. 12 to 14 inches tall and wide. Zones 5–10.

5 **BLUE DART SLENDER RUSH** (*J. tenuis*) Quick-growing, upright, blue-tone foliage. Part sun. Adapted to standing water or drought. Space closely together as a low-maintenance groundcover. Use in containers as a replacement for cordyline. 14 to 16 inches tall, 10 to 12 inches wide. Zones 5–10.

6 **'BLUE MOHAWK' SOFT RUSH** (*J. inflexus*) Foliage thriller with upright leaves in a blue tint. For a water garden in submerged pots or as a marginal plant. Spreads by rhizomes; contain by sinking potted plants into soil. 2 to 3 feet tall, 8 to 12 inches wide. Zones 5–9.

PURPLE FOUNTAIN GRASS (*Pennisetum setaceum*)
In Western states, check with local native plant societies to discover invasive potential of this upright, arching grass.

purple fountain grass varieties:

7 **'RUBRUM'** Dark purple leaves. Burgundy-tinted flower heads. Feathery bottlebrush plumes 1 foot above foliage. Winter interest. Full sun; well-drained soil. Tolerant of part shade, drought, heat, and high humidity. Use in containers as a thriller; use odd-numbered groups in a landscape. 3 to 5 feet tall, 2 to 4 feet wide Zones 9–11.

8 **'FIREWORKS'** Variegated leaves striped in white, green, burgundy, and hot pink. 24 to 36 inches tall, 18 to 24 inches wide. Zones 9–11.

9 **'RED RIDING HOOD'** Dwarf form dark purple-red leaves. 18 to 30 inches tall, 12 to 20 inches wide. Zones 9–11.

ORNAMENTAL CORN (*Zea mays*)
Leaves appear solid green, then add variegation after roughly three weeks in full sun. Use as a thriller plant in container combinations or as a screen or central upright element in the landscape. Pair with tall tropicals, such as banana and canna, and underplant with mounded plants, such as celosia, pentas, and lantana. 4 to 6 feet tall, 18 to 24 inches wide. Annual.

ORNAMENTAL MILLET (*Pennisetum glaucum*)
Strong, upright growth. Leaves in a variety of hues. Flower heads—stiff bottlebrushlike plumes 9 to 12 inches long—in early summer. Seed heads good for fresh or dried arrangements. Full sun to part shade. Average, moist, well-drained soil. In landscapes, adds drama or serves as a low-maintenance planting. Space 10 to 12 inches apart. In containers, use as a thriller. 3 to 4 feet tall, 18 to 24 inches wide. Zones 10–11.

ornamental corn & millet varieties:

10 **'FIELD OF DREAMS'** (*Z. mays*) Wavy green leaves display varying white stripes and pink tinges and edges. Plants branch well and add a strong textural element to plantings. This corn produces ears with dark kernels that can be used for popcorn. 4 to 5 feet tall, 24 to 28 inches wide.

11 **'TRICOLOR'** (*Z. mays*) Wavy rose, cream, and green leaves. Small ears, covered with multicolor kernels. 4 feet tall, 2 feet wide.

12 **'PURPLE MAJESTY'** (*P. glaucum*) Deep violet leaves, stems, and seedheads. Thrives in high heat, along a driveway or foundation. 3 to 4 feet tall, 18 to 24 inches wide.

13 **'JESTER'** (*P. glaucum*) Leaves emerge bright chartreuse and fade as they age, changing to red, bronze, and burgundy-purple. Best color in full sun. 3 to 4 feet tall, 10 to 14 inches wide.

Heliotrope
(*Heliotropium* spp.)

An old-fashioned cottage garden favorite, heliotrope combines ease of care with enticing fragrance. Tiny blooms in purple, lavender, rose, or white open in big showy bunches from summer to fall. Deep green foliage serves as a counterpoint to flower color on this deer-resistant plant.

Best site

Plant in soil that offers consistent moisture, high organic content, and good drainage. In containers, use a soilless potting mix containing coir, which helps maintain even soil moisture levels. Site in full sun. Provide afternoon shade in regions with sizzling summers or intense sun, such as in high altitudes.

Growing

Prune plants while they're young to stimulate branching and bushy growth. Continue to pinch and shape plants over time. Remove spent blooms to encourage new flower buds to form and maintain a tidy appearance.

Flowers open alternately in the cluster, from side to side, starting near the center and working outward. Eventually, the cluster shows a brown, spent interior with individual star-shape blooms opening toward cluster edges. It's okay to remove spent clusters before every blossom opens.

Keep the soil consistently moist but not waterlogged. Plants in dry soil are more susceptible to powdery mildew. Fertilize regularly using a water-soluble bloom booster according to package directions or blend a slow-release fertilizer into the soil when planting.

Design ideas

An old-fashioned cottage garden plant, heliotrope suits contemporary themes equally well. Its fragrance makes it ideal for planting near sitting areas or porches where you can savor the perfume. Use it in containers as a filler, surrounding it with pink baby's breath or calibrachoa. Mix with pentas, lantana, and nierembergia to create a butterfly or hummingbird buffet.

varieties:

❶ **AZURE SKIES** (*H. amplexicaule*) Creeping groundcover heliotrope with lavender blooms. Good heat tolerance. 12 to 14 inches tall, 2 to 3 feet wide. Zones 7–11.

❷ **GARDEN HELIOTROPE** (*H. arborescens*) Deep purple or lavender blooms; dark foliage. 18 to 24 inches tall, 12 to 15 inches wide. Zones 10–11.

❸ **'ALBA'** Pure white flowers; deep green foliage. Scent like baby powder or vanilla. 18 to 24 inches tall, 12 to 15 inches wide. Zones 10–11.

❹ **'ATLANTA'** Also sold as 'Atlantis'. Violet-blue blooms; compact plant. Strong heat tolerance. 6 to 12 inches tall, 10 to 14 inches wide. Zones 9–11.

❺ **SIMPLY SCENTSATIONAL** Star-shape blooms with golden centers surrounded by a white band edged in lavender. Salt-tolerant. 24 to 30 inches tall, 10 to 14 inches wide. Zones 9–11.

Hibiscus
(*Hibiscus* spp.)

Beloved for its tropical blossoms, Chinese hibiscus (*H. rosa-sinensis*) infuses settings with flamboyant style. The exotic flowers linger for a day or two in shades of red, gold, pink, white, and other hues. Use a different hibiscus for its stunning bronze-red foliage: *Hibiscus acetosella*.

Best site

Plant hibiscus in full sun in well-drained soil enriched with organic matter. Provide consistent and ample moisture. Protect Chinese hibiscus from strong winds to prevent stems from breaking. It is frost-tender. Zones 7–10.

Growing

Chinese hibiscus: Lightly pinch tips of growing stems in spring and midsummer to increase branching and flower numbers.

Fertilize monthly using an all-purpose product. Plants don't respond to bloom-booster fertilizers. They need extra potassium for maximum flowering.

Keep soil consistently moist. Overwinter indoors in a cool spot near a sunny window.

In spring, prune one-third of old wood.

Hibiscus acetosella: Prune as needed to maintain size and shape. In southern regions where growth is vigorous, prune monthly to encourage a full, bushy plant. If the spread is too great, pull the stems from soil, roots and all.

As new growth appears, fertilize with a slow-release product containing more nitrogen and potassium than phosphorus or mulch with compost to slowly feed plants.

Water every few days until established, then water every 7 to 10 days if no rainfall occurs.

In areas where plants are hardy, stems die to the ground following a freeze. Mulch to protect plants through winter. Don't remove dead stems even if they're unsightly. This could trigger new growth, which won't survive winter. Prune stems to 6 inches in early spring in southern gardens.

Design ideas

Chinese hibiscus blossoms lure butterflies and hummingbirds. In cool climates, this is an ideal container plant, with standard-type specimens as a thrillers. Underplant with petunias, purple heart, or sweet potato vine. Where Chinese hibiscus is hardy, it makes a great seasonal hedge.

H. acetosella also works as a thriller in a container. The dark color pairs well with lime green or variegated foliage. In the landscape, plants die back at the end of the season.

varieties:

❶ **'MAHOGANY SPLENDOR'** (*H. acetosella*) Purple-to-burgundy foliage, with best color in full sun. In part shade, color becomes rusty brown and green. Coarse-textured leaves with deeply serrated edges. Grows in standing water. 3 to 5 feet tall, 24 to 30 inches wide Zones 8–11.

❷ **'DAINTY DAIQUIRI'** (*H. rosa-sinensis*) Frilly, salmon-edged blooms with shades of lavender and pinkish-red centers. Blooms up to 7 inches across. 3 to 11 feet tall, 2 to 4 feet wide. Zones 9–11.

❸ **'TIKI TEMPTATION'** (*H. rosa-sinensis*) Flowers in yellow tones surrounding a hot pink bull's-eye center up to 7 inches across. 3 to 11 feet tall, 2 to 4 feet wide. Zones 9–11.

Impatiens
(*Impatiens* spp.)

Impatiens, America's top bedding plant, is the go-to pick for quick shade color with constant blooms in all but blue. New Guinea types, which have burgundy, purple, bronze, or variegated foliage and large flowers, can take a bit more sun. SunPatiens, similar to New Guinea types, thrive in full sun.

Best site

All impatiens grow well in evenly moist and well-drained soil enriched with organic matter. In containers, use a soilless peat-based mix.

Different types of impatiens thrive in varying light levels. Site traditional bedding impatiens (*I. walleriana*) and New Guinea impatiens (*I. hawkeri*) in part to full shade. A location with morning sun and afternoon shade is ideal. SunPatiens perform in full sun (morning or afternoon sun) to part shade. Avoid placing SunPatiens in deep shade because plants stretch and become leggy.

Hardiness varies, but all succumb to a hard frost. Zones 9–11, depending on type.

Growing

All impatiens flower vigorously from planting until frost melts plants. Some New Guinea impatiens cycle in and out of flower, although newer types offer consistent blooming.

Provide all impatiens with even soil moisture. In full-sun conditions in the South, SunPatiens require daily watering; avoid growing them in areas with watering restrictions. In northern regions, full sun demands daily watering but less water volume than in the South.

In containers, all impatiens require almost daily watering. Once summer heat arrives, New Guinea impatiens in hanging baskets can be hard to keep well watered. Impatiens grown in terra-cotta pots require more frequent watering than other types of containers. Mulch in-ground plantings to reduce water needs. Use a 2- to 3-inch layer to slow water evaporation and lower the soil temperature.

Fertilize impatiens regularly during the growing season. Bloom-booster products work well to stimulate flower formation. For in-ground plantings, blend slow-release fertilizer

sunpatiens hybrid varieties:

❶ COMPACT WHITE Large white flowers. Good choice for the Deep South. 24 to 36 inches tall and wide in planting beds, 18 to 24 inches in containers. Zone 11.

❷ VIGOROUS MAGENTA BOLD Magenta blooms. Vigorous plants for beds. Good choice for northern gardens with shorter growing seasons because plants grow quickly after planting. 36 to 48 inches tall and wide in planting beds, 24 to 36 inches in containers. Zone 11.

❸ SPREADING SALMON Variegated foliage and salmon blooms. Later flowering than other SunPatiens. Pairs with blue or lavender plants, such as trailing scaevola or upright blue salvia. 36 to 48 inches tall and wide in planting beds, 24 to 36 inches in containers. Zone 11.

into the soil prior to planting. Topdress beds in midsummer for all but SunPatiens, which are light feeders.

Impatiens don't require pruning except to control plant size and promote branching. If you prune in summer, fertilize plants to stimulate growth. SunPatiens in part shade usually need pruning in midsummer. Prune anytime you notice plants stretching.

Bedding impatiens have become afflicted with a deadly fungal disease called downy mildew that kills plants. It can overwinter on infected plant parts. Symptoms include pale or stippled leaves, stunted growth, and white or light gray fuzz on leaf undersides. Leaves eventually fall off, leaving bare stems.

Pull and bag infected plants on the spot to prevent disease spread by wind. Preventive fungicide sprays help slow disease spread, but once mildew is present in a plant, it moves throughout the entire plant.

At the end of the growing season, even if you haven't had disease present, gather all impatiens residue, and bag and destroy it. Avoid placing impatiens in the same planting bed year after year. Downy mildew problems have occurred on both coasts and in the Midwest.

SunPatiens and New Guinea impatiens show strong resistance to downy mildew.

Design ideas

Impatiens form blooming mounds of color in the landscape. In containers, they hold their own as solo plantings. Impatiens pair well with sun- or shade-loving coleus, depending on each type. Other partners for shade to part shade include caladium, lobelia, polka-dot plant, and wishbone flower. With SunPatiens in a sunny location, select calibrachoa, moss rose, verbena, or trailing vinca as colorful edgings.

Names to watch for

IMPATIENS HYBRIDA 'Fusion Sunset' Apricot blooms with maroon centers. Heat and humidity tolerant. Grow in morning sun and afternoon shade. Use in containers or landscapes. No deadheading required. 10 to 16 inches tall and wide. Zones 9–11.

bedding impatiens varieties:

4 **'FIESTA STARDUST PINK'** (*I. walleriana*) Fully double roselike blossoms streaked with pink and stippled with white. Deep green leaves. Deadheading not necessary. Part to full shade. 10 to 16 inches tall, 10 to 12 inches wide.

5 **'XTREME LILAC'** (*I. walleriana*) Large 2½-inch-wide lilac flowers almost hide foliage. Blooms from planting until frost. Heat-tolerant in southern climates. Part to full shade. 8 to 10 inches tall and wide.

6 **ROCKAPULCO ROSE** (*I. walleriana*) Double blooms resemble rosebuds. Site in part to full shade. Thrives in heat and humidity. 10 to 20 inches tall, 1 foot wide. Zones 10–11.

new guinea impatiens varieties:

7 **INFINITY BLUSHING CRIMSON** (*I. hawkeri*) Large light pink petals brushed with vibrant crimson. Deep green foliage. No deadheading necessary. Part or full shade. 10 to 14 inches tall, 6 to 8 wide. Zones 10–11.

8 **'MAGNUM PINK'** (*I. hawkeri*) Clear pink flowers; dark green leaves. Part to full shade. 10 to 20 inches tall by 20 to 30 inches wide. Zones 10–11.

Iresine
(*Iresine herbstii*)

Iresine brings continuous color all season long to the garden party. Leaves sizzle with exotic hues, including lime green, hot pink, and electric yellow. These versatile plants grow in light levels from full sun to shade and don't demand intense care.

Best site

Plant in almost any light condition. The ideal is morning sun followed by light afternoon shade. Soil should be enriched with organic matter and well-drained. In heavy clay soils, work 3 to 4 inches of organic matter into the soil before planting or build raised beds you can fill with fertile soil. Zones 10–11.

Growing

Feed iresine monthly with light applications of an all-purpose, balanced fertilizer. Plants stand up to heat, and grow strong even through southern summers. Pinch stems after planting to promote branching and bushy growth. Prune or pinch plants at any time during the growing season to curtail or shape growth or promote branching. Plants typically grow 12 to 20 inches tall and 16 to 20 inches wide.

Design ideas

This foliage plant enhances the landscape with intense color. Iresine thrives in planting beds or containers.

The calypso colors blend well with tropical plants, such as banana, canna, elephant's ear, and hibiscus. Or mix and match leaf hues with sweet potato vine, New Guinea impatiens, and grasslike plants for strong combinations.

Plants tucked into light shade beneath trees seem to glow when sunlight filters through the tree canopy and splashes on the leaves.

The groundcover variety 'Purple Lady' provides a bright edging for beds and also shines in hanging baskets or containers. Plant it with ageratum and marigold for a vivid combination.

varieties:

❶ **'BLAZIN' ROSE'** Quilted foliage in green, bronze, or deep burgundy with vibrant pink veins. 18 to 30 inches tall, 16 to 20 inches wide.
❷ **'PURPLE LADY'** Heat-loving groundcover with bright cranberry and maroon leaves with dark burgundy stems. 6 to 8 inches tall, 2 to 3 feet wide.
❸ **'BLAZIN' LIME'** Lime-green leaves with cream-colored veins and fuchsia stems. Heat tolerant. Best in part sun to full shade. 12 to 18 inches tall, 16 to 20 inches wide.

Lantana
(*Lantana camara*)

Summer can turn up the heat and humidity, but when lantana is in the garden you'll still enjoy outstanding color. Because blossoms change colors as they age, the clusters of tiny flowers often display several shades of pink, orange, yellow, purple, or white at the same time.

Best site

Lantana flowers best in full sun but grows in part shade in average, well-drained soils. It tolerates poor soil and drought but prefers soil with medium moisture. Zones 9–11.

Growing

Lantana tops the chart for low-maintenance attractiveness. Plants tolerate heat, humidity, and drought. Established landscape plants need little supplemental irrigation; too much water and fertilizer diminish flower number. However, container plantings benefit from water and bloom-booster fertilizer.

Pests and diseases don't typically attack. Lantana needs no deadheading. After the first flush of flowers, prune plants. Otherwise, prune anytime to promote branching and more flowers.

A tender perennial reaching 3 to 4 feet tall and 1 to 3 feet wide, lantana dies to the ground at 28°F, but grows back from the roots in warm zones, where it forms a shrub. In these zones, apply midsummer fertilizer.

Lantana has escaped cultivation and become a problem plant in South Florida, Texas, Hawaii, and along the Gulf Coast. Buy named varieties to avoid planting a potential invader.

Leaves and any unripe fruits have a toxic effect on pets or livestock.

Design ideas

In the landscape, plants form bright swaths of color that offer a consistent presence all season. Use as a groundcover at the feet of taller plants, such as canna, banana, or grasslike plants. Lantana tolerates salt spray; use it in beach plantings. In containers, use lantana as a filler or spiller plant. The flowers beckon butterflies, hummingbirds, and all kinds of pollinators.

varieties:

1. **BANDANA CHERRY SUNRISE** Yellow centers and bands of apricot and pink flowers ringed with deep-crimson blooms, resembling a sunrise. Sets little seed. 1 to 2 feet tall, 1 to 3 feet wide.
2. **BANDANA ROSE** Sunny yellow blooms change to rose. Sets little seed. 12 to 26 inches tall, 12 to 24 inches wide.
3. **LANDMARK CITRUS** Gold flowers turn apricot and tangerine. Best in landscapes. 15 to 20 inches tall, 18 to 24 inches wide.
4. **LUSCIOUS GRAPE PURPLE** Numerous purple flower clusters nearly obscure foliage. 10 to 16 inches tall, 2 to 3 feet wide.
5. **'SAMANTHA'** Variegated leaves with irregularly marbled hues of medium green, chartreuse, and cream. Gold flowers. Pair with purple salvia. 10 to 16 inches tall, 24 to 30 inches wide.

Licorice Plant
(*Helichrysum* spp.)

Felted silver leaves add a frosted look to plantings in the heat of summer. Drought-tolerant and heat-loving licorice plant infuses any design with elegance. Stems spread and cascade, splashing silver throughout plantings. Plants grow vigorously; you'll need only one for most containers.

Best site

Plant in full sun to part shade in average, well-drained soil. Plants do best in dry to moderately moist soils but tolerate poor soil. Drainage is vital to success with licorice plant. In containers, use a soilless planting mix. Zones 9–11 except where noted.

Growing

Licorice plant is susceptible to root rot in poorly drained soils. Avoid overwatering in landscape situations. Plants in containers require more frequent watering, but avoid maintaining consistently wet soil. Licorice plant doesn't require much fertilizer. If it's in soil containing slow-release fertilizer, that's sufficient.

Plants branch freely, but you can pinch the growing tips at planting time to promote branching and bushiness. When adding licorice plant to container combinations, tuck it in front of the thriller but toward the center of the pot. Aim the stems in different directions so the new growth winds between surrounding plants. Planted in this fashion, use one licorice plant per 16-inch or smaller pot viewed from one side. For 16-inch or larger containers viewed from multiple sides, invest in two plants per pot.

Design ideas

Silver is a go-with-anything color. It blends with dark shades such as maroon, purple, and bronze. Pastels shine next to silver, and bold reds and oranges sizzle. No matter where you place licorice plant in the garden, you won't go wrong.

Excellent partners include Persian shield, a fineleaf purple verbena, orange New Guinea impatiens, cherry red zonal geranium, burgundy petunia, and coleus in black tones.

varieties:

❶ LEMON LICORICE (*H. petiolare*) A hint of yellow in leaves. Pair with purple verbena or burgundy calibrachoa. 8 to 12 inches tall, 20 inches wide.

❷ 'VARIEGATA' (*H. petiolare*) Irregular patterns of gold, silver, and green on leaves. Use in containers; pair with pink and deep blue. 12 to 18 inches tall, 15 to 18 inches wide

❸ 'SILVER MIST' (*H. microphyllum*) Small leaves with silver intensify with more sun. Forms a cushion in planting beds; winds through container plants. 6 to 8 inches tall, 18 to 24 inches wide.

❹ 'ICICLES' (*H. thianschanicum*) Narrow, linear leaves with an anise scent. Use in containers as a filler. Tuck among succulents in a xeriscape design. 8 to 16 inches tall, 18 to 24 inches wide. Zones 8–11.

Lobelia
(*Lobelia erinus*)

Intensely colored blooms earn lobelia a place in any garden. Look for flowers in shades of purple, blue, lavender, rose, white, and blends. A naturally trailing habit makes this charmer the perfect choice for hanging baskets and window boxes. The fan-shape blossoms display a large lower lip.

Best site

Plant in well-drained soil enriched with organic matter. The soil must drain well because plants are susceptible to root rot. Site in full sun to part shade. In southern regions, plants grow better in partly shaded situations. Zones 10–11 unless listed as otherwise.

Growing

Lobelia typically flowers strongest from late spring to early summer, declining as summer heat and humidity arrive. Night temperatures in the upper 70s and higher trigger a cessation in flowering although foliage continues to look fine. In areas with cool summers, lobelia shines. Choose newer heat-tolerant varieties for hot-summer regions. If flower numbers and growth dwindle, cut plants back to spur autumn bloom.

Always allow soil to dry out between waterings to avoid root rot. Regularly fertilize plants in containers using a bloom-booster product. In landscape plantings, lobelia benefits from compost or a slow-release fertilizer worked into soil prior to planting. There's no need to remove spent flowers. Prune plants at any point during the growing season as needed.

Design ideas

Trailing forms cascade from hanging baskets, window boxes, and containers. Upright forms create mounds of color in containers or planting beds. Plant lobelia as an edging or tuck it into rock gardens or small spaces. Lobelia attracts butterflies. Deep blue flowers tend to disappear in partly shady areas. Choose lighter-color forms for low-light areas.

Pair with nemesia, diascia, or pansy in spring and flowering cabbage or kale in fall.

varieties:

1 LUCIA DARK BLUE True blue blooms. Good in containers and hanging baskets. 6 to 8 inches tall and wide.

2 'MAGADI BLUE WITH WHITE EYE' Brilliant blue blooms with a white central eye. Heat-tolerant. 8 to 12 inches tall, 6 to 10 inches wide.

3 TECHNO HEAT WHITE White blooms. Heat tolerant. 6 to 12 inches tall, 8 to 12 inches wide.

4 'REGATTA ROSE' Early season rose-colored bloom with a white eye. Blooms nearly obscure foliage. 6 to 8 inches tall, 10 to 12 inches wide.

5 LAGUNA HEAVENLY LILAC Lavender blooms. 8 to 10 inches tall, 6 to 10 inches wide. Zones 9–11.

Mandevilla
(*Mandevilla* spp.)

Lusciously colored funnel-shape blooms unfurl in shades of red, pink, or white on this tender woody vine. Mandevilla enhances an exotic ambience in outdoor settings. Flowers open up to 6 inches across and showcase throats in contrasting hues.

YOU SHOULD KNOW
An easy way to tell if mandevilla vines need water is leaf color. When plants are dry, the glossy sheen on leaves becomes dull.

Best site
Mandevilla thrives in moist, well-drained soil. Give plants full sun to light shade. In the hottest regions, provide light afternoon shade. Moisture is key during the growing season, but be sure soil drains well to avoid root rot. In containers, use a moisture-retentive potting mix. Some are root-hardy to Zone 8, otherwise Zones 10 and 11.

Growing
Plants climb by twining stems around supports. Provide an adequately anchored support, especially for vines planted in the landscape in warmer zones. Mandevilla requires consistent moisture but plants can survive short droughts. In planting beds, it develops an enlarged root system that retains water. Plants in containers require more frequent watering.

Pinch vines at planting and as needed through the growing season to control growth and promote branching (and more flowers). Fertilize plants in containers on a regular basis with a bloom-booster product. Mix slow-release fertilizer into beds at planting time.

Mandevilla offers moderate salt tolerance and survives in seaside locations when planted behind the first line of dunes. In Zones 8–9, the tops of plants are usually killed by frosts, but some varieties may resprout from the roots in spring. All parts of this plant are poisonous.

Design ideas
In the Deep South, mandevilla is the classic lamppost or mailbox vine. In other parts of the country, train it to climb a trellis or lattice. This vine is a fast grower in warmer zones and quickly creates a living screen. In colder regions, grow mandevilla in pots to add tropical color to outdoor living settings.

varieties:

❶ SUN PARASOL CRIMSON (*M. × amabilis*) Deep green leaves and 4- to 6-inch-wide red blooms with orange throats. 10 to 15 feet tall, 2 to 3 feet wide. Zones 10–11.

❷ SUN PARASOL STARS AND STRIPES (*M. × amabilis*) Red petals streaked with white. 6 to 8 feet tall, 2 to 3 feet wide. Zones 10–11.

❸ BOLIVIAN MANDEVILLA (*M. boliviensis*) Large white blooms with contrasting yellow throats 3 to 4 inches across. Native to Bolivia and Ecuador. 3 to 10 feet tall, 3 to 6 feet wide. Zones 10–11.

❹ 'RED RIDING HOOD' (*M. sanderi*) Fragrant 3-inch-wide deep pink flowers with golden throats. Vines do not trail readily. 6 to 8 feet tall, 3 to 5 feet wide. Zones 10–11.

Marguerite Daisy
(*Argyranthemum frutescens*)

Fill the cool-season garden with the unbeatable look of old-fashioned summer daisies. Marguerite daisies offer deep green, fine-texture foliage along stems topped with masses of blooms in shades of pink, white, yellow, or lavender. Butterflies can't resist them.

Best site
Plant in full sun in average, well-drained soil. In containers, use a soilless peat-based potting mix. Most hardy in Zones 9–11.

Growing
Consistent soil moisture ensures a strong flower show. Mix a slow-release fertilizer into beds before planting. Fertilize containers with a bloom-booster product. Prune growing tips to increase branching and flower number.

Remove spent blooms if the plant tag specifies it's necessary. An easy way to do this is by snipping or shearing the plant back; it will branch and flush into flower again. New varieties don't require deadheading.

Marguerite daisy thrives with cool night temperatures. In regions where summer evening temperatures go above the upper 70s, plants continue to grow but may stop flowering. Before autumn's cool nights arrive, shear plants lightly to encourage branching, which also increases flower number.

Design ideas
Use marguerite daisy as an upright filler in combinations or use it solo in pots. It mounds over the pot edges to create a cushion of bloom. Incorporate marguerite daisy into butterfly gardens. It also performs well in landscape beds. Pair it with flowers or foliage in contrasting or complementary colors to stir interest. Red-blossomed varieties look stunning planted with gold foliage or purple flowers. Use white varieties to bridge gaps in the garden between potentially clashing hues. Pastel-tone varieties make natural partners for pansies and sweet alyssum.

varieties:

❶ **'LIPSTICK'** Fully double hot pink blooms. 12 to 18 inches tall, 15 to 18 inches wide. Zones 9–11.

❷ **'BUTTERFLY'** Lemon yellow blooms open steadily through summer heat. No deadheading needed. 18 to 36 inches tall, 12 to 14 inches wide. Zones 10–11.

❸ **MADEIRA RED** Red blooms with gold centers. Pair with purple or yellow flowers or bronze sedge. 12 to 18 inches tall, 16 to 20 inches wide. Zones 9–11.

❹ **COBBITY DAISY 'SUMMER MELODY'** Cheery pink flowers don't demand deadheading. 14 to 16 inches tall, 12 to 14 inches wide. Zones 9–11.

❺ **'COMET WHITE'** Classic white daisies with yellow centers. 12 to 18 inches tall, 15 to 18 inches wide. Zones 9–11.

Marigold
(*Tagetes* spp.)

If you're looking for a strong garden performer, consider marigolds. They boast quick growth, continuous color, and drought resistance. These reliable bloomers infuse plantings with vivid color in shades of gold, orange, red, yellow, and blends.

Best site

Plant in average, well-drained soil in full sun. Provide light afternoon shade in areas with hot summers. Use a soilless potting mix in containers. Moderately moist soil is ideal. Marigolds don't grow well in high humidity or wet conditions. Site taller types in locations protected from heavy winds. Zones 9–11.

Growing

Pinch young marigolds, especially French types, at planting time to encourage branching. Snap off lower leaves on tall types and plant them deeply to anchor the plant. Mix slow-release fertilizer into planting beds and pots, or fertilize containers twice monthly with liquid plant food. Temperatures above 90°F stall flower formation, especially in African types.

Deadhead African marigolds to promote a second flush of flowers. It's not vital to remove spent blooms on French, signet, or triploid marigolds, but it keeps plants looking neat.

Design ideas

Use marigolds in containers with other plants to add nonstop flowers to outdoor living areas. Combine with blue, purple, and red tones.

Butterflies swarm to marigolds. Great plants for children to sow and grow, marigolds are sturdy enough to withstand season-long care by a five-year-old.

The petals of all marigolds are edible, but not all are tasty. 'Lemon Gem' signet marigold offers the best flavor, according to taste trials.

In the landscape, use marigolds in mass plantings. Their pomponlike blooms combine well with taller, spiky plants, such as salvia, celosia, or grasses.

AFRICAN MARIGOLD (*T. erecta*)
Tall, sturdy plants usually grow to 3 feet tall, although dwarf types exist. Blossoms are larger than French types, but open for a shorter time span. Deadhead African marigolds to encourage more flowers.

african marigold varieties:

❶ **'TAISHAN GOLD'** Double gold flowers handily shed water. 10 to 12 inches tall, 8 to 10 inches wide.
❷ **'VANILLA'** Bushy, extra-sturdy plant with 3-inch creamy flowers. The first white hybrid marigold. 2 feet tall, 8 to 10 inches wide.
❸ **'MOONSTRUCK DEEP ORANGE'** Many 3- to 4-inch pompon heads hide foliage. Blooms last longer, thanks to tightly packed petals that shed rain. 10 to 15 inches tall, 8 to 10 inches wide.

YOU SHOULD KNOW

Marigold leaves release an aroma that some gardeners like and others find unpleasant. The good news is that the odor contributes to the plant's deer and rabbit resistance. Roots produce a substance that deters root-damaging nematodes, which attack some vegetable crops. Many gardeners incorporate marigolds in vegetable plantings to repel nematodes and attract pollinators.

marigold

FRENCH MARIGOLD (*T. patula*)
Small bushy plants typically grow 6 to 12 inches tall, opening 2- to 3-inch flowers in yellow, orange, and bronze to maroon. Blooms may have single hues or bicolor blends. Plants flower continuously until frost.

french marigold varieties:

④ 'BONANZA BOLERO' Golden yellow blooms splashed with dark red. Earliest-flowering crested French marigold. Heat tolerant. Pair with deep burgundy sun-loving coleus. 10 to 12 inches tall, 6 to 8 inches wide.

⑤ 'HERO BEE' Large flowers with bright yellow petals with red splotches at their bases. Pair with burgundy alternanthera for a heat- and humidity-tolerant combination. 10 to 12 inches tall, 8 to 10 inches wide.

⑥ 'SAFARI YELLOW' Sunny yellow anemone-type flower with almost flat petals surrounding a center of upright petals. 8 to 12 inches tall and 12 inches wide.

⑦ 'STRIPED MARVEL' Bright golden yellow stripe crossing the center of each deep burgundy-red petal, for a pinwheel effect. 18 to 30 inches tall, 15 to 18 inches wide.

TRIPLOID MARIGOLD (*T. erecta × patula*)
These sterile hybrids result from crossing French and African types. Plants flower without ceasing until frost, opening 3-inch blooms. Colors are bright and bold: yellow, gold, red, and russet.

triploid marigold varieties:

⑧ 'ZENITH RED' Red petals edged in gold. Full, double flowers 3 to 4 inches wide. Bushy, vigorous plants good for mass plantings. Plants don't produce seed; no need for deadheading. 12 to 14 inches tall, 6 to 10 inches wide.

SIGNET MARIGOLD (*T. tenuifolia*)
Finely divided leaves produce a lacy appearance and have a citrusy aroma. Plants typically grow 10 to 12 inches tall. Flowers open in the usual marigold shades (orange, gold, red, yellow) but are smaller, about the size of a signet ring (less than 1 inch). Bloom petals are edible and open steadily until frost.

signet marigold varieties:

⑨ 'LEMON GEM' Single, dainty blossoms. Finely divided, lemon-scented foliage. Petals edible when grown organically; spicy flavor with tarragon overtones. 6 to 12 inches tall, 8 to 10 inches wide.

⑩ 'RED GEM' Red petals edged in orange. Citrus-scented foliage. 8 to 10 inches tall, 12 to 15 inches wide.

Melampodium
(*Melampodium paludosum*)

Often overlooked, this tough-as-nails plant produces daisylike blooms throughout the summer despite sizzling heat or seasonal downpours. Plants form neat mounds of medium green leaves that contrast prettily with the flowers. Best of all, rabbits and deer typically aren't interested in this easy-to-grow plant.

Best site
Plant in average, well-drained soil in full sun. Plants prefer consistent moisture but need good drainage. In clay, add 3 to 4 inches of organic matter to soil before planting. Zones 10–11.

Growing
For landscape plantings, blend a slow-release fertilizer into beds prior to planting. Topdress beds about four weeks after planting and also in midsummer. In containers, fertilize using a bloom-booster product (slow-release or liquid) according to label instructions.

Melampodium requires consistent but moderate soil moisture to prevent wilting. Mulch planting beds to help sustain soil moisture. Plants are drought tolerant but appreciate irrigation during prolonged dry periods. When severe drought or extended wet conditions occur, leaves shrivel and growth is stunted.

Deadheading isn't required unless you want to do so late in the season to stave off a host of volunteer seedlings.

Design ideas
This rugged summer performer belongs in every garden. Use compact varieties in containers as fillers. In beds, short varieties work well edging paths or in front of taller plants to hide stems.

Blooms attract butterflies. Melampodium's self-seeding nature makes it a good fit for cottage gardens. In beds or containers, pair melampodium with other heat-loving plants such as blue-purple ageratum, angelonia, blue salvia, and purple petunias. In a container, the flower sizes of melampodium and calibrachoa complement one another. Melampodium's yellow blooms pair well with pinks and reds, such as salvia, petunia, begonia, cosmos, and vinca.

varieties:

❶ **'DERBY'** Golden yellow 1-inch flowers. 8 to 12 inches tall, 9 to 12 inches wide

❷ **'MEDALLION'** The tallest melampodium with 1-inch blooms. Tends to flop if not supported. En masse, plants support each other. 2 to 3 feet tall, 12 to 16 inches wide. Can grow taller in southern climates and with ideal moisture.

❸ **'MELANIE'** Bright gold, 1-inch blooms. 12 to 14 inches tall, 12 to 16 inches wide.

❹ **'LEMON DELIGHT'** Nickel-size flowers in shades of sunny lemon yellow. 8 to 10 inches tall, 12 to 14 inches wide.

Mexican Petunia
(*Ruellia* spp.)

Heat and humidity don't faze this tender perennial, which opens brilliant purple, white, or pink trumpet-shape, upward-facing flowers. The plant shrugs off pests and diseases, growing quickly. Nectar-laden blooms lure swarms of butterflies. New red-blossom types attract hummingbirds.

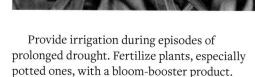

YOU SHOULD KNOW Mexican petunia tolerates both wet and dry soil, making it a good candidate for a rain garden.

Best site
Plants grow in full sun to part shade, but blossom numbers increase the more sunlight plants receive. Mexican petunia grows in fertile or poor, wet or dry soil. Ideal growth occurs in soil that's consistently moist. Plants survive in standing water and can be grown as pondside marginal plants. Zones 8–10. Plant dies to the ground in Zone 7 but may return in spring if mulched.

Growing
Plants are generally pest- and disease-free. There's no need to remove spent blooms to encourage further flowering, but trimming plants increases the blossom numbers. For tall varieties, after the first flush of flowers, cut stems back by half to promote branching and a new set of blooms. Blossoms last one day, but many open in succession, creating a steady show of color.

Provide irrigation during episodes of prolonged drought. Fertilize plants, especially potted ones, with a bloom-booster product.

Mexican petunia spreads by seed and underground stems. When moisture is abundant, it can spread and overtake native plant species. In parts of the South, including Florida, it invades waterways and meadows.

The species typically grows 3 to 4 feet tall and 2 to 3 feet wide. Dwarf varieties are available.

Design ideas
Dwarf varieties work well to edge beds and infuse any setting with steady summer color. In cold regions, taller types thrive in containers, filling the thriller role. All types beckon butterflies. Pair them with pentas, lantana, red salvia, or trailing verbena for a butterfly nectar supply.

varieties:

❶ **MEXICAN PETUNIA** (*R. brittoniana*) Lavender-blue, 2-inch blossoms nonstop from summer till frost. 3 feet tall; indefinite width.

❷ **'KATIE'** (*R. brittoniana*) Dwarf variety with 2-inch-wide lavender blooms. Not as invasive as the species. Use as an edging for planting beds or in containers. Also in white or pink. 6 to 12 inches tall and wide.

❸ **'PURPLE SHOWERS'** (*R. brittoniana*) Greenish-purple stems with loads of lavender blossoms. Heat and humidity tolerant. In colder zones, grow in large containers. Spreads in warm regions. 3 to 4 feet tall, 2 to 3 feet wide.

❹ **'RAGIN' CAJUN'** (*R. elegans*) Five-petaled, scarlet red blooms on tall, delicate stems. Not as invasive as the species. 1 foot tall, 2 feet wide; a Zone 7 North Carolina garden grew three-year-old clumps 4 feet tall, 8 feet wide.

Mimulus
(*Mimulus* spp.)

Playful funnel-shape blooms display a kaleidoscope of colors, including cream, yellow, orange, purple, and many other hues and bicolor blends. Plants stage an exceptional container show, forming a rich mound of cool-season color. Mimulus tolerates—and even demands—soil that is constantly wet.

Best site
Plant in moist but well-drained soil enriched with ample organic matter. Site in full sun to part shade. This cool-season bloomer requires light shade as spring slips into summer, especially in regions with warm summers. Zones 7–11.

Growing
In native habitats, mimulus is often found growing alongside streams. Plants thrive in soil that is constantly damp, and they grow even in an inch or two of standing water.

Mimulus shines in spring and tolerates late frosts. Color continues in regions with cool summers, but in warmer zones, move plants to a location with filtered light or morning sun or a spot along a northern wall.

Air circulation defeats fungal diseases, which claim plants if given a chance to take hold. As flowering dwindles, water less frequently.

Design ideas
This unusual bloomer serves exceptional color that flourishes where many annuals cannot: in damp, shady spots. Mimulus thrives in areas along the north side of a home where the sun rarely shines, small city gardens where tall buildings block sunlight, and damp, shady areas of a yard.

Companion plants include other shade-loving annuals such as impatiens, begonia, and wishbone flower. It also grows well with sweet alyssum, pansy, and snapdragon, its cousin. Mimulus is probably at its best grown in window boxes, hanging baskets, and pots.

varieties:
❶ **'MYSTIC CREAM WITH SPOTS'** (*M.* × *hybridus*) Creamy-ivory petals with contrasting wine red spots. 6 to 12 inches tall, 6 to 10 inches wide. Zones 7–9.

❷ **'BOUNTY ORANGE'** (*M.* × *hybridus*) Large tubular blossoms in sizzling orange. Pair with purple violas or sweet alyssum. 6 to 12 inches tall, 6 to 10 inches wide Zones 7–9.

❸ **'MYSTIC IVORY'** (*M.* × *hybridus*) Ivory flowers and fresh green foliage. 6 to 12 inches tall, 6 to 10 inches wide. Zones 7–9.

❹ **CURIOUS RED BOLD** (*M. aurantiacus*) Solid red blooms. Attracts early-season pollinators. Needs well-drained soil enriched with organic matter kept evenly moist. 12 to 18 inches tall and wide. Zones 9–11.

Moss Rose
(*Portulaca* spp.)

Hot and dry conditions are no problem for resilient moss rose. Blossoms that resemble little roses punctuate this durable groundcover's cylindrical, water-hoarding foliage. Flowers open in response to sunlight and close when clouds gather. There's a bloom color to please every palette.

Best site

Grow this succulent bloomer in poor to average well-drained soil that can be gravelly, sandy, or even loamy, as long as it drains well. Amend heavy clay soil by digging in 3 to 4 inches of organic matter. In containers, use a commercial soilless mix. Site moss rose in full sun for best flowering. Annual, except as noted.

Growing

Once established, moss rose offers strong drought tolerance, but plants flower most intensely when they receive regular irrigation. Avoid overhead watering, which can damage blooms. Fertilize plants every four to six weeks to fuel steady growth. A bloom-booster fertilizer is especially helpful for container-grown plants.

Watch out for aphids on new growth early and late in the season. If root-knot nematodes are a problem, purchase resistant plants.

Design ideas

Choose moss rose for trouble spots where poor soil and hot sun cause other plants to fizzle. Ground-hugging growth and heat tolerance makes moss rose a terrific plant for roadside planting areas. Mass single colors in the landscape for a stunning color show.

Use moss rose as a groundcover, a path edging, or a rock garden plant. It roots easily in the cracks of a rock wall. Plants don't tolerate foot traffic but can prove useful to cover ground between stepping-stones. This trailing bloomer cascades beautifully over rock walls or along dry slopes.

Moss rose works well in hanging baskets and window boxes. It looks elegant in contemporary containers and is the perfect choice for terra-cotta pots. Great planting partners include lantana, purple heart, angelonia, and ruby grass.

varieties:

1. **'SUNSEEKER RED'** (*P. grandiflora*) Double, 2-inch red blooms; open on cloudy days. 6 to 12 inches tall, 6 to 9 inches wide.
2. **'HAPPY HOUR COCONUT'** (*P. grandiflora*) Semidouble white blooms flower earlier in the season than other moss roses. Open on cloudy days. 8 to 10 inches tall, 10 to 12 inches wide.
3. **'SUNDIAL PEPPERMINT'** (*P. grandiflora*) Double blooms with white petals splashed with hot pink; open on cloudy days. 6 inches tall, 14 to 16 inches wide.
4. **'FAIRYTALES CINDERELLA'** (*P. grandiflora*) Ruffled magenta pompon center, flat golden petals. Shade tolerant. 4 to 8 inches tall, 14 to 16 inches wide. Zones 10–11.
5. **'PAZAZZ SALMON GLOW'** (*P. oleracea*) Salmon with yellow center; open on cloudy days. 3 to 6 inches tall, 12 to 16 inches wide. Zone 11.

Nemesia
(*Nemesia* spp.)

Cool-season nemesia grows quickly, filling containers or baskets with head-turning color. Plants flower into autumn where summers are cool, although new varieties withstand warmer temperatures. Look for blossoms in a rainbow of hues, including wonderful bicolors and blends.

Best site

Plant in evenly moist, well-drained soil enriched with organic matter. In containers, use a soilless potting mix that includes coir for water retention. If possible, provide a slightly acidic soil (peat accomplishes this, as does oak leaf-based compost).

Nemesia performs best in full sun in spring. Maintain a full-sun exposure in regions with cool summers. In warmer regions, provide afternoon shade, especially when summer begins to heat up. Zones 9–11.

Growing

Nemesia puts on its best show in places with cool summer days and nights. When night temperatures remain in the upper 70s and above, plants stop flowering, resuming when night temperatures drop. Prune plants lightly to spur branching and increase flower number.

Many varieties of nemesia never need to be deadheaded. Read the plant tag before purchase.

Plants require consistent moisture. Allow soil to barely dry out between waterings. Blend slow-release fertilizer into the soil when planting. In containers, apply liquid bloom-booster fertilizer to plants according to label directions.

Design ideas

In warmer regions, count on nemesia for lovely cool-season color to kick off the growing year. Tuck plants into pots, window boxes, or hanging baskets for portable blossoms you can showcase in outdoor living areas and on porches. In planting beds, pair nemesia with pansy, poppy, sweet alyssum, larkspur, or bachelor's button.

YOU SHOULD KNOW Many gardeners prune nemesia aggressively after the first flower flush to encourage future blossom formation.

varieties:

❶ **SERENGETI UPRIGHT PURPLE** (*N.* × *hybrida*) Magenta-and-rose blooms with maroon-and-purple throats. Heat tolerant. 12 to 14 inches tall; 10 to 12 inches wide.

❷ **'DARK BLUE'** (*N.* × *hybrida*) Midnight blue-purple petals with a bright yellow lip on lower petals. 14 to 16 inches tall, 10 to 12 inches wide.

❸ **JUICY FRUITS KUMQUAT** (*N.* × *hybrida*) Bloom blend of orange, red, fuchsia, salmon, and gold. 8 to 12 inches tall and wide.

❹ **ANGELART FRUIT PUNCH** (*N.* × *hybrida*) Red, pink, and coral blooms with purple overtones. Heat tolerant. Butterfly magnet. 12 to 18 inches tall, 9 to 12 inches wide.

❺ **INNOCENCE OPAL** (*N. fruticans*) Rosy-pink, creamy-ivory, and lavender blooms. No deadheading needed. Frost-tolerant to 25°F. 12 to 16 inches tall, 6 to 8 inches wide.

New Zealand Flax
(*Phormium tenax*)

A striking form and colorful foliage earn this plant rave reviews, but its drought tolerance, deerproof foliage, and rugged personality also make it a winner. Sword-shape leaves feature varying hues, including bronze, purple, pink, orange, and gold. It's easy to grow and makes a great addition to containers.

Best site

Plant in average, well-drained soil in full sun to part shade. Plants with variegated leaves develop the prettiest tints in part sun. Provide afternoon shade in hot regions and at higher elevations.

Plants are winter hardy in Zones 9 to 11, but roots may survive in the ground in a protected location in Zones 7 and 8 with winter mulch.

Growing

New Zealand flax grows in dry soil and hot wind. It survives extended periods without irrigation but looks best when it receives occasional water. In containers, keep soil consistently moist. New Zealand flax in planting beds doesn't require heavy moisture.

Fertilize plants in containers according to label directions if using a liquid product, or mix a slow-release food into the soil prior to planting.

Mature plants produce a flower stalk topped with tubular red or yellow blooms in regions that don't freeze. Occasionally New Zealand flax with colorful leaves produce shoots with a different—often unwanted—hue. Cut these shoots at the base. If newer growth is most colorful, remove older leaves as plants grow. Choose from 1-foot dwarfs or selections 6 feet tall.

Design ideas

New Zealand flax works as a thriller in pots. Surround it with fine-textured foliage and flowers. Varieties with dark leaves pair exquisitely with lime or chartreuse foliage or with pink or orange flowers. Mounding plants, such as lantana, coleus, New Guinea impatiens, and euphorbia, pair well with this upright grower. Trailers such as petunia and calibrachoa offer a wide array of colors to complement or contrast with New Zealand flax leaf shades.

varieties:

❶ **'DARK DELIGHT'** Deep reddish-brown leaves. 3 to 4 feet tall, 4 to 6 feet wide.

❷ **'GOLDEN RAY'** Green leaves with creamy-yellow margins set off by a fine, orange-red edge. Leaf tips tend to arch downward. 4 to 5 feet tall and wide.

❸ **'SUNDOWNER'** Strongly upright growth habit. Bronze-green leaves with wide rose pink margins and streaks that age to cream in summer. 5 to 8 feet tall, 3 to 5 feet wide.

❹ **'TAYA'** Young leaves emerge with green-and-burgundy coloration, maturing to purple-chocolate with a silver-gray underside. Upright with a broader leaf blade. 3 to 4 feet tall, 18 to 30 inches wide.

Nierembergia
(*Nierembergia scoparia*)

Cup-shape flowers feature a five-pointed starry look in shades of white, purple, and blue. Narrow leaves back blossoms with a fine texture in a handsome gray-green hue. Highlight this bloomer in containers to showcase its cascading color show.

Best site

Plant in moist, well-drained soil in full sun to part shade. In landscape plantings, nierembergia requires good drainage. Enrich the soil with organic matter to aid in moisture retention. In containers, use a moisture-retentive soilless mix with coir. Hardiness varies by variety.

Growing

Nierembergia flowers best in regions where summers stay cool. Provide light afternoon shade for strong blooming. Mulch prevents the soil from heating up and helps preserve flowering. In warm regions, blooms may stall and stop opening. When this occurs, shear plants to encourage branching and more flowers when temperatures tumble with autumn's arrival. New varieties boast strong flowering during summer heat and humidity.

Fertilize plants in containers regularly with a bloom-booster product.

Design ideas

Nierembergia exhibits a natural trailing growth that makes it a good spiller in pots, hanging baskets, and window boxes. When nierembergia is planted solo, its mounding, trailing habit forms a blanket of color that may obscure the pot.

White-flowered varieties work with many other plants. Use blue nierembergia in purple-and-blue plantings. Employ a pink type for a pastel fest, or red for an electric combination.

Newer nierembergia varieties feature strongly mounding forms that work well as edging along paths, planting beds, or patios.

varieties:

❶ **'PURPLE ROBE'** Violet-blue blooms sparkle among gray-green foliage. Plant beneath upright red salvia. 3 to 9 inches tall, 6 to 12 inches wide. Zones 7-10.

❷ **'MONT BLANC'** Snow-white flowers. 6 to 12 inches tall by 6 to 9 inches Zones 10–11.

❸ **'BLUE EYES'** (*N.* × *hybrida*) Silvery lilac-blue blossoms with deep purple eyes. Heat and humidity resistant. 8 to 10 inches tall, 18 to 24 inches wide. Zones 7-10.

❹ **AUGUSTA BLUE SKIES** Large, vibrant violet-blue flowers; blossoms strongly in heat. Good partner for pink mounding or upright bloomers, such as verbena, pentas, and angelonia. 8 to 12 inches tall and wide. Zones 9–11.

Ornamental Pepper
(*Capsicum annuum*)

Festive and fun, ornamental peppers add a quirky, colorful presence to outdoor settings. Fingerlike fruit types explode in multicolored fireworks, and darkleaf types lend drama to plantings. Peppers are easy to grow, thrive in containers or planting beds, and tolerate heat and humidity.

YOU SHOULD KNOW

Fruits left on ornamental peppers ripen and dry in place. In warmer regions, some ornamental peppers self-sow if fruits are allowed to ripen on plants and drop to the ground. If you plan to save seeds from peppers, wear protective gloves.

Best site

Plant in well-drained soil enriched with organic matter. The soil needs to be moisture-retentive but well-drained. In a container, use a soilless mix that includes coir. Site peppers in full sun. Zones 9–11 unless otherwise noted.

Growing

Pinch plants when they're young to encourage branching, which leads to more fruits. Feed peppers with a complete fertilizer higher in phosphorus to promote fruiting. This means the middle number shown on the package should be higher, such as 10-20-10. Avoid high-nitrogen fertilizer (which has a higher first number); it promotes leafy growth over pepper formation. Fertilize peppers in containers with a water-soluble product according to label instructions.

Ornamental peppers attract thrips. These sucking plant pests attack roses and other ornamental plants and also transmit diseases to plants. Site peppers away from problem areas.

Choose varieties that don't bear hot fruits or grow them in hanging baskets where young children could pick and nibble the peppers.

Some ornamental peppers are edible but most pack scorching heat. Purchased transplants may have been treated with chemicals, so keep this in mind if you want to taste the fruits.

Design ideas

Ornamental peppers blend beautifully with potted tropical plants such as palm, banana, cordyline, and hibiscus. Use ornamental pepper as a filler in container combinations.

varieties:

1. **'BLACK PEARL'** Semiglossy, deep purple-black leaves. Heat, humidity, and drought tolerant. Spicy hot, round black fruits ripen to red. 18 to 36 inches tall, 12 to 16 inches wide.
2. **'CHILLY CHILI'** Upright, blunt-nosed peppers protrude above deep green foliage. Not hot to the taste. Peppers ripen from chartreuse to orange to deep red, often with all three colors at the same time. 9 to 10 inches tall, 13 to 14 inches wide.
3. **'PURPLE FLASH'** Near-black leaves splashed with bright purple. New leaves emerge white. Small round, glossy jet-black fruit. Heat tolerant. 13 to 15 inches tall, 19 to 21 inches wide.
4. **'NEW SANGRIA'** Bright purple fruits mature to red. Plants flower for roughly four weeks, fruits continue until frost. Fruits aren't spicy hot. 10 to 12 inches tall, 16 to 18 inches wide. Zones 10–11.

Pansy
(Viola × wittrockiana)

True cool-season plants, pansies are at their best in early spring and fall in much of the country. Newer varieties boast heat tolerance and extend the flower show well into summer. In warmer regions, pansies bloom all winter. These versatile players work equally well in containers or landscapes.

Best site

Pansies thrive in consistently moist, well-drained soil rich in organic matter. If your native soil is hard clay or light sand, mix in 2 to 3 inches of compost prior to planting to improve soil drainage and aeration. For containers, choose a soilless peat-based mix.

Site in full sun to part shade. Plants growing in full sun melt sooner as hot summer weather settles in, although newer varieties withstand sun and heat better. Provide afternoon shade to lengthen pansy performance into summer. Pansies grow in deep shade but won't flower nearly as well.

Avoid planting pansies in the same landscape bed for more than three years in a row because a fungus disease, pythium, tends to build up in soil. Zones 6–10.

Growing

Pansies are planted in the spring in cool regions and in both spring and fall in warm regions. In mild parts of the South and West, fall-planted pansies flower through winter and kick off spring with an early blossom show. Ideal day temperatures for growth and flowering are 40°F to 60°F. In warm zones, pansies can freeze solid during winter cold snaps and thaw the next day without missing a blooming beat.

In landscape settings, space plants 7 to 12 inches apart, based on the mature planting size listed on plant tags. At planting time, blend a slow-release fertilizer into the soil and remove flower buds to promote root formation. Pinch growing tips to encourage branching and greater flower numbers. Mulch to keep the soil cool in spring and warm in fall and winter.

pansy varieties:

❶ **'DELTA PREMIUM YELLOW WITH BLOTCH'** Pretty yellow petals with burgundy blotch; blooms well into summer. 6 inches tall, 4 to 6 inches wide.

❷ **'DELTA COTTON CANDY MIX'** Pastel-tinted mix. Heat tolerant. Blooms in low light conditions. 6 inches tall, 4 to 6 inches wide.

❸ **'KARMA TRUE BLUE'** Large blue flowers. Compact plants 6 to 8 inches tall and wide.

❹ **'FRIZZLE SIZZLE YELLOW'** Yellow blossoms with ruffled petal edges and classic pansy whiskers. 6 to 8 inches tall, 8 to 10 inches wide.

pansy

Pansies like consistently moist soil. Avoid watering during late afternoon or evening to discourage diseases. With fall and winter plantings, water during dry periods and when air is above freezing. Irrigate pansies if a freeze is predicted; well-hydrated plants survive freezing better than drought-stricken ones.

For spring-planted landscape pansies, fertilize at planting and then throughout the growing season using a slow-release bloom-booster product blended into the soil. In containers, blend slow-release bloom-booster fertilizer into soil mix prior to planting; supplement with liquid fertilizer according to label instructions.

For fall and winter pansies, fertilize at planting time, followed by regular applications of liquid food in fall. When winter sets in, fertilize during any warm spells.

Remove spent blossoms to extend flowering. If plants get leggy, shear them back and fertilize to jump-start growth. When plants fade in summer heat, pull them and add to the compost pile. Replace with heat-loving quick color plants.

Design ideas

Versatile pansies shine in planting beds, pots, hanging baskets, and window boxes. In early spring, strategically place containers of pansies to brighten entries, patios, and porches with lively color.

Use pansies as an edging plant in borders and along paths or driveways. In planting beds, tuck pansies between spring-flowering bulbs to complement bulbs and fill in the scene after bulb blossoms fade and before summer color kicks in. For greatest impact in the landscape, plant pansies in swaths of single colors.

The flowers are edible when grown organically. Add to salads, or use to decorate desserts. For a longer-lasting treat, crystallize blossoms with sugar or freeze in ice cubes.

Types

LARGE-FLOWERED. Blooms reach 3 to 4 inches across.

MEDIUM-FLOWERED. Blooms reach 2 to 3 inches across.

MULTIFLORA. Small-flowered pansies; blooms 1 to 2 inches across.

TRAILING. Small, multiflora-type blooms open on plants with trailing stems that work well as a groundcover, as spiller plants in container combinations, or in hanging baskets.

pansy varieties:

⑤ 'FIZZY LEMONBERRY' Frilly yellow petals with deep purple splotches and whiskers and grape-purple accents on petal edges. Petals ruffle in cool growing conditions. 6 to 8 inches tall, 8 to 10 inches wide.

⑥ COOL WAVE FROST Medium-size white petals with frosted blue and faint whiskers. Use in hanging baskets or to form a spreading cool-season groundcover. Cool Wave series pansies return early in spring where hardy. 6 to 8 inches tall, 24 to 30 inches wide.

⑦ 'MATRIX COASTAL SUNRISE MIX' A blend of shades including midnight purple, deep rose, light pink, lavender, peach, and pale yellow. 8 inches tall, 8 to 10 inches wide.

⑧ 'MATRIX ORANGE' Extra-large, 3½-inch clear tangerine blossoms. 6 to 8 inches tall, 18 to 24 inches wide.

⑨ 'PANOLA DEEP BLUE BLOTCH' Blue petals with midnight blue blotch. Multiflora. Outstanding landscape performance. Plants don't stretch in the South. Good growth in early spring in areas where hardy. 6 to 8 inches tall, 8 to 10 inches wide.

Pentas
(Pentas lanceolata)
Plant this quick color bloomer, and butterflies will come—guaranteed. Nectar-laden flowers open in clusters above deeply veined, dark green leaves. Look for pink, white, rose, scarlet, lavender, and bicolor blossom hues. Plants grow fast as temperatures rise and humidity builds.

Best site
Pentas grows quickly and easily in average, well-drained soil. Best growth happens in soil that is rich in organic matter such as compost. In containers, use a soilless potting mix containing coir to retain moisture. Plants flower best in full sun but tolerate part shade. Zones 8–11, except as indicated differently.

Growing
Prior to planting, mix a slow-release fertilizer into soil in pots or planting beds. Plants grow quickly and are heavy feeders. If using water-soluble bloom-booster fertilizer, feed plants in beds monthly; in containers, twice a month.

This bloomer prefers consistently moist soil. Allow the soil to dry slightly between waterings. Mulch plants in landscape settings to conserve soil moisture as summer heats up.

Pentas doesn't require deadheading. Spent blooms fall from plants. Some varieties tend to sprawl. Prune pentas as needed during the growing season to curtail or direct growth.

Design ideas
The floral abundance of pentas makes it highly useful in the garden and growing in containers. In a container, blend pentas with short gomphrena, scarlet salvia, compact lantana, 'Victoria Blue' salvia, and trailing nierembergia for a butterfly garden. Alone in a container, pentas display graceful mounds.

For impact in planting beds and borders, arrange pentas in mass plantings of a single color. For a butterfly-beckoning landscape, plant pentas with butterfly bush, lantana, and trailing petunia.

varieties:
❶ **'GRAFFITI LIPSTICK'** Red flower clusters. Short variety good for containers. 13 inches tall and wide.
❷ **'NORTHERN LIGHTS LAVENDER'** Soft lavender blooms. Grows in cooler temperatures of northern gardens; tolerant of acidic soil. 20 to 24 inches tall, 1 to 2 feet wide.
❸ **'STARS AND STRIPES'** Clusters of scarlet blooms with pink centers. Creamy, variegated foliage, developing best variegation in full sun. 12 to 24 inches tall and wide. Zones 9–11.
❹ **'BUTTERFLY WHITE'** Snow-white blossom clusters to 3 inches across. In cool weather, flowers blush pale pink. Heat and humidity tolerant. 12 to 22 inches tall, 10 to 18 inches wide.

Perilla
(*Perilla frutescens* Magilla)

Very much a coleus lookalike, Magilla perilla is an easy-to-grow annual that blends exotic appeal with durability. Brightly tinted variegated leaves are splashed with green, deep plum, magenta, and cream. Unlike the straight species, Magilla is sterile, so it is not at all invasive.

Best site

Grow in moist, loose, well-drained soil enriched with organic matter. In containers, use a moisture-retentive potting mix. Site in full sun to light shade. Best leaf coloring occurs in full sun or bright, filtered sunlight. Annual.

Growing

Arrange plants in groups of three or five, spaced 15 inches apart, to create a mass of mounding landscape color. Follow the same care as for Persian shield. Pinch growing tips to promote branching and curtail growth. Remove blossom spikes as they appear.

Design ideas

Magilla perilla thrives in planting beds and pots. Blend with vibrant bloomers for a festive look. Use to skirt bananas, cannas, purple fountain grass, or ornamental millet for garden sizzle.

Persian Shield
(*Strobilanthes dyerianus*)

Native to Asia, this foliage beauty outshines many bloomers. Richly tinted seersucker leaves display variegated purple-pink and dark green overlaid with a silvery sheen. Leaf undersides are blushed with purple. Iridescent foliage shrugs off heat, humidity, and deer.

Best site

Plant in well-drained soil enriched with organic matter. Site in full sun (cool-summer climates) to part shade (hot regions). Provide afternoon shade in southern areas to prevent leaf scorch. The best leaf color occurs in part shade. Zones 10–11; root-hardy in Zone 9 with winter mulch.

Growing

Pinch growing tips to promote branching and bushy growth. Keep the soil consistently moist. Remove flowers as they appear. Fertilize at planting and again in midsummer with a slow-release product high in nitrogen.

Design ideas

Combine Persian shield with pink verbena, lime green licorice plant, and purple calibrachoa. Use it as a thriller in containers or as a filler when planted with banana.

varieties:
1 MAGILLA 2 to 3 feet tall and wide.

varieties:
1 STROBILANTHES DYERIANUS 1 to 3 feet tall and wide.

Petunia
(*Petunia* × *hybrida*)

Fast growing and fabulous, petunias paint the garden with colors in every shade but brown. Blooms boast assorted shapes and patterns, including bicolors, stripes, speckles, and picotee edges. Petunias prove versatile, looking gorgeous in pots, window boxes, hanging baskets, and landscape plantings.

Best site

Plant in average, well-drained soil. Petunias tolerate poor soil as long as it drains well. Site in full sun to light shade. Best flowering occurs in sunny settings. Zones 10–11; grown as annuals by gardeners in nearly every zone.

Growing

At planting time, pinch the tips of plants to encourage branching and bushiness. In planting beds, blend an all-purpose, slow-release fertilizer (10-10-10) into the soil prior to planting. Follow label instructions to determine the rate.

As summer heat arrives, fertilize with a liquid product every three weeks (weekly for spreading types). In containers, mix slow-release fertilizer into the soil at planting, or feed every two to three weeks with liquid bloom-booster fertilizer.

Petunias are heat tolerant but require consistent watering. In landscape plantings, all but spreading types can get by with less frequent watering (weekly in cooler zones, twice weekly in warmer ones). Spreading types need to be watered several times a week. Water plants in containers when the the soil is dry to the touch.

Plants may decline in midsummer. Prune to stimulate branching and new growth, but remove no more than 20 percent of growth. Fertilize after pruning. Repeat the process again in late August if stems become straggly.

In hot regions, petunias are often planted in cooler seasons so plants are established before serious summer heat arrives.

Although petunias are not always recognized for attracting butterflies and hummingbirds, the funnel-shape blossoms, many with a floral perfume, may draw these winged garden friends.

YOU SHOULD KNOW

Watch for a new type of petunia called a "Potunia." These plants have a bubble-shape growth habit that neatly curls around the edge of containers and hanging baskets and creates an eye-catching mound of color in planting beds. Potunia flowers through summer and offers moderate drought tolerance.

petunia varieties:

❶ FANTASY PINK MORN' Milliflora. Pale pink blooms with darker pink edges and yellow throats. Good for containers. No midsummer pruning needed. 10 to 12 inches tall, 10 to 24 inches wide.

❷ HURRAH BLUE VEINED Multiflora. Patterned lavender flowers with purple veins. Heat and humidity tolerant. 10 to 12 inches tall, 12 to 14 inches wide.

❸ BLACK VELVET Novelty. The first black petunia. Pair with orange marigold, white euphorbia, lime green coleus, or pink vinca. 8 to 12 inches tall, 10 to 12 inches wide.

❹ SUN SPUN BLUE Novelty. Deep purple-blue, 2-inch blooms with a velvet texture. Vigorous; good weather resistance. 6 to 10 inches tall, 8 to 10 inches wide.

petunia

Design ideas

Petunias shine in hanging baskets and window boxes, where their trailing habits fit perfectly. Use them as spiller plants in container combinations. In the landscape, petunias can function as flowery groundcovers or edging plants. Be sure to select the right size and type of plant to fill your intended use in the garden. For instance, if the garden space is small, select one with a tidy habit instead of a spreading petunia.

The vast color range in petunia blossoms means that combining them can be as artistic an endeavor as you want to make it. Focus on color echoes or complementary or contrasting hues to arrange striking compositions. Upright, mounding, and spiky plants all pair well with petunias, introducing simple contrasting elements that are pleasing to the eye.

Types

GRANDIFLORA. Large flowers measure 3 to 4 inches across. Blossoms may be single or double and feature various colors and patterns, including solid, bicolor, veined, striped, and edged. Plants thrive in cooler temperatures. Use for mass landscape plantings or in containers.

MULTIFLORA. Smaller flowers measure 1½ to 3 inches across, but plants possess greater flower power than grandifloras, opening large numbers of blooms simultaneously and continuously. Plants stand up to intense summer weather conditions (heat, humidity, and rain) with no decrease in flower number. Various blossom colors and patterns are available, including mostly single, but some double types. Use for mass landscape plantings or in pots, hanging baskets, and window boxes.

MILLIFLORA. Miniature, compact plants grow about two-thirds the size of traditional petunias. Flowers 1 to 1½ inches across occur in large numbers to the point of nearly obscuring foliage. Plants continue to bloom without a midsummer shearing. Use in containers and small planting beds or as an edging plant.

SPREADING. Also called groundcover petunias, these plants stay on the short side—4 to 6 inches tall—and spread up to several feet. These petunias have large appetites and require sufficient fertilizer and water to reach their full potential. Flowers 2 to 3 inches across come in an array of colors. Use as a flowering groundcover or as a trailer in containers.

petunia varieties:

⑤ SUPERTUNIA WHITE RUSSIAN Spreading. Antique-white petals contrast with chocolate veins and chocolate eyes. Supertunias work well in baskets and window boxes. Use as a groundcover in planting beds. Deadheading not necessary. 6 to 10 inches tall, 2 to 3 feet wide.

⑥ 'RHYTHM AND BLUES' Spreading. Deep purple blossoms with scalloped edges dipped in white. Pair with white bacopa, euphorbia, white mealycup sage, and lime green helichrysum. 8 to 12 inches tall, 12 to 16 inches wide.

⑦ 'SHOCK WAVE CORAL CRUSH' Spreading. Coral blooms with yellow throats. Small-flowers. 7 to 10 inches tall, 30 to 36 inches wide.

⑧ 'SWEET SUNSHINE COMPACT LIME' Multiflora. Chartreuse petals fade to white edges on ruffled double flowers 2½ inches across. No deadheading needed. Pair with purple, burgundy, or orange annuals. 10 to 12 inches tall, 20 to 24 inches wide.

⑨ 'SWEET SUNSHINE BURGUNDY' Multiflora. Deep burgundy, ruffled double flowers. Use in containers, hanging baskets, or small planting beds. Deadheading not required. 10 to 12 inches tall, 12 to 18 inches wide.

⑩ 'TAFFY WATERMELON' Spreading. Watermelon pink blooms 3 inches wide with a touch of salmon. Use in baskets or containers, or plant in beds for a carpet of color. 6 to 12 inches tall, 30 to 39 inches wide.

Phlox
(*Phlox drummondii*)

Annual phlox delivers fragrant quick color. Flowers kick off the season with a spring appearance that lingers into summer. Drought tolerant, the plants frequently bloom anew when fall's cool air arrives. The perfumed, 1-inch flowers in pink, red, white, or lavender attract butterflies.

Best site

Plant in well-drained soil enriched with organic matter. Phlox grows in sandy soil; add organic matter to improve moisture-holding capacity. Adequate water fuels a strong flower show.

Provide full sun to part shade; afternoon shade is necessary in the warmest zones. In a container, use a soilless mix with coir to enhance moisture retention. Established plants hardened off to cold can withstand light frost. A hard freeze (25°F) kills plants. Zones 10–11.

Growing

Mix slow-release fertilizer into beds and pots prior to planting. A bloom-booster fertilizer encourages flower formation.

Space plants 8 inches apart in landscape beds. Pinch growing tips at planting time to promote branching and full, bushy plants. Protect young plants from rabbits with a barrier or repellent.

Remove spent flowers to spur continuous blooming; newer phlox hybrids don't require deadheading. When temperatures remain above 85°F, flowering stalls. Shear plants lightly and continue to water and fertilize. Growth and flowering should resume with cool air. In regions with cool summers, plants bloom prolifically. In the warmest areas, plant this phlox in fall.

Design ideas

Plant annual phlox in window boxes, hanging baskets, and pots. It serves as a filler in container combinations with other cool-season bloomers, such as tall snapdragon and trailing lobelia.

Phlox creates a carpet of color in cool-spring regions, and from fall to winter in warmer areas.

varieties:

❶ **INTENSIA BLUEBERRY** Blue-purple blooms with a contrasting deep purple eye. Good heat tolerance; flowering through summer; deadheading not necessary. 10 to 12 inches tall, 8 to 10 inches wide.

❷ **INTENSIA CABERNET** Deep pink petals add snap to plantings. Heat tolerant; strongest bloom occurs in spring and fall. Deadheading isn't necessary. 10 to 18 inches tall, 10 to 12 inches wide.

❸ **INTENSIA WHITE** White flowers blanket foliage. Heat tolerant; blooming all summer. Deadheading isn't necessary. 10 to 12 inches tall, 8 to 10 inches wide.

❹ **ASTORIA BLUE** Blue-tone blossoms with darker blue veins. 8 inches tall, 15 inches wide.

Polka-dot Plant
(*Hypoestes phyllostachya*)

Speckles, splotches, and spots decorate the foliage of this easy-growing beauty. Vivid colors include white, pink, wine red, and carmine red. Count on polka-dot plant to dress a shady spot with deer-resistant, fuss-free color. It can double as a houseplant, but give it bright, indirect light indoors.

Best site

Plant in rich, well-drained soil with medium moisture. Add organic matter to the soil to improve fertility and water-holding ability. Polka-dot plant requires consistent moisture for best growth. In containers, use a soilless mix with coir to retain moisture. Site in part to full shade in warmer regions. Morning sun with afternoon shade is ideal. In cooler areas, plants withstand part sun. Zones 10–11.

Growing

In landscape beds, mix slow-release fertilizer into the soil prior to planting. Do the same in containers, or fertilize twice a month with a liquid product. Use an all-purpose fertilizer to promote foliage formation.

At planting time, pinch growing tips to encourage branching and bushiness. Pinch or prune to control plant growth and size.

Small flower spikes may appear as summer heat builds, but most gardeners remove them. In the warmest regions, plants readily self-sow but won't overtake an area.

Design ideas

Use this spotted charmer for quick color in shady spots. Use in mass plantings in front of shrubs or other plants. The speckled leaves make an attractive edging along beds, paths, and patios.

In containers, use polka-dot plant as a filler. Plants start the season as a rounded mound that grows into a more upright form as the season progresses. Great partners for polka-dot plant include asparagus fern, wax begonia, impatiens, and shade-loving coleus. In the landscape, place white polka-dot plant in front of Dragon Wing begonia for a beautiful combination.

varieties:

❶ **'SPLASH SELECT PINK'** Clear pink zones are so large that leaves appear to be pink with green veins. 10 to 18 inches tall, 12 to 14 inches wide.

❷ **'SPLASH SELECT WHITE'** Dark green leaves with large white splotches. 10 to 18 inches tall, 12 to 14 inches wide.

❸ **'SPLASH SELECT RED'** Green leaves with deep pink spots. 10 to 18 inches tall, 12 to 14 inches wide.

❹ **'CONFETTI PINK'** Pink sprinkles or blotches on deep green leaves. 4 to 8 inches tall, 4 to 6 inches wide.

Purple Heart

(Setcreasea pallida; syn. *Tradescantia pallida)*

Drought-tolerant and tough, purple heart serves as a groundcover in hot, dry sites or as a spiller plant in container combinations. Succulent stems and leaves display purple, pink, or green tones. This sprawling, deer-resistant plant is a native of eastern New Mexico.

Best site

Purple heart thrives in various soils, including sandy, rocky, and organically enriched. The soil must be well-drained for the plants to survive. Site in full sun to part shade. Best leaf coloration typically occurs in full sun. In hot regions, provide afternoon shade. Zones 8–11; frequently returns from roots in Zone 7 when the plant crown is protected with mulch.

Growing

Drainage is key to success. Plants are susceptible to root rot in poorly drained soils. Irrigate new plantings until they show consistent new growth. Established plants require watering only during extended periods of drought.

Avoid planting in windy locations. Constant exposure to strong winds can break stems, which tend to be brittle. This is more of a problem with container plants.

Remove spent flowers easily with a light shearing. Prune at any time to curtail growth or shape plants. If a freeze threatens, cover plants.

Design ideas

Purple heart is a tough, colorful groundcover. Its broad leaves blend well with annuals, tropicals, and succulents. This sturdy plant enhances rock gardens or fills dry spots in the landscape, such as beneath eaves and awnings.

Strong heat tolerance makes it a natural for balcony and rooftop gardens. In arid, ultra-bright desert settings, grow it in raised planters or in a shaded atrium or shade garden. Good planting partners include lantana, angelonia, purple fountain grass, and vinca, all offering sturdy personalities and plant forms that blend well with purple heart.

varieties:

❶ **'PINK CORAZON'** Purple-tone leaves dazzle with hot pink streaks. Grow in full to part sun. Pair with blue-flowered plants like salvia. 8 inches tall, 16 inches wide. Zone 11.

❷ **'PALE PUMA'** Leaves are green on the stems ends, fading to purple at outer edges. Foliage turns solid purple in bright sun. Look for white blooms in late summer. 1 foot tall, 3 feet wide. Zones 7–10.

❸ **'BLUE SUE'** Purple edges outline foliage that ranges from chartreuse to blue-green. Pink flowers complement leaf coloration. 6 to 8 inches tall, 16 inches wide. Zones 7–11.

Quick Color Perennials

Long revered for their versatility and durability in the garden, perennials can play seasonal display roles in quick color combinations. Grown from seed, these perennials offer an affordable alternative to traditional nursery stock, competing with annuals on price point. Plants that are perennial in warm Zones may perform as annuals in colder areas, but you can find quick color perennial candidates that are hardy in every region.

Best site

Perennials thrive in many growing conditions; some require intense soil fertility, but others thrive with only a little compost mixed into the soil. Read plant tags carefully so you provide ideal growing conditions. See variety descriptions for hardiness information.

Growing

There are two options with quick color perennials: Treat them as annuals and dispose of them after one season, or grow them as true perennials, saving them from year to year. The perennials on these pages flower from seed in their first season of growth or provide steady foliage color. Deadheading is probably the most important grooming task for most perennials in the course of a growing season.

Design ideas

When using perennials in a container or small space, plant annuals, such as baby's breath, impatiens, or calibrachoa to cover bare soil until the perennials fill out.

Recruit perennials with colorful foliage to anchor plantings you change from season to season. Their foliage adds steady color through the seasons as other plantings peak and wane.

FOLIAGE When it comes to foliage variety, perennials earn top marks. Plants bear leaves in many shapes, shades, and textures. The immense variety expands the palette of possibilities for dreaming up quick color designs. You can find a perennial with foliage that shines all season long, rivaling the color of annual flower power.

foliage varieties:

❶ **'MELTING FIRE' CORALBELLS** (*Heuchera micrantha*) Bright red new growth matures to purple-maroon ruffled leaves with red tones. Full sun in cool areas; afternoon shade in warm zones. 9 to 18 inches tall and wide. Zones 4–8.

❷ **HENS-AND-CHICKS** (*Sempervivum* spp.) Evergreen succulent grows slowly outward, forming ground-hugging clusters. Leaves whorled in rosettes. Needs sharp drainage to thrive. Tolerates air pollution, drought, and deer. 6 to 12 inches tall, 6 to 18 inches wide. Zones 3–8.

❸ **'ANGELINA' SEDUM** (*S. rupestre*) Electric gold leaves cluster tightly on stems that creep along the ground. Requires good drainage. Tolerates heat, drought, deer, and rabbits. In cold regions, leaves burnish golden orange in fall. 3 to 6 inches tall, 1 to 2 feet wide. Zones 5–8.

PRAIRIE Native prairie plants boast tough-as-nails personalities dressed with pretty blossoms to beckon pollinators. In the garden, prairie perennials adapt to border or container culture with ease and make every garden a butterfly banquet. With deadheading, many of these bloomers continue to form flower buds throughout the growing season.

prairie varieties:

4 **'POWWOW WILDBERRY' CONEFLOWER** (*Echinacea purpurea*) Intense rose-purple petals encircle an orange-brown center cone. Remove spent blooms for the most flowers. Plants tolerate many soil types and resist deer. 2 to 3 feet tall, 12 to 18 inches wide. Zones 3–8.

5 **'EARLY SUNRISE' COREOPSIS** (*C. grandiflora*) Bright yellow, semidouble blooms from late spring to fall. Short-lived perennial self-sows freely; deadheading prevents some spread. 18 to 24 inches tall and wide. Zones 4–9.

6 **'PAPILLION PINK' GAURA** (*G. lindheimeri*) Wands of pink butterflylike blooms form a misty haze of color. Bright green leaves. Tolerates drought and heat. 15 to 18 inches tall, 10 to 12 inches wide. Zones 5–9.

7 **BELIEVER ASTER** (*A. novi-belgii*) Mounded plants resemble small shrubs blanketed with deep violet-blue blooms from late summer to fall. Pinch plants in early summer to reduce final flowering height. 10 to 12 inches tall, 1 to 2 feet wide. Zones 4–9.

COTTAGE When you're in the mood for flower-filled bowers, you want cottage-style perennials. They toss open blossoms with carefree abandon, creating quick color that's perfect for picking and arranging in bouquets. In containers or planting beds, the floral finery continues all season. Cottage plants include tender bulbs that survive in cold regions only when provided indoor winter storage, plus herbs that pull double duty in household and culinary uses.

cottage varieties:

8 **DALMATIAN PEACH FOXGLOVE** (*Digitalis purpurea*) Pale peach blooms glow as they cluster along upright stems; amazing planted in drifts. Site in full sun to part shade in acidic, moist, well-drained soil. 3 to 4 feet tall, 15 to 18 inches wide. Zones 4–9.

9 **'BISHOP'S CHILDREN' DAHLIA** (*D.* × *hybrida*) Dark, nearly black foliage underpins armloads of single and semidouble flowers in solids and bicolors of pink, yellow, orange, and purple. Dig tubers for winter storage in cold Zones. 30 to 36 inches tall, 12 inches wide. Zones 8–10.

10 **'LADY' LAVENDER** (*Lavandula angustifolia*) Fragrance-packed gray-green foliage with purple flower wands to 12 inches long. Flowers and foliage work in all traditional applications—culinary, household, medicinal. Well-drained, neutral to alkaline soil. 10 to 18 inches tall, 10 inches wide. Zones 6–9.

11 **'SHEFFIELD PINK' GARDEN MUM** (*Chrysanthemum spp.*) Also called 'Sheffield'. Daisylike apricot-pink blooms in late fall. Group for drifts of color. Plant in rich, well-drained soil in full to part sun. Provide afternoon shade in the South. 30 to 36 inches tall, 3 feet wide. Zones 5–9.

Salvia
(*Salvia* spp.)

Variety and flower power earn salvia a spot in every quick color garden. Heat-tolerant and deer-resistant plants thrive in pots or planting beds. Blossoms whorl around showy spikes in shades of blue, purple, red, or white and many hues in between. Most are perennial in warm zones, but work well as annuals elsewhere.

Best site

Plant in full sun in well-drained, moderately fertile soil. Although apparently drought tolerant, plants grow best with consistent moisture. In containers, use a soilless commercial mix. Hardiness varies by species.

Growing

Salvias typically mature to form loose bushes. Pinching plants when they're young encourages branching and increases flower number. Because brittle stems break easily, it's a good idea to stake in windy locations, especially scarlet sage (*S. coccinea*) and Mexican bush sage (*S. leucantha*).

Fertilize landscape plants by mixing slow-release fertilizer into the soil prior to planting. Supplement with a midsummer topdressing as needed. In containers, use a slow-release product blended into the soil or a liquid-soluble food. Bloom-booster fertilizer works well.

Remove faded flowers by snipping or breaking the flower stem at the base. Some varieties don't require deadheading; read plant labels for proper care. Flowers open along the spike, so blossoms at the base fade before those at the top. Plants are generally pest free, although whiteflies prefer the greenleaf types. Plant size varies by species.

Design ideas

Many salvias bloom all season, including mealycup (*S. farinacea*), scarlet (*S. coccinea* and *S. splendens*), culinary sage (*S. officianalis*), and blue anise sage (*S. guaranitica*). Mexican bush sage waits for late summer to burst into bloom. Plant bedding salvia types in landscape beds for a strong display. All types except Mexican bush sage work well in containers as fillers or thrillers. Salvias, especially red-flowered types, attract butterflies and hummingbirds.

varieties:

❶ **'BLACK AND BLUE'** (*S. guaranitica*) Deep blue blooms, black-purple calyces. 2 to 4 feet tall, 2 to 3 feet wide. Zones 7–11.

❷ **'EVOLUTION'** (*S. farinacea*) Lilac-purple blooms. Drought and heat tolerant. 18 inches tall, 14 to 18 inches wide. Zones 8–11.

❸ **'SUMMER JEWEL RED'** (*S. coccinea*) Bright red flowers against dark green leaves. 20 inches tall, 11 to 16 inches wide. Zones 9–11.

❹ **'BRAZILIAN PURPLE'** (*S. splendens*) Purple-black calyces, bright purple petals, and medium green foliage. 2 to 4 feet tall, 2 to 3 feet wide. Zones 9–11.

❺ **MEXICAN BUSH SAGE** (*S. leucantha*) White blooms, purple calyces, and gray-green foliage with woolly white undersides. Drought-tolerant. 2 to 4 feet tall and wide. Zones 8–11.

Scaevola
(Scaevola aemula)

Add low-maintenance, nonstop color to the garden with scaevola, also known as fan flower. The plant forms a spreading mound and bears blossoms with five petals arranged in a semicircle, resembling a hand fan. Heat- and drought-tolerant flowers bloom in white, pink, or lavender-blue tones.

Best site

Plant in average, well-drained soil for best growth. Scaevola tolerates sandy soils. In containers, use a peat-based soilless mix.

Site in full sun to part shade. Provide afternoon shade in the hottest regions. Plants tolerate light frosts and salt spray. Hardiness varies by species.

Growing

Scaevola boasts natural heat and drought tolerance but benefits from consistent watering throughout the growing season, especially during extended drought. Plants in containers require water when the soil is dry.

During the growing season, feed scaevola with a plant food high in nitrogen. Bloom-booster fertilizers also feed plants while fueling flower formation. Plants flower continuously without deadheading.

Design ideas

In containers, scaevola is at its best grown in hanging baskets and window boxes, tumbling out of pots in the role of a spiller. Use scaevola solo in a container to focus on the unusual fanshape blooms, or pair it with flowers in similar or complementary shades.

The blue tones of scaevola always look good with pink-tinted flowers and silvery leaves. They also blend beautifully with dark burgundy, purple-black, and bronze tones. The plant has a coarse texture that sings with fine-textured sedges and ornamental grasses.

In the landscape, tuck scaevola into rock gardens, where its rugged personality easily holds its own, or plant it along the top of a wall to allow stems to cascade over the edge. Use the bloomer as a groundcover in seaside gardens.

varieties:

1 **'TOPAZ PINK'** Clear pink flowers. 8 to 12 inches tall, 12 to 18 inches wide. Zones 10–11.

2 **'DIAMOND'** White petals edged in lavender. 6 to 8 inches tall, 8 to 15 inches wide. Zones 10–11.

3 **'COMPACT BLUE'** Flowers appear to blanket foliage because of short stems. Ideal for hanging baskets and trailing from containers. 4 to 12 inches tall, 2 to 5 feet wide. Zones 9–11.

4 **'BOMBAY DARK BLUE'** Lavender-blue flowers. Pair with bronze-tone foliage. 6 to 10 inches tall, 14 to 18 inches wide. Zones 10–11.

5 **'WHIRLWIND WHITE'** Snow-white blooms and medium green foliage. 8 to 14 inches tall, 10 to 12 inches wide. Zones 10–11.

Shamrock
(*Oxalis* spp.)

A favorite St. Patrick's Day emblem, shamrock brings a petite, tidy form to the quick color scene. Leaves feature the classic three-lobe form in hues of green, purple-black, chartreuse, or orange. Flowers open in white, pink, or yellow. Both leaves and flowers fold at night and open with the dawn.

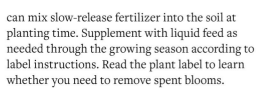

Best site

Plant in moisture-retentive, well-drained soil enriched with organic matter. For containers, choose a moisture-retentive soilless mix that includes coir. Site in part to full shade; sun scorches leaves. However, if the light is too low, plants tend to stretch and fall open. Zones 5–11, depending on species.

Growing

Drainage is key to growing shamrock, often called by its botanical name, oxalis. Roots need moist soil, but soggy conditions lead to rot. Supply even moisture. Leaves grow from a thick, bulblike root. If it takes constant watering to keep the soil moist, dig and divide the plant. New varieties have sterile flowers, which limits their spread by seed. Many are non-invasive.

Fertilize plants monthly using an all-purpose product. In containers or planting beds, you can mix slow-release fertilizer into the soil at planting time. Supplement with liquid feed as needed through the growing season according to label instructions. Read the plant label to learn whether you need to remove spent blooms.

To overwinter oxalis in containers, bring pots inside after the first freeze, which should kill leaves. Store the pots in a cool spot for winter without water. In spring, place them in a bright window, water well, and add liquid fertilizer to jump-start growth.

Design ideas

Use oxalis as a ground cover in moist, shady areas. Tuck individual plants into containers or group plantings. Oxalis works well in shady gardens as a filler. Pair them with shade-loving coleus for drama.

varieties:

❶ 'MOLTEN LAVA' (*O. vulcanicola*) Leaves glow in chartreuse tones in low light and turn rich orange in sunnier settings. 6 to 10 inches tall, 10 to 12 inches wide. Zones 9–11.

❷ 'ZINFANDEL' (*O. vulcanicola*) Black-purple foliage contrasts with bright yellow blooms. 6 to 10 inches tall, 10 to 12 inches wide. Zones 9–11.

❸ 'CHARMED VELVET' (*O. regnellii*) Blush pink blooms and dark purple-black leaves. Pair with lime or chartreuse foliage. 12 to 16 inches tall, 12 to 14 inches wide Zones 8–11.

❹ GARDEN HARDY PINK (*O. crassipes*) Pink blooms glow among bright green leaves. 5 to 8 inches tall, 12 to 14 inches wide Zones 5–10.

❺ 'VELVET SUNSET' (*O. siliquosa*) Fuchsia stems and golden flowers. Plant in full sun or full shade. 8 inches tall, 12 inches wide. Zones 8–10.

Snapdragon
(*Antirrhinum majus*)

Dragon-shape, two-lip blossoms in nearly every hue except true blue whorl around flower stems. When squeezed, flower jaws gape open like a great maw. This old-fashioned favorite is a classic cottage garden plant. Breeding advances include heat tolerance, creating plants that flower through summer.

Best site

Plant in moist, well-drained soils high in organic matter. Snapdragon tolerates part shade, but flowers best in full sun.

Snapdragon is used as an annual although technically it is a short-lived perennial in Zones 7 to 11; well-mulched plants may overwinter unreliably in colder Zones.

Growing

Older varieties perform best where summers are cool; they fade in summer heat and must be replaced by midsummer. New heat-tolerant varieties flower strongly in summer heat, bearing blooms all season while retaining frost tolerance. Read plant tags carefully to know which type of snapdragon you should purchase.

At planting time, pinch stem tips of plants to encourage branching and bushiness. Avoid planting snapdragons too deeply to prevent stem rot. Remove spent blooms to promote more flowers. If flowering stops after the first bloom period, prune back plants and fertilize to promote fresh growth. Stake tall varieties.

In warm Zones, snapdragons are planted in fall for winter color, blooming as long as temperatures remain above freezing.

Snapdragons grow to varying sizes, from dwarf forms 6 to 12 inches tall, to intermediate types 1 to 2 feet tall, to tall cutting varieties 2 to 3 feet tall.

Design ideas

Dwarf snapdragons edge beds and paths or add color to window boxes, containers, and rock gardens. Intermediate sizes work well in containers and mixed borders. Use tall varieties in bouquets; snip stems when one-third of the flowers are open.

varieties:

❶ **'SNAP DADDY'** Clear yellow flowers. Leaves are narrow and edged in creamy tones. 16 inches tall, 8 to 10 inches wide.

❷ **'FLORAL SHOWERS WHITE'** White blossoms with splashes of yellow at the base. Uniform, extra-dwarf plant branches from the base. Good for landscape designs. 6 to 8 inches tall, 5 to 8 inches wide.

❸ **'FLORAL SHOWERS FUCHSIA'** Coral pink-and-white blooms sometimes display a gradation of shades. Extra-dwarf plant. Heat-tolerant. Mound-forming. 6 to 8 inches tall, 5 to 8 inches wide.

❹ **'TWINNY PEACH'** Twin blossoms in a blend of apricot, peach, and soft lemon. Tolerates heat. Good for bouquets. 12 to 15 inches tall, 8 to 10 inches wide.

Stock

(*Matthiola incana*)

Fill cool-season scenes with the rich clove scent of flowering stock. This pretty bloomer opens flowers in shades of red, yellow, white, or purple on upright spikes. Gray-green stems and leaves contrast nicely with blossom colors. Plants thrive in cool weather, pairing well with pansy and viola.

Best site

Plant in moist, well-drained soil enriched with organic matter. Use a soilless mix for containers. Site in full sun or light shade. Stock is technically a biennial, Zones 7–10, but most gardeners grow it as an annual.

Growing

Remove spent blooms to encourage flower formation. In the warmest Zones, plant in fall for winter color. Stock fades when the temperature reaches 80°F.

Design ideas

Flowering stock adds cool-season color. This fragrant plant grows well in containers and planting beds. Plant it near entries and outdoor seating areas where its fragrance can be savored. In cool summers, stock may flower all season, rebounding in autumn with a strong show.

varieties:

❶ 'VINTAGE LAVENDER' Double blooms unfurl in lavender shades. 15 to 20 inches tall, 12 to 14 inches wide.

Strawflower

(*Bracteantha bracteata*, syn. *Xerochrysum bracteatum*)

Sometimes called paper daisy, strawflower bursts into brilliant bloom, revealing papery petals in saturated shades that include gold, orange, red, purple, and bronze. Plants thrive where summers are long and hot, opening blooms until fall frosts arrive.

Best site

Plant in average, well-drained soil. In sandy or gravelly soil, water more frequently. Plants rot in heavy clay soil. Site in full sun for best flowering; strawflower tolerates light shade. Zones 8–11.

Growing

Fertilize with a bloom-booster to promote flower formation. Varieties range from 1 to 5 feet tall and 6 to 18 inches wide. Stake tall types.

Design ideas

This bloomer fits well in many spots in the garden. Use smaller varieties as bed edging or in window boxes; taller forms fit in container combinations or planting beds. Strawflower's stiff petals dry without losing color or shape and last indefinitely. To harvest larger but fewer blooms, remove side shoots on stems. Cut just as flowers begin to open; hang upside down to dry.

varieties:

❶ 'MOHAVE FIRE' Blazing orange blossoms with bright yellow centers. Pair with blue or purple flowers, such as ageratum or angelonia. 14 to 16 inches tall and wide.

Sunflower
(*Helianthus annuus*)

A familiar and beloved bloomer, sunflower weaves magic into a garden. Larger-than-life flowers turn their heads to follow the sun across the sky each day. New varieties offer shorter stature and blooms with no pollen, in colors that include yellow, mahogany, bronze, burgundy, purple, red, and orange.

Best site
Plant in well-drained soil of any fertility, even in poor soil with low moisture. Sunflower prefers slightly alkaline soil; add lime to acidic soils. Site in full sun. The weight of the flower heads often topples plants. Annual.

Growing
Mix slow-release fertilizer into the soil prior to planting; rotted manure or compost also nourishes plants. Sow seeds after danger of frost is past. Place taller varieties in a spot protected from strong winds or stake their skyscraping stems. Water freely for the greatest growth. Sunflowers thrive in high temperatures. Varieties range about 3 to 10 feet tall and 1 to 3 feet wide.

Design ideas
Add taller versions of these cheerful flowers to planting beds. The larger varieties can overpower small gardens, but they work well at the back of a vegetable garden or along a fence as a seasonal screen. Dwarf varieties are suited for mixed planting beds and containers.

Sunflowers are a natural choice for butterfly, cottage, and native plant gardens. The big seeds are easy for children's small fingers to plant. For a double color show, place morning glory seeds at the base of sunflowers. Hunt for pollen-free varieties to use in cutting gardens for bouquets.

Birds and squirrels feast on ripe seeds. To save seeds for winter bird feeding, cover seed heads with netting to prevent wildlife access. To harvest seeds, cut the flower head when the back is brown with no hint of green remaining and hang upside down in a dry, warm, well-ventilated place. When the back of the flower head dries to a papery texture, use a ridged surface such as an old-fashioned washboard to scrape off the seeds.

varieties:

1 **'EVENING SUN'** Large, 6-inch blossoms in orange, red, and burgundy with contrasting dark centers. 6 to 8 feet tall, 2 to 3 feet wide.

2 **'GLORIOSA'** Single gold petals with maroon inner centers. Flowers resemble gloriosa daisies. Multiple flower heads. 6 to 10 feet high, 8 to 12 inches wide.

3 **'TEDDY BEAR'** Fluffy, fully double 6-inch golden blooms. Short plants with sturdy, well-branched stems. Good for containers. 2 to 3 feet tall, 14 to 16 inches wide.

4 **'VALENTINE'** Pale lemon yellow blooms with dark centers. Plants branch well, bearing multiple flowers. 4 to 6 feet tall, 18 to 24 inches wide.

Swan River Daisy
(Brachyscome iberidifolia)

Delicate lacy leaves contrast beautifully with sparkling daisylike blooms that open in shades of blue-purple, pink, rose, or white. Plants stage the strongest show during cool times of the year, when flower numbers can be so intense they nearly obscure the foliage.

Best site

Plant in well-drained soil. Heavy and clay-filled soils can lead to rot. Plants don't do well in poor soils. Blend rotted manure or compost into soil prior to planting. In containers, choose a commercial soilless mix.

Site in full sun to part shade. Light shade can help extend bloom time as summer heat starts to build. Zones 10–11.

Growing

Swan river daisy flowers best in cool seasons. Plant for spring and fall color in northern regions. In frost-free areas, autumn plantings can provide color all winter long.

Blend slow-release fertilizer into the soil at planting time.

Shear plants after the first flush of bloom and feed using a liquid soluble bloom-booster fertilizer to promote further flower bud formation. Newer varieties offer a strong flowering habit through summer months, but most plants cease blooming in summer heat.

Prune plants as needed to control size, direct growth, or promote flowering.

Design ideas

This petite-flowered plant makes a fantastic addition to container gardens. Plant it solo in a pot and let it mound and cascade over container edges. It creates a muffin-top effect, completely engulfing a pot. Swan River daisy tumbles gracefully from hanging baskets and window boxes. Use it in container combinations as a spiller plant. Pair with other cool-season beauties, such as pansy, viola, stock, sweet alyssum, nemesia, or flowering cabbage.

varieties:

1 **'SURDAISY PINK'** Large, showy pink blooms. Deep green leaves with fatter, nonferny texture. 6 to 10 inches tall, 10 to 20 inches wide. Zones 10–11.

2 **'BLUE ZEPHYR'** Lavender blossoms with golden centers. 9 to 15 inches tall, 12 to 16 inches wide. Zones 9–11.

3 **'SURDAISY WHITE'** Miniature white flowers with chartreuse eyes. Deadheading isn't necessary. 6 to 12 inches tall and wide. Zones 9–11.

4 **'TOUCAN TANGO'** Light purple petals and a chartreuse center. 8 to 12 inches tall, 8 to 10 inches wide. Zones 9–11.

Sweet Alyssum
(*Lobularia maritima*)

You can't beat the beauty of sweet alyssum in full bloom. Plants boast a low profile, forming dense mats of color fueled by dainty blossoms that release a sweet honey scent and attract butterflies. Look for flowers in white as well as varying shades of purple, pink, or apricot.

Best site

Plant in well-drained soil that's moderately fertile. Gritty, loam-enriched soil yields strong growth. Soggy soil tends to rot roots, so in containers use a soilless mix.

Site sweet alyssum in full sun, although plants tolerate light shade. In hottest regions, provide afternoon shade for most types. Some newer varieties and hybrids withstand full sun. Read plant tags to learn the best growing conditions.

Although hardy in Zones 9 to 11, this mat-forming bloomer is usually grown as an annual because plants become rangy in subsequent years.

Growing

With the exception of newer varieties and hybrids, sweet alyssum performs best where summers are cool. If plants wane during the hottest period of summer, shear by half, and fertilize when the weather cools off. In warm zones, plant sweet alyssum in fall for winter color. Trim plants lightly after flowering to encourage subsequent bloom. Newer types may not require that treatment.

Water plants when the soil is dry. Fertilize with a bloom-booster product. Use a slow-release type mixed into the soil or a water-soluble formulation for plants in pots. Sweet alyssum typically grows 4 to 9 inches tall and 6 to 12 inches wide.

Design ideas

Use this self-sowing plant in rock gardens and between flagstones to create a carpet of color. Sweet alyssum also performs well as a bed-edging plant. In containers, it fills the spiller role. Partner it with other cool-season bloomers, such as pansy, sweet William, stock, and nemesia.

varieties:

❶ **'EASTER BONNET'** Blooms in shades of lavender, white, deep pink, violet, lemonade, or peach. More compact and tidier than other varieties. 4 to 10 inches tall, 10 to 12 inches wide. Zones 10–11.

❷ **'CLEAR CRYSTAL LAVENDER SHADES'** A blend of purple, violet, and lavender blooms. Vigorous plants. Blossoms open all season. 6 to 10 inches tall, 12 to 14 inches wide. Zones 10–11.

❸ **'ORIENTAL NIGHTS'** Dark violet flowers open from spring until frost. 2 to 4 inches tall, 6 to 12 inches wide. Zones 10–11.

❹ **SNOW PRINCESS** Large white blooms. Heat and humidity tolerant. Requires evenly moist soil. Prune as needed to curtail vigorous growth. 4 to 8 inches tall, 8 to 10 inches wide. Zones 9–11.

Sweet Potato Vine (*Ipomoea batatas*)

Colorful, adaptable, and easy growing, sweet potato vine is the go-to plant when you really need to cover ground. This vine roots as it grows, reaching up to 3 feet per week in warm regions. It cascades 8 to 10 feet over a wall, forming a lush curtain. Foliage colors include chartreuse, red, bronze, pink, black-purple, and variegated blends. Leaf patterns vary greatly; some leaves resemble hearts while others are lacy, three-lobed forms.

Best site

Plant sweet potato vine in well-drained soil enriched with organic matter. The soil must drain well to prevent root rot. Organic matter enhances the soil's ability to retain moisture in a way that's available to plant roots without damaging them. Set plants at the same depth that they're growing in their pots. Site plants in full sun to mostly shade. Many types color best in full sun. Zones 10–11, unless indicated otherwise.

Growing

Blend slow-release fertilizer into landscape beds and containers prior to planting. For in-ground plantings, supplement this fertilizer throughout the growing season according to instructions on the product label. In containers, fertilize throughout the growing season.

Stems root as they grow, so prepare planting beds accordingly to encourage rooting. If you start with one plant in a window box, as vines grow you can snip and stick the pieces into soil and they'll root. This is an easy way to create a lush, full planting on a budget. Keep the soil moist while stems root. Rooting occurs faster in warm soil. You can also dip stem ends into rooting hormone to spur root formation.

Sweet potato vine doesn't guzzle water; the underground tuber stores enough water to help plants survive short drought periods. In containers, water more frequently, especially as vines grow larger. Adding water-retentive crystals to the soil can increase time between irrigations. Leaves droop when the soil is too dry, but they recover quickly upon receiving water.

Prune vines as needed throughout the growing season to control growth and curtail spread. In containers, this prevents vines from overrunning other plants. Pinching the vines increases branching. Sweet potato vines grow quickly in summer heat and humidity. In the South, they may grow 3 feet per week. Read plant tags to purchase the right vine; some varieties have shorter sprawls than others.

Sweet potato whiteflies can infest vines in summer. If vines are growing near container plants you plan to overwinter indoors, inspect carefully before taking the plants inside. Flea beetles may chew holes in leaves. These beetles reproduce quickly. Treat with an appropriate pesticide at the first sign of a problem.

Sweet potato vines melt with frost. Cover plants during cool weather to prolong the growing season. In cold regions after frost nips vines, dig tubers and store them indoors for winter in a cool, dry place. Repot them indoors in early spring but wait to set plants out until all danger of frost has passed.

Design ideas

Chartreuse-tone varieties brighten shady areas. Dark leaf types add contrast to light-colored plantings. Mingle or alternate different color sweet potato vines for a beautiful display.

Cascading vines are ideal for hanging baskets or window boxes. In containers, choose varieties like the Illusion series that won't overpower other plants. In the landscape, you can fill a 3- to 4-foot-wide area with solid color for just a few dollars. In northern regions, use sweet potato vine to fill bare areas along driveways and streets where snow gets piled in winter.

Plant sweet potato vine with canna or coleus for a calypso-style scene. Try this winning combination: dark leaf sweet potato vine, white or hot pink trailing zinnia (Profusion type) or trailing vinca, celery-green asparagus fern, and Tropicanna canna.

varieties:

1 SWEET CAROLINE 'SWEETHEART RED' Heart-shape leaves (shown at bottom of photo) emerge chartreuse, then turn a range of hues including bronze, purple-veined bronze, purple-veined green, and red as they age. Shown with Dipt in Wine coleus, Versa Crimson Gold coleus, and Zahara Yellow zinnia. 6 to 8 inches tall, 3 to 4 feet wide.

2 'DESANA COMPACT RED' Leaves open red and mature to green; maroon veins on mature leaves. Blossoms in pale pink. 8 to 10 inches tall, 2 to 4 feet wide.

3 ILLUSION GARNET LACE Deeply lobed leaves emerge chartreuse, then deepen to bronze-red before turning burgundy-brown. The Illusion series sweet potato vine doesn't overpower other plants in a container. 6 to 10 inches tall, 2 to 3 feet wide.

4 ILLUSION EMERALD LACE Chartreuse leaves display enlarged middle lobe flanked by two smaller lobes, creating a filigree effect. Pair with dark flowering or foliage plants. 6 to 10 inches tall, 2 to 3 feet wide.

5 ILLUSION MIDNIGHT LACE Deeply cut leaves in shades of purple-black. Pair with pink angelonia and a goldleaf sun-loving coleus. 6 to 10 inches tall, 2 to 3 feet wide.

6 SWEET CAROLINE RAVEN Glossy, three-lobed leaves in deep purple-black tones. Pair with any lime green sweet potato vine. 6 to 8 inches tall, 3 to 4 feet wide.

7 SOUTH OF THE BORDER 'CHIHUAHUA' Chartreuse leaves; compact growth habit. To 8 inches tall, 36 inches wide. Zones 8–11.

Verbena
(*Verbena* spp.)

Grow verbena for long-season color that beckons butterflies. This flower-covered beauty offers variety, forming shrubby mounds, trailing mats, or open, airy plants. Small blossoms appear in clusters up to 3 inches across in many shades, including pink, purple, red, yellow, and apricot.

Best site

Plant in average well-drained soil. Verbena tolerates poor or sandy soil as long as it drains well. Water until plants are established, when plants adapt to drought conditions. In containers, use a soilless mix.

Site in full to part sun. Verbena flowers performs best in full sun. In warm regions, shade them during midday. Hardiness varies by type.

Growing

At planting time, pinch growing shoots of plants to promote branching and bushiness. Mix slow-release fertilizer into planting beds and containers; supplement with additional bloom-booster fertilizer through summer according to package directions. Nutrition needs vary. Read plant labels for best fertilizing practices.

Remove spent blooms to encourage more flower buds. With some plants, lightly shearing stems after flowering is the easiest way to deadhead. Some hybrids don't need dead flowers removed; read plant labels to learn proper care.

Verbena benefits from consistently moist but not soggy soil. Overhead watering can lead to powdery mildew outbreaks; newer hybrids boast disease resistance. For landscape plantings that have automatic overhead irrigation, plant mildew-resistant varieties.

Prune as needed to curtail plant spread and direct growth. If plants languish, cut back and fertilize to fuel new growth. In warm Zones, you may need to do this twice, as needed.

Design ideas

In the landscape verbenas serve as ground covers and edging plants. It performs well in containers and hanging baskets. Include verbena in butterfly or wildlife gardens.

varieties:

1 LANAI LAVENDER STAR Lavender petals striped in white. 4 to 10 inches tall, 12 to 18 inches wide. Zones 7–11.

2 LASCAR BIG EYE RASPBERRY White centers on raspberry-pink flowers. Heat-tolerant, mildew-resistant. 12 to 14 inches tall by 12 to 16 inches wide Zones 7–11.

3 'TAPIEN SALMON' Deep salmon flowers; fernlike leaves. 3 to 8 inches tall by 1 to 3 feet wide. Zones 8–11.

4 'ROCCO BURGUNDY' (*V. tenera*) Fully double, deep-burgundy-purple blossoms. Lacy leaves. High mildew tolerance; heat tolerant. 9 inches tall, 2 feet wide. Zones 9–11.

5 BRAZILIAN VERBENA (*V. bonariensis*) Lavender-pink blooms. Self-sows. Drought-tolerant. 2 to 4 feet tall, 18 to 36 inches wide. Zones 7–11.

Vinca
(*Catharanthus roseus*)

No matter how high the mercury soars, vinca endures. This tough plant displays intense flower power during summer's hottest days. Contrasting against glossy foliage, blooms open to five flat petals in many shades, including red, purple, pink, and white. Look for compact, upright, and trailing types.

Best site
Plant in poor or sandy, well-drained soil. Drainage is crucial; in heavy clay or poorly drained soils, plants stall and roots rot. In too-fertile soil, foliage thrives at the expense of flowers. In containers, use a soilless potting mix. Site in full sun to part shade. Zones 9–11; varieties here are all Zone 11.

Growing
At planting time, pinch growing tips to promote branching and a fuller, flower-filled plant. There's no need to remove spent blooms.

Once established, plants display moderate drought tolerance. If possible, provide consistent moisture for top growth, but avoid overwatering. Vinca won't tolerate overwatering; plants die quickly in waterlogged soil.

Use drip irrigation or soaker hoses to deliver water directly to roots and avoid wetting foliage.

Vinca is susceptible to fungal diseases that attack and multiply quickly on wet leaves. If using overhead irrigation, water plants early in the day so leaves dry before dusk. New varieties display good disease resistance. In humid growing areas, select resistant varieties for best success.

In warm regions, leaves may curl during the hottest part of the day but typically return to normal as evening's cooler temperatures arrive and dew falls.

Design ideas
Vinca fills containers with color and rolls out a bloom-spangled carpet in planting beds. Use upright vinca in window boxes and pots; choose trailing varieties for hanging baskets. Shorter upright varieties make a wonderful edging for paths and planting beds. Plants are deer and rabbit resistant. The flowers beckon butterflies.

varieties:

1 MEDITERRANEAN 'HOT ROSE XP' Overlapping vivid rose petals on large blossoms. 4 to 6 inches, 20 to 30 inches wide.

2 MEDITERRANEAN 'STRAWBERRY XP' Blush pink, overlapping petals with deep pink center. 4 to 6 inches tall, 20 to 30 inches wide.

3 'RASPBERRY COOLER' Overlapping petals on large raspberry-tinted flowers with white eyes. Plants perform well in cool, wet, or hot weather. 12 to 14 inches tall, 6 to 8 inches wide.

4 'CORA LAVENDER' Lavender 2-inch-wide blooms. Resistant to aerial *Phytophthora* fungus. Grows in damp conditions. 14 to 16 inches tall, 22 to 25 inches wide.

5 'TITAN APRICOT' Coral pink blossoms open with deep pink-apricot centers. 14 to 16 inches tall, 10 to 14 inches wide.

Viola
(*Viola* spp.)

Dress the cool-season garden with the smiling faces of perky violas. These pansy cousins shrug off frost and display petals in a variety of tones, including pastels and deep, rich hues. New varieties endow plants with heat tolerance, so they can toss open new flowers all summer long.

Best site

Plant in moist, well-drained soil that's been enriched with organic matter. Blend 2 to 3 inches of compost or rotted manure into light sand or hard clay to improve drainage and soil aeration. For containers, use a soilless peat-based potting mix.

Site in full sun to part shade. In the warmest Zones, place violas in morning sun and afternoon shade. Plants in full shade don't flower as strongly. Violas grow best in temperatures ranging from 30°F to 80°F. Zones 6–11.

Growing

In landscape beds and containers, mix a slow-release fertilizer into the soil at planting time. In planting beds, add mulch to maintain soil moisture and reduce soil temperature. Remove spent flowers to spur further blossom formation. Flowering typically dwindles when summer temperatures soar above 90°F. Prolonged heat often kills plants. To save plants for fall, cut them to 3 to 4 inches tall and continue to water and fertilize. Plants should rebound with the return of cooler temperatures.

Choose a planting location with good air circulation to avoid fungal diseases, including botrytis and powdery mildew.

Design ideas

Tuck violas in containers, such as pots and window boxes. Use trailing types in hanging baskets or atop a garden wall. Spring planting partners include nemesia, sweet William, snapdragon, and flowering bulbs. In warmer Zones, plant viola in fall for winter color. Viola blossoms are edible when grown organically. Do not eat blooms from purchased plants that may have been chemically treated by a nursery.

varieties:

1 **'SORBET COCONUT DUET'** Lavender-white lower and deep purple upper petals, yellow center, purple dimple on lower petals. Heat and cold tolerant. 6 to 8 inches tall and wide. Zones 6–11.

2 **'PENNY YELLOW'** Golden yellow petals with purple-tinted whiskers. Good heat and cold tolerance. 4 to 6 inches tall and wide. Zones 4–8.

3 **'PENNY PRIMROSE PICOTEE'** Whiskered yellow 1-inch faces, purple-edged petals. Cold tolerant. 4 to 6 inches tall and wide. Zones 4–8.

4 **'PENNY ALL SEASON MIX'** A mixture of flower colors in shades of blue, orange, yellow, or white. 4 to 6 inches tall and wide. Zones 4–8.

5 **'VELOCITY BABY BLUE'** (*Viola × williamsii*) Lavender blooms with deep purple whiskers, yellow centers. Add extra moisture in full sun. 4 to 6 inches tall, 6 inches wide. Zones 6–11.

Wishbone Flower
(Torenia fournieri)

Light up shady areas with the richly tinted, velvety-petaled blooms of wishbone flower. This heat-loving, deer-resistant plant holds its own in shade, opening 1-inch blossoms in a range of colors, from purple to pink, burgundy, gold, and white. The blooms attract hummingbirds.

Best site

Plant in rich, well-drained soil. Add compost or rotted manure to beds as needed to retain the moisture wishbone flower requires. In containers, use a peat-based soilless mix.

Site in part shade to almost full shade. Morning sun and afternoon shade provide nearly ideal growing conditions in warmer Zones. In regions with cool summers, wishbone flower withstands full sun. It is a tender perennial that won't tolerate temperatures below 40°F. Torienias hardiness varies by species from Zones 6 to 11; varieties shown here are Zones 10-11.

Growing

Mix a slow-release fertilizer into landscape beds or containers at planting time. Fertilize plants in containers throughout the growing season using a bloom-booster product.

Wishbone flower prefers consistently moist soil. Water when the soil is dry. Add mulch to planting beds to maintain soil moisture and reduce soil temperature. Remove spent flowers to spur blossom formation. Newer varieties don't always require deadheading, so check plant tags.

Pinch wishbone flower at planting time to encourage branching and bushiness.

Design ideas

Wishbone flower provides steady, reliable color in shady areas. In the warmest areas, gardeners and landscapers consider wishbone flower a hot-weather substitute for pansies. In all Zones, this heat-tolerant bloomer thrives in planting beds and as a filler plant in containers.

Use wishbone flower in window boxes and hanging baskets. Trailing types work well in hanging baskets. This colorful annual fits perfectly into shade and woodland gardens.

varieties:

❶ SOLARINA WHITE VEIL Silvery white with hints of lavender; purple throat. 6 to 10 inches tall, 18 to 36 inches wide.

❷ 'PURPLE MOON' Varying purple tones. Trailing growth works well in hanging baskets. 6 to 8 inches tall, 14 to 16 inches wide.

❸ 'LOVELY PUNKY VIOLET' Raspberry to mauve petals with lavender edges. 8 to 10 inches tall, 6 to 16 inches wide.

❹ 'LOVELY YELLOW' Unusual lemon yellow flowers with burgundy throats. 8 to 10 inches tall, 6 to 16 inches wide.

❺ 'LOVELY ROSY CHEEK' Flowers in pink shades with yellow splotch on lower petals. Trailing type for landscape beds or hanging baskets. 8 to 10 inches tall, 6 to 16 inches wide.

Zinnia (*Zinnia* spp.)

An old-fashioned favorite, zinnia brings easy-growing beauty to quick color displays. Flowers open in nearly every shade, including hot pink, chartreuse, peach, cream, red, and vivid bicolor blends. The only hues missing are blue and brown. Blossoms grow in a variety of forms, from simple singles to luxurious doubles 1 to 6 inches across. Zinnia is a versatile garden performer, thriving in containers or planting beds.

Best site

Plant in evenly moist, well-drained soil. In heavy clay or sandy soil, work 2 to 3 inches of organic material such as rotted manure or compost into the soil prior to planting. In containers, use a moisture-retentive soilless potting mix.

Site zinnia in areas that receive full sun. In hottest regions, plants benefit from morning sun and afternoon shade. Some pastel-tinted varieties, like pale green 'Envy', grow and flower in light shade, although sun is preferable. Read plant tags to provide the ideal conditions for your zinnias. Native to Mexico, plants are true tropicals and don't tolerate frost. Annual.

Growing

In landscape beds, blend in slow-release fertilizer prior to planting. Mixing organic matter into the soil feeds plants for a portion of the summer. In midsummer, supplement with water-soluble fertilizer or a granular type worked into the top few inches of soil. Plants in containers benefit from regular applications of a bloom booster.

Pinch zinnia at planting time to encourage branching. Remove spent blooms regularly to encourage more flower buds to form. To coax super-large blossoms to form on tall cutting types, remove all side shoots so the plant's energy goes into producing one single bloom.

Once plants are established, they're fairly drought tolerant. Consistent watering produces maximum growth. Avoid overhead watering. Drip irrigation or soaker hoses are best. If you must use overhead watering for landscape plantings, water early in the day so foliage can dry before dusk. In pots, apply water directly to the soil.

Zinnias are susceptible to several fungal leaf diseases, typically during humid summer days. Prevent disease by planting in spots with good air circulation. Don't crowd plants in the garden or containers; follow recommended spacing on plant labels. Avoid getting leaves wet when watering. Some zinnia species, including thinleaf zinnia (*Z. angustifolia*) and Mexican zinnia (*Z. haageana*), are more resistant to leaf diseases than others. Profusion (*Z. hybrida*) and Zahara (*Z. marylandica*) types also have good resistance. Avoid overhead watering and provide good air circulation for all zinnias.

Container-grown zinnias add instant color, but they also grow quickly and easily from seed. Enhance and extend the display by sowing zinnia seeds at 2- to 3-week intervals through early summer. Sow seeds of similar types or choose unusual forms to spice up the flower show.

Design ideas

Zinnias are a traditional choice for cottage and cutting gardens. Include zinnia in wildlife and butterfly planting designs.

These carefree annuals grow in a variety of sizes, from petite and tidy dwarf types, to rounded mound plants, to tall, waist-high types. Choose the right size for the right place.

Dwarf zinnias serve as edging plants along beds and paths and fit into window boxes and containers. Rounded mound types play a filler or spiller role in containers and make a low-maintenance addition to planting beds. Profusion and Zahara varieties provide a color-filled edging treatment for large beds. Plant taller zinnias in the backs of planting beds, as companion plants in vegetable gardens, and in cutting gardens.

All zinnias make good cut flowers that last about 7 to 10 days in a vase. Snip stems early in the day, choosing ones that aren't fully open. Strip any lower leaves that would be under water. Any tightly closed buds that have been harvested won't open indoors.

varieties:

❶ NARROWLEAF ZINNIA (*Z. angustifolia*) Single, 2-inch flowers in shades of gold, orange, white, or yellow. Narrow leaves with excellent disease resistance. Plants flower strongly through summer heat and humidity. Ideal for edging beds or in containers. 8 to 14 inches tall, 8 to 12 inches wide

❷ 'BENARY'S GIANT LIME' (*Z. elegans*) Chartreuse blooms shrug off rain and hold up in summer heat. Fully double blossoms measure 4 to 6 inches across. Plants offer some mildew resistance. 3 to 4 feet tall, 9 to 12 inches wide.

❸ 'SWIZZLE SCARLET & YELLOW' (*Z. grandiflora*) Large, fully double 3- to 4-inch gold flowers with scarlet centers and pencil-thin red edges. Narrow, disease-resistant leaves. Use in containers or landscape beds. 10 to 12 inches tall and wide.

❹ PROFUSION (*Z. hybrida* Profusion Series) Orange, red, yellow, white, or pink blooms 2 to 3 inches across. Hybrid that bears the flower power of *Zinnia elegans* and the disease resistance of thinleaf zinnia. No deadheading needed. New landscape double-flowered types perfect for landscape use. 10 to 18 inches tall, 12 to 15 inches wide.

❺ 'ZAHARA STARLIGHT ROSE' (*Z. marylandica*) Bicolor blooms with white petals and splashes of pink. Petal coloring varies with growing conditions. Best coloration develops with high light, consistent fertilization, and cool nights. Low water needs once established. 12 to 18 inches tall and wide.

❻ 'CUT & COME AGAIN MIX' (*Z. pumila*) Red, salmon, yellow, orange, or white fully double 2½-inch flowers. Plants are susceptible to fungal diseases. 24 to 30 inches tall, 8 to 10 inches wide.

USDA Plant Hardiness Zone Map
Many quick color plants are hardy in the warmest Zones but need winter protection elsewhere to survive freezes.

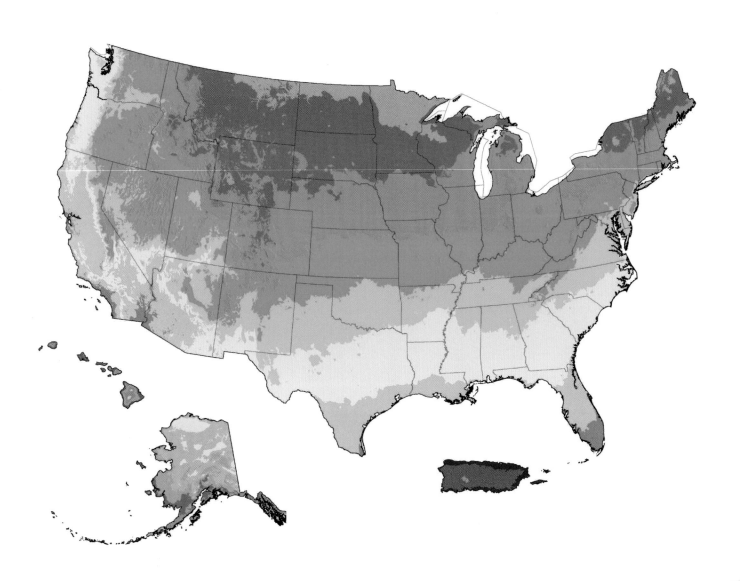

Average annual extreme minimum temperature for each Zone

3	Zone 3: -40 to -30°F (-40 to -35°C)
4	Zone 4: -30 to -20°F (-34 to -29°C)
5	Zone 5: -20 to -10°F (-29 to -23°C)
6	Zone 6: -10 to 0°F (-23 to -18°C)
7	Zone 7: 0 to 10°F (-18 to -12°C)
8	Zone 8: 10 to 20°F (-12 to -7°C)
9	Zone 9: 20 to 30°F (-7 to -1°C)
10	Zone 10: 30 to 40°F (-1 to 4°C)
11	Zone 11: 40 to 50°F (4.5°C to 10°C)

Source: U.S. Department of Agriculture

Spring Frost Map
The average date of the last spring frost is a valuable guide for determining when to plant many quick color plants.

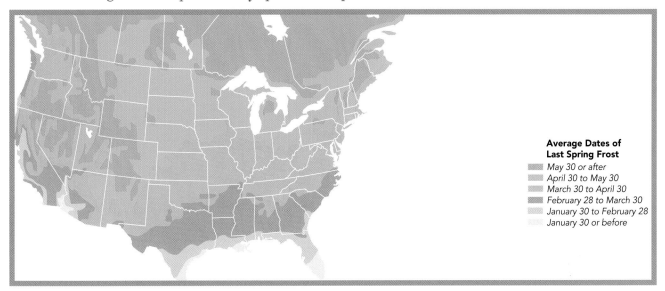

Average Dates of Last Spring Frost
- May 30 or after
- April 30 to May 30
- March 30 to April 30
- February 28 to March 30
- January 30 to February 28
- January 30 or before

Tropical plants such as banana and mandevilla vine and heat-loving quick color favorites such as lantana and cleome are usually planted after the last spring frost. Cool-season plants such as sweet alyssum and pansy can be planted three to four weeks before the average frost date. Learn about annuals that thrive in cool weather on page 33.

Many factors determine the actual date for planting in your garden. Weather, plus the contours and orientation of your landscape, are major contributors. More often than not, if you time plantings by following the average date of last spring's frost for your area, your quick color plants will thrive.

Fall Frost Map
The average date of the first autumn frost is helpful in deciding when to plant late season quick color for fall and winter displays.

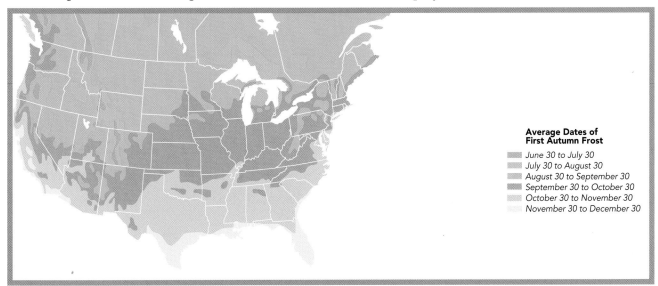

Average Dates of First Autumn Frost
- June 30 to July 30
- July 30 to August 30
- August 30 to September 30
- September 30 to October 30
- October 30 to November 30
- November 30 to December 30

For fall and winter color, set plants into the ground two to three weeks before the first frost arrives. When garden centers start stocking plants, it's generally the right time to purchase and plant. Timing is more critical in regions where winters are harsh. Even frost-tolerant plants in these areas must be established before hard freezes arrive.

Knowing when frost occurs is also useful when you grow tropical plants that you intend to overwinter. For some tropicals, wait to dig roots until after a freeze occurs. You may want to move potted tropicals indoors before frost arrives. To review what to do with tropicals and tender perennials when fall frost arrives, see page 122.

Mail-order quick color plants

If you can't find the plants you want locally, try mail order specialists—companies that grow plants or seeds for shipping.

ANNIE'S ANNUALS
www.anniesannuals.com
888.266.4370
Seeds and plants: annuals, perennials

BLUESTONE PERENNIALS
www.bluestoneperennials.com
800.852.5243
Perennials, succulents, tender perennials

BRENT AND BECKY'S BULBS
www.brentandbeckysbulbs.com
877.661.2852
Bulbs, tropicals

THE COOK'S GARDEN
www.cooksgarden.com
800.457.9703
Seeds and plants: annuals, tender perennials

GURNEY'S SEED & NURSERY COMPANY
www.gurneys.com
513.354.1491
Seeds and plants: annuals, perennials, grasses

HENRY FIELD'S SEED & NURSERY CO.
www.henryfields.com
513.354.1494
Seeds and plants: annuals, perennials, tropicals

HIGH COUNTRY GARDENS
www.highcountrygardens.com
800.925.9387
Grasses, perennials, prairie plants, succulents

JOHNNY'S SELECTED SEEDS
www.johnnyseeds.com
877.564.6697
Seeds: annuals, perennials, tender perennials

J.W. JUNG SEED COMPANY
www.jungseed.com
800.297.3123
Seeds & plants: annuals, perennials, bulbs, grasses

MCCLURE & ZIMMERMAN
www.mzbulb.com
800.546.4053
Tropicals, bulbs

NICHE GARDENS
www.nichegardens.com
919.967.0078
Perennials, tender perennials, succulents, tropicals

NICHOLS GARDEN NURSERY
www.nicholsgardennursery.com
800.422.3985
Seeds: annuals

PARK SEED COMPANY
www.parkseed.com
800.845.3369
Seeds and plants: annuals, tender perennials, grasses, tropicals

PLANT DELIGHTS
www.plantdelights.com
919.772.4794
Perennials, tender perennials, succulents, tropicals

PRAIRIE NURSERY
www.prairienursery.com
800.476.9453
Seeds and plants: grasses, perennials, prairie plants

PROVEN WINNERS
www.provenwinners.com
877.865.5818
Annuals, tender perennials, grasses, succulents, tropicals

RENEE'S GARDEN
www.reneesgarden.com
888.880.7228
Seeds: annuals, perennials

SEED SAVERS EXCHANGE
www.seedsavers.org
563.382.5990
Seeds: annuals, grasses, prairie plants

SOUTHERN EXPOSURE SEED EXCHANGE
www.southernexposure.com
540.894.9480
Seeds: annuals, tender perennials, grasses

TERRITORIAL SEED COMPANY
www.territorialseed.com
800.626.0866
Seeds and plants: annuals, tender perennials, grasses

**THOMPSON & MORGAN
SEEDSMEN, INC.**
www.tmseeds.com
800.274.7333
Seeds: annuals, tender perennials, grasses, tropicals

W. ATLEE BURPEE & COMPANY
www.burpee.com
800.888.1447
Seeds and plants: annuals, tender perennials, grasses

WAYSIDE GARDENS
www.waysidegardens.com
800.213.0379
Perennials, tender perennials, succulents

WHITE FLOWER FARM
www.whiteflowerfarm.com
800.503.9624
Annuals, perennials, tender perennials, succulents, tropicals

YUCCA DO NURSERY
www.yuccado.com
979.542.8811
Perennials, tender perennials, succulents, tropicals

Brand-name quick color plants

Some quick color plants bear branded plant tags or pots. These suppliers provide growing instructions and combination ideas.

HORT COUTURE
www.hortcoutureplants.com
517.542.4548
Annuals, tender perennials, tropicals, grasses, herbs, succulents

MONROVIA
www.monrovia.com
Plants: annuals, perennials, tropicals

PROVEN WINNERS
www.provenwinners.com
877.865.5818
Annuals, tender perennials, tropicals, grasses, succulents

SIMPLY BEAUTIFUL
www.simplybeautifulgardens.com
Annuals, tender perennials, tropicals, grasses, succulents

VIVA! GARDEN
www.vivagarden.com
Annuals, tender perennials, tropicals, grasses

Tools, stakes, fertilizer, and supplies

Find the gear you need to grow beautiful quick color displays.

A.M. LEONARD
www.amleo.com
800.543.8955

GARDENERS SUPPLY
www.gardeners.com
888.833.1412

GARDENS ALIVE!
www.gardensalive.com
513.354.1482

GOODS FOR THE GARDEN
www.goodsforthegarden.com
800.663.3158

KINSMAN COMPANY
www.kinsmangarden.com
800.733.4146

LEE VALLEY TOOLS
www.leevalley.com
800.267.8735

SPRAY-N-GROW
www.spray-n-grow.com
800.323.2363

index

index

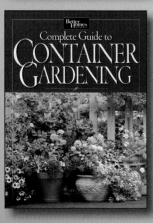

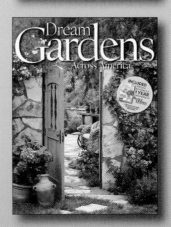